KB143050

토익영문법

지은이 **나병모**

한남대학교 영어영문학과(문학사)
고려대학교 대학원 영어영문학과(문학석사, 문학박사)
대진대학교 영어영문학과 교수

주요 저서
『구구조의 생성』 1988(공역)
『현대언어학의 흐름』 1991(역서)
『장벽이론과 논리형태』 1992(저서)
『영어통사론』 1995(저서)
『언어학의 이해』 1996(공역)
『영어의 구조』 2001(저서)
『영어구문분석』 2008(저서)
『핵심영문법』 2011(저서)
『Advanced VOA Listening』 2013(저서)
『Basic VOA Listening』 2013(저서)
『English Words and Their Stories』 2015(저서)

최근 논문
「인터넷을 통한 영작문 교육」 1998
「최소주의와 단일점검원리」 1999
「인터넷을 통한 영문법 평가」 1999
「웹기반수업에 대한 태도 분석」 1999
「대용어의 해석과 재구」 2003
「VPC의 최소주의적 접근」 2004

토익영문법

발행일 2016년 3월 15일
지은이 나병모 **발행인** 이성모
발행처 도서출판 동인 / 서울시 종로구 혜화로 3길 5 118호
등 록 1-1599호
전 화 (02)765-7145 **팩스** (02)765-7165
이메일 dongin60@chol.com

ISBN 978-89-5506-697-5 **정가** 18,000원

※ 잘못 만들어진 책은 바꾸어 드립니다.

토익영문법

나병모 지음

도서출판 동인

Contents

Chapter 01

Subjects

영어 문장은 주어(S) + 동사(V) + 목적어(O)의 어순을 가지며, 주어 자리에는 명사, 명사구, 부정사, 동명사, 명사절이 나타나야 한다.

SECTION 1-1

문장

Grammar Focus 1: 문장

영어의 문장은 주어(S)와 동사(V)로 이루어지며, 목적어(O), 보어(C), 수식어가 따르기도 한다.

- <u>The door</u> <u>opened</u>.
      S   V

  그 문이 열렸다.

- <u>The man</u> <u>opened</u> <u>the door</u>.
      S   V   O

  그 사람이 그 문을 열었다.

- <u>The cat</u> <u>saw</u> <u>a rat</u> in the garden.
      S   V   O

  그 고양이가 정원에서 쥐를 보았다.

- <u>The gentleman</u> <u>was</u> <u>very tall</u>.
         S   V   C

  그 신사는 매우 컸다.

접속사 다음에는 주어와 동사가 하나씩 나타난다.

- The dogs saw a cat **and** (they) chased it.
     S   V   S   V

  그 개들이 고양이를 보았으며, 뒤쫓았다.

- The rats ran away **when** they saw a cat.
     S   V   S   V

  그 쥐들이 고양이를 보았을 때 달아났다.

주격관계대명사에 이끌리는 절은 주어가 불필요하다.

- John wants to marry a girl **who/that** has blond hair and blue eyes.

  John은 금발과 파란 눈을 가진 여자와 결혼하고자 한다.

- Bill works for a company **which/that** sells cars.

  Bill은 자동차를 판매하는 회사에서 일한다.

Grammar Focus 2: 절의 종류

명사절은 문장에서 주어, 목적어, 보어 역할을 하는데, 주로 접속사인 that이나 whether로 시작되며, 의문사로 시작되기도 한다.

- He demonstrated **that he was a valuable member of this community**.

  그는 이 사회의 귀중한 구성원이라는 것을 증명하였다.

- **How he feels** is his business not mine.

  그가 어떻게 느끼는가 하는 것은 내 문제가 아니라 그의 문제야.

형용사절은 명사를 수식하는 절로 관계대명사나 관계부사로 시작된다.

- The book **which I bought** is regarded as one of the classics of American book design.

  내가 산 그 책은 미국 책 디자인의 고전 중의 하나로 여겨진다.

- Are there any parts of the city **where you live** *which you are afraid to visit after dark*?

  네가 사는 도시에서 어두워진 뒤 방문하기 두려운 곳이 있니?

부사절은 시간, 조건, 이유, 양보 등을 나타내는 절로 동사, 형용사, 부사, 문장을 수식한다.

- **When it comes to divorce**, British dads are at a disadvantage no matter how involved they've been in their children's lives.

  이혼 문제에 이르면, 영국의 아빠들은 아이들의 삶에 아무리 열중하였다 하더라도 불리하다.

- **Although he has been aggressive on domestic policy**, Kim's attitude toward foreign policy has taken a defensive tone.

  Kim이 국내 문제에 공격적이었지만, 대외정책에 대한 그의 태도는 방어적 논조를 취해왔다.

SECTION 1-2

주어

Grammar Focus 3: 주어

명사나 대명사가 주어로 쓰인다.

- **Cats** like boxes.

  고양이는 상자를 좋아한다.

- **They** like to sleep in boxes and other warm places.

  그들은 상자와 다른 따뜻한 곳에서 자는 것을 좋아한다.

명사구, 부정사, 동명사가 주어로 쓰인다.

- **The man next door** walked around his house naked.

  이웃집 남자가 벌거벗은 채 그의 집 주위를 걸어 다녔다.

- **To know** is one thing, and **to teach** is another.

  아는 것과 가르치는 것은 다르다.

- **Studying** in the United States can be expensive.

  미국에서 공부하는 것이 비용이 많이 들 수 있다.

that절과 의문사절이 주어로 쓰인다.

- **That the earth is round** is obvious to everyone.

  지구가 둥글다는 것은 모든 사람에게 명백하다.

- **How long they stay in the United States** depends on many things.
  미국에서 얼마나 오래 머무를 것인가는 많은 요인이 있다.

Point 1

문장은 주어를 가져야 하며, 명사, 대명사, 부정사, 동명사, 명사절 등이 주어로 쓰인다.

---

001 **Sit up** late is not good for the health.

어구 │ sit up 안 자다

002 In effect, **learn** the meaning of things is better than learning the meaning of words.

어구 │ in effect 사실상

003 _____ found four-leaf clover is considered a lucky sign.

(A) It is rarely   (B) Rarely

(C) The rarely   (D) Despite its being rarely

004 _____ have been discovered on top of peaks in the Rockies and the Appalachians, as far as a thousand miles from the nearest ocean.

(A) Fossils of sea creatures

(B) There are fossils of sea creatures

(C) Fossils of sea creatures that

(D) For fossils of sea creatures

어구 │ fossil *n.* 화석   creature *n.* 생물, 사람

005 _____ is of comparatively modern development.

(A) It is the game of tennis

(B) The game of tennis

(C) Though the game of tennis

(D) Like the game of tennis

어구 comparatively *adv.* 비교적, 꽤

006 _____ are eventually destroyed by the sea.

(A) Rocky shores lack beaches

(B) Rocky shores that lack beaches

(C) Rocky shores that are lack beaches

(D) Rocky shores that lacks beaches

어구 eventually *adv.* 결국   shore *n.* 해안

007 _____ dog was the first animal to be domesticated is generally agreed upon by authorities in the field.

(A) Until the   (B) It was the

(C) The   (D) That the

어구 domesticate *v.* 길들이다   authority *n.* 권위자

Point 2

접속사로 연결되지 않았을 때 문장에는 주어가 하나만 나타나야 한다.

---

008 Government library collections **they are** geared chiefly toward serving the need of government officials.

어구 gear *A* toward *B* B에 적합하도록 A를 맞추다   government official 공무원, 관료

009 **My professor he** says that the history of philosophy is simply a series of footnotes to Plato's works.

010 Dancer Isadora Duncan **who rebelled** against the rigid, formal training of classical ballet and created an individualistic form of expression.

어구 rebel *v.* 반대하다   individualistic *a.* 개인주의적

011 James Farmer, an American civil rights leader, **he** helped establish the Congress of Racial Equality, an organization that is dedicated to the principle of nonviolence.

어구 civil *a.* 시민의   establish *v.* 설립하다   congress *n.* 의회, 회합   equality *n.* 평등   dedicate *v.* 헌신하다, 바치다   nonviolence *n.* 비폭력

012 **It** took only 60 days to complete the merger is an extraordinary feat.

> 어구 merger *n.* 합병   feat *n.* 위업, 재주

013 **What** both astrology and alchemy may be regarded as fundamental aspects of thought is indicated by their apparent universality.

> 어구 astrology *n.* 점성술   alchemy *n.* 연금술   universality *n.* 보편성

014 _____ on water depends on the density of both the object and the water.

(A) An object floats   (B) Whether an object floats

(C) Does an object float   (D) So an object floats

> 어구 density *n.* 밀도

015 _____ the Mayan civilization declined is still a mystery but as with all mysteries there are a lot of theories.

(A) Why   (B) Since

(C) Because   (D) That

> 어구 civilization *n.* 문명   decline *v.* 쇠퇴하다

016 _____ made the first United States flag is widely believed.

(A) When Betsy Ross   (B) That Betsy Ross

(C) Betsy Ross   (D) Whether Betsy Ross

017 _____ often considered both a science and an art.

(A) Navigation is　　(B) It is navigation

(C) Navigation, which is　　(D) Navigation that is

어구 navigation *n.* 항해, 항법　　art *n.* 예술, 기술

018 _____ an increasing international exchange of educational films.

(A) It is　　(B) There is

(C) Though there is　　(D) Although it is

어구 exchange *n.* 교환

019 _____ a bicameral, or two-chamber, parliament.

(A) Canada has　　(B) Having Canada

(C) Because Canada　　(D) That Canada is having

어구 bicameral *a.* 상하 양원제의　　parliament *n.* 의회

PRACTICE TEST

020 The mediator in the labor dispute was replaced when her _____ was called into question.

(A) neutrality　　(B) neuter

(C) neutral　　(D) neutron

어구 mediator *n.* 중재자　　labor dispute 노동분쟁　　call into question 의문을 제기하다　　neutrality *n.* 중립성　　neuter *n.* 중성의　　neutron *n.* 중성자

021 In the second half of the nineteenth century, textiles from the south-western United States, particularly fabrics woven by the Navajo people, _____.

(A) began to be used as rugs　　(B) rugs began to be used

(C) as rugs began to be used　　(D) began to use them as rugs

textile *n.* 직물, 옷감   fabric *n.* 직물, 천   weave *n.* 짜다

022 _____ a lonely and rugged life, far from home and family.

(A) However the early gold prospector often lived

(B) The early gold prospector often lived

(C) Not only did the early gold prospector often live

(D) The early gold prospector often living

prospector *n.* 탐사자   rugged *a.* 누추한

023 _____ is rooted in experiments in iron and steel conducted in the nineteenth century.

(A) While the history of twentieth-century architecture

(B) The history of twentieth-century architecture

(C) That the history of twentieth-century architecture

(D) Both twentieth-century architecture and its history

024 _____ economic change by investigating the fluctuations in the relationship between workers' wages and their buying power.

(A) Economists gauging   (B) Economists gauge how

(C) Economists gauge   (D) Whenever economists gauge

investigate *v.* 조사하다   fluctuation *n.* 변동, 동요   wage *n.* 임금   buying power 구매력   gauge *v.* 측정하다

Chapter 02

Predicates

동사가 술부의 중심인데, 주어를 갖기 위해서는 시제 동사가 필요하다. 동사는 시제와 관계 없이 목적어, 보어를 가질 수 있으며, 수식어는 필수 요소가 아니다.

SECTION 2-1

시제동사

Grammar Focus 4: 시제동사

문장은 반드시 시제 동사를 가져야 한다.

- The sun **rises** in the east.
  해가 동쪽에서 뜬다.

- I **played** the piano in the afternoon with Lucy.
  나는 Lucy와 함께 그날 오후에 피아노를 쳤다.

- Peter **will come** to the party.
  Peter가 파티에 올 것이다.

Point 5

문장은 반드시 시제동사를 하나 가져야 한다.

025 Although Emily Dickinson is now a well-known American poet, only seven of her poems were published while she **alive**.

026 **It necessary** to contact the firm within a week or the contract will become ineffective.

027 Margaret Fuller was not active in the women's rights movement, but she **asking** for a fair chance for women in her book, *Woman in the Nineteenth Century*.

어구 | movement *n.* 운동   fair *a.* 공정한

028 **Being** sure to complete the evaluation form before you leave the seminar.

어구 | evaluation form 평가지

029 The grasslands of all continents **supporting** populations of grazing animals feeding on the grasses.

어구 | grassland *n.* 목초지   population *n.* 인구, 집단   grazing animal 방목 동물

030 Marilyn Monroe, a US film actress widely known as a sex symbol, **starring** in many adroit comedies.

어구 | adroit *a.* 손재주가 있는, 재치 있는

031 The nineteenth-century historian Harriet Maxwell Converse **having been** a tireless and effective lobbyist on behalf of American Indians.

어구 | on behalf of 대신하여

032 The mission of the museum is to display objects and highlight significant events that **reflecting** the city's cultural and industrial history.

어구 | mission *n.* 임무   highlight *v.* 강조하다, 집중조명하다

033 The office manager _____ supplies through a Web site that offers a wide range of products.

(A) purchase

(B) purchasing

(C) purchases

(D) to purchase

어구 | office manager *n.* 사무장, 사무실 관리자   supplies *n.* 물품   a wide range of 다양한

034 With affection and humor, poet Phyllis McGinley _____ of ordinary life.

(A) the virtues were praised   (B) praised the virtues

(C) she praised the virtues   (D) her praise of the virtues

035 The large compound eyes of the dragonfly _____ to see moving objects almost eighteen feet away.

(A) to enable it   (B) enabling it

(C) it enables   (D) enable it

036 Some economists maintain that fluctuations in the economy _____ from political events.

(A) resulting   (B) which result

(C) these result   (D) result

> **Point 6**
>
> 하나의 주어에 하나의 시제동사만 나타나야 한다.

037 A paragraph is a portion of a text **consists** of one or more sentences related to the same idea.

038 People **return** home after extended periods abroad often experience a number of problems connected with cultural gap.

039 Ducks have been domesticated for many centuries _____ commercially for their meat and eggs.

(A) raised   (B) and are raised

(C) raised as   (D) are raised

040 William Walker's mural, "Wall of Respect," _____ an outdoor wall in Chicago, deals with social issues.

(A) covers

(B) covers it

(C) which covers

(D) which it covers

Section 2-2

목적어

Grammar Focus 5: 목적어

명사나 대명사가 목적어로 쓰인다.

- The cat chased **a rat**.
  그 고양이가 쥐를 뒤쫓았다.

- The cat was running after **it**.
  그 고양이가 그것을 뒤쫓고 있었다.

명사구, 부정사, 동명사가 목적어로 쓰인다.

- The cat bit **the mouse's tail** off.
  그 고양이가 생쥐의 꼬리를 물어뜯었다.

- Bill wanted **to watch the movie**.
  Bill은 그 영화를 보기를 원했다.

- The mechanic finished **fixing the car**.
  그 정비사가 차 수리를 마쳤다.

that절과 whether/if절, 의문사절이 목적어로 쓰인다.

- Who believed **that Earth was the center of the Universe**?
  누가 지구가 우주의 중심이라고 믿었나요?

- I didn't know **whether she was going to start crying or hitting me**.
  나는 그녀가 울기 시작할지, 아니면 나를 때릴지 알 수 없었다.

- He wondered **if his father was still awake**, and **if he would beat him again**.

  그는 그의 아버지가 아직 깨어 있으신지, 그리고 아버지가 그를 다시 때리실지 궁금했다.

- He wondered **whose bike it was**, because he had never seen it before.

  그는 전에 그것을 본 적이 없었기 때문에 그게 누구의 자전거인지 궁금했다.

Grammar Focus 6: 가주어, 가목적어, 분리주어

주어나 목적어가 길 때 원래의 자리에 it을 쓰는데, 이를 가주어 또는 가목적어라 한다.

- **It** was hard **for him to live on his small pension**.

  그는 적은 연금으로 살기가 힘들었다.

- I must leave **it** to your own judgement **to decide whether you should offer your resignation**.

  나는 네가 사표를 내야 할 것인지를 결정하는 것을 너의 판단에 맡겨야 한다.

- Do you think **it** odd **that I should live alone**?

  내가 혼자 살아야 하는 것이 이상하다고 생각하니?

가주어-진주어 구문에서 부정사의 주어가 주절의 주어로 이동하여 주어가 나누어지는 구문이 있는데, 이러한 주어를 분리주어라 한다.

- **The baby** seems **to be asleep**.

  그 아이는 잠을 자고 있는 것 같다.

- **My inquiries** appear **to have been resented**.

  나의 질문이 분노를 샀었던 것 같다.

Point 7

동사의 목적어로는 명사, 대명사, 부정사, 동명사, 명사절이 쓰인다.

---

041 Responsibilities of this position include **achieve** sales goals and promoting cooperation between the regional bureaus.

어구 cooperation *n.* 협력   bureau *n.* 사무국

042 One of the tenets of New Criticism is that a critic need not tell readers **how to** think about a story.

> 어구 | tenet *n.* 주장　 new criticism *n.* 신비평

043 Pele, a Brazilian athlete, won **famous** as the greatest soccer player of his time and the most recognized athlete in world sports.

> 어구 | athlete *n.* 운동선수　 recognized *a.* 인정받는

044 Oliver Ellsworth, the third chief justice of the United States Supreme Court, was the author of the bill that **was established** the federal court system.

> 어구 | chief justice 대법원장　 Supreme Court 대법원　 bill *n.* 법안, 고지서

045 During adolescence many young people begin to question _____ held by their families.

(A) the values　　　　　　(B) of the values

(C) the values are　　　　(D) are the values

> 어구 | adolescence *n.* 청소년기

046 Animals obtain their energy from _____.

(A) eat their food　　　　(B) their food to eat

(C) the food they eat　　 (D) they eat the food

047 We often ask _____ the proper standard for making our decisions.

(A) that pleasure is　　　 (B) whether pleasure is

(C) what is pleasure　　　(D) which is pleasure

Point 8

명사나 동명사는 가목적어-진목적어 구문에 쓰이지 않는다.

---

048 The combination of two lenses makes **it** possible greater magnification than can be achieved with a single lens.

> 어구 | magnification *n.* 확대

049 Frederick Jones invented a refrigerator unit that **made it possible** the transportation of frozen foods by truck.

> 어구   transportation *n.* 운송

SECTION 2-3

보어

Grammar Focus 7: 보어

명사나 형용사가 보어로 쓰인다.

- The man is **a fool**.
  그 사람은 바보다.

- The man is **foolish**.
  그 사람은 바보스럽다.

부정사와 동명사가 보어로 쓰인다.

- Our job is **to make life better for our fellow Americans**, and **to help them to build a future of hope**.
  우리의 임무는 우리 미국인들의 삶을 개선하고, 그들이 희망찬 미래를 만드는 것을 도와주는 것이다.

- For me, seeing is **believing when it comes to SQL Server performance issues**.
  나에겐 SQL 서버 수행 문제에 관한 한 보는 것이 믿는 것이다.

that절과 whether절이 보어로 쓰인다.

- A final perspective is **that the crisis is the consequence neither of financial fragility nor of mistakes by important central banks**.
  최종적 견해는 그 위기가 중요한 중앙은행들의 재정적 취약성이나 실수의 결과가 아니라는 것이다.

- The real question is **whether their religion has helped them to prosper or even just survive**.
  현실적인 의문은 그들의 종교가 그들이 번성하는 데, 심지어 생존하는 데 도움이 되었느냐는 것이다.

Point 9

주어나 목적어를 서술해주는 요소가 필요할 때는 보어를 쓴다.

050 You need about forty different nutrients to stay **healthily**.

   어구   nutrient *n.* 영양소

051 The Red Wagon on Main Street is known for its impressive array of learning materials that encourage children to be **creativity**.

   어구   array *n.* 배열, 정렬

052 Traders became **more caution** as the finance department began to review the rules governing bond sales.

   어구   finance department 재무부   bond *n.* 공채

053 Coffee mixed with chicory is likely to taste _____ to a person not used to it.

   (A) sweetly   (B) bitter

   (C) bitterly   (D) well

   어구   chicory *n.* 치커리, 꽃상추

054 A politician can make a legislative proposal more _____ by giving specific examples of what its effect will be.

   (A) to understand   (B) understandably

   (C) understandable   (D) when understood

   어구   legislative *a.* 입법의   understandable *a.* 당연한

055 The chief objectives of American Federation of Teachers _____ professionalism in teaching and to secure appropriate wages, better working conditions, and job security for its members.

(A) to promote   (B) are promote

(C) are promoting   (D) are to promote

어구   objective *n.* 목적   federation *n.* 연합   professionalism *n.* 전문적 기술   secure *v.* 확보하다   wage *n.* 임금

SECTION 2-4

수식어

> **Grammar Focus 9: 수식어**
>
> 형용사나 분사가 명사를 전치 수식한다.
>
> - The citizenry will come up with **effective** solutions.
>   그 시민들이 효과적인 해결책을 제시할 것이다.
>
> - Parents should not be tempted to leave their **sleeping** babies in the car seat.
>   부모들은 잠자는 아기를 차의 좌석에 남겨두고 싶은 유혹을 받아서는 안 된다.
>
> - A ceremony was held to honor **fallen** soldiers at the National Cemetery.
>   국립묘지에서 죽은 병사를 기리기 위해 의식이 거행되었다.
>
> 전치사구, 분사구, 관계절 등이 명사를 후치 수식한다.
>
> - I met a pretty girl **with long hair**.
>   나는 긴 머리를 한 예쁜 소녀를 만났다.
>
> - He heard about the man **searching for his car keys under a streetlight**.
>   그는 가로등 아래서 자동차 열쇠를 찾고 있던 남자에 대해 들었다.
>
> - I met a pretty girl **who had long hair**.
>   나는 긴 머리의 예쁜 소녀를 만났다.
>
> 형용사와 부사는 부사의 수식을 받는다.

- Love is **so short**, and oblivion **so long**.

  사랑은 매우 짧고, 망각은 매우 길다.

- I ran **so fast that time and youth at last ran out**.

  내가 너무 빨리 달려서 시간과 젊음을 다써버렸다.

부사절이 문장을 수식한다.

- **When I was young** I believed in equality as a guiding principle in life.

  내가 어렸을 적에 평등을 삶의 지표라고 믿었다.

- **Although he was now a student** he still taught six to seven hours a day, six days a week, to support himself, his wife, and children.

  그가 그 당시에 학생이었지만 자신, 아내, 자식을 부양하기 위해 여전히 일주일에 6일간 매일 7시간씩 가르치고 있었다.

Point 10

명사는 형용사의 수식을 받는다

---

056 Ken Demino is such a **well** professor that his class has very little withdrawal.

> 어구   withdrawal *n.* 취소

057 Mr. Hazel analyzed his **personally** income to see if he could afford to rent a bigger house.

058 Seldom has the mathematical theory of games been of **practically** use in playing real games.

059 When the focus of a pair of binoculars is adjusted, **distance** objects can be brought into view.

> 어구   binoculars *n.* 쌍안경

060 The only flaw to her otherwise _____ travel was a little airsick-ness on the plane.

(A) perfection   (B) perfecting

(C) perfect   (D) perfected

어구 flaw *n.* 결점   airsickness *n.* 비행기 멀미

061 Staff _____ in the building after 10 PM are requested to use the rear exit when leaving.

(A) will remain   (B) remaining

(C) remain   (D) have remained

어구 rear *a.* 후방의

062 The maintenance shop has confirmed that _____ assessments of the engine, brakes and tires are done for all delivery trucks.

(A) frequent   (B) frequently

(C) frequents   (D) frequency

어구 maintenance shop 정비공장   delivery truck 화물 배달 트럭

Point 11

부사는 동사, 형용사, 부사, 문장을 수식한다.

---

063 The company's travel budget has been reduced **substantial**, so our executives will not be attending as many conferences as in the past.

어구 budget *n.* 예산   substantial *a.* 상당한

064 We are **regrettable** unable to forward the document you asked for about the project the other day.

어구 forward *v.* 전송하다

065 Obsidian, an uncommon volcanic rock, **polishes good** and makes an attractive semiprecious stone.

어구 obsidian *n.* 흑요석   volcanic *a.* 화산의   polish *v.* 닦다, 닦이다   semiprecious stone 준보석

066 If it were too far from the Sun, the Earth would be **too much** cold to support any living thing.

어구 support *v.* 지지하다, 살게하다

067 A liter is **scientific** defined as the volume of one kilogram of water at its maximum density.

어구 volume *n.* 양, 용적   density *n.* 밀도

068 He is _____ working in the same department after 20 years.

(A) already   (B) still

(C) before   (D) after

069 The security expert recommended that closed-circuit cameras hang _____ from the celling behind the store's cash registers.

(A) lowers   (B) lowly

(C) low   (D) lowest

어구 security expert 보안 전문가   recommend *v.* 권장하다   closed-circuit 폐쇄회로   cash register 금전등록기

070 Springwater is _____ clean, since it has been filtered through permeable rocks, but all spring water contains some dissolved minerals.

(A) generally fair   (B) generally fairly

(C) in general fair   (D) general and fair

어구 springwater *n.* 샘물   permeable *a.* 스며들 수 있는   dissolved *a.* 용해된

071 If the computer system had been shutdown _____, the loss of data could have been avoided.

(A) correct   (B) correctly

(C) correction   (D) correctness

072 Ms. Agrawala, the representative who went to the trade show, was instructed to report all new orders _____ to headquarters.

(A) direction   (B) directing

(C) directly   (D) directive

어구 │ representative *n.* 대표   trade show 시사회   instruct *v.* 명령하
         다   headquarter *n.* 본부

073 Geysers are found near rivers and lakes, where water drains through

the soil _____.

(A) surface below the deep   (B) deep below the surface

(C) the deep below surface   (D) the deep surface below

어구 │ geyser *n.* 간헐온천   drain *v.* 흘러 나가다

PRACTICE TEST

074 Seaweed nurtures numerous communities of living things, which are
protected under the wet coverings of the weeds while the tide out.

어구 │ seaweed *n.* 해조, 해초   nurture *v.* 양육하다

075 After only five years in Hollywood, the man able to buy a house in
the Beverly Hills and retired for life.

어구 │ retire *v.* 퇴직하다

076 The crocuses which bloom as the winter snow recedes and are

harbingers of approaching spring.

어구 │ crocus *n.* 크로커스(영국에서 봄에 제일 먼저 피는 꽃)   harbinger *n.* 선
         구자

077 Sociology, the study of humans in their collective aspect, _____ :

economic, social, political, and religious.

(A) and examines all group activities

(B) examines all group activities

(C) which examines all group activities

(D) examining all group activities

어구 sociology *n.* 사회학   collective *a.* 집단적인   aspect *n.* 양상

078 Fairs that were held to improve farming methods have been _____ in the agricultural history of the United States.

(A) much importance   (B) very important

(C) very importantly   (D) very importance

어구 fair *n.* 박람회, 품평회

079 The _____ result of the negotiation will be announced sometime next week.

(A) finalize   (B) final

(C) finally   (D) finalist

어구 negotiation *n.* 교섭

080 According to researchers Katharine Payne and Linda Guinee, the long, complex songs of the humpback whale _____ that appear to be similar to rhymes.

(A) containing sounds   (B) sounds contain

(C) which contain sounds   (D) contain sounds

어구 humpback whale 혹등고래   rhyme *n.* 각운

081 Potential dehydration is _____ that a land animal faces.

(A) the often greatest hazard   (B) the greatest often hazard

(C) often the greatest hazard   (D) often the hazard greatest

어구 dehydration *n.* 탈수증   hazard *n.* 위험

082 "Do you think that the labor bill will be passed?"

"Oh, yes. It's _____ that it will."

(A) almost surely   (B) very likely

(C) near positive   (D) quite certainly

어구 bill *n.* 법안

083 Mr. Kobayashi spoke quite _____ while he was making sales presentation.

(A) exciting

(B) excitable

(C) excitement

(D) excitedly

084 With the start for the penny papers in the 1830's, the number of people _____ a newspaper rose considerably.

(A) regularly reading

(B) were reading regularly

(C) regularly reading what

(D) who reading regularly

어구 considerably *adv.* 상당히, 꽤

085 At present production levels, _____ deposits of bauxite can provide the world with aluminum for hundreds of years.

(A) known

(B) known are

(C) they are known

(D) what is known

어구 deposit *n.* 매장층   bauxite *n.* 보크사이트

Chapter 03

Word Order

동사는 목적어의 유무에 따라 자동사와 타동사로 나뉘며, 주요 어순은 주어+동사+목적어이지만, 문두에 오는 요소에 따라 어순이 바뀌기도 한다.

┌─ **SECTION** 3-1 ─────────────────────────
│
│ 자동사
│
└───

Grammar Focus 10: 자동사

제1형식(주어+자동사)

- The moon **rose**.
  달이 떴다.

- He was **breathing** slowly and deeply.
  그는 천천히 그리고 깊이 숨을 쉬고 있었다.

제2형식(주어+자동사+보어)

- He **was** silent.(상태동사)
  그는 아무 말도 하지 않고 있었다.

- He **grew** silent.(상태변화동사)
  그는 조용해졌다.

- The soup **tasted** horrible.(감각동사)
  수프가 끔찍한 맛이 났다.

Point 12

자동사는 목적어를 취하지 못하며, 목적어를 취하려면 전치사가 필요하다.

086 The most explosive issue which the government must **deal** is deregulation of the aviation industry.

> 어구 explosive *a.* 폭발적인, 논쟁을 일으키는   deregulation *n.* 규제 해
> 제   aviation industry 항공 산업

087 In general, prawns **live shallow** coastal waters or in streams.

> 어구 prawn *n.* 참새우(lobster보다 작고 shrimp보다는 큰 것)

088 Her untiring energy _____ her obvious success.

(A) resulted   (B) have resulted

(C) resulted from   (D) resulted in

> 어구 untiring *a.* 불굴의, 지치지 않는

089 A lunar eclipse _____ the earth passes between the sun and the
moon, causing the moon to become dark.

(A) occurs   (B) that occurs

(C) which occurs   (D) occurs when

> 어구 lunar eclipse 월식

Point 13

자동사는 목적어를 취하지 못하므로 수동태를 쓰지 못한다.

090 Though smaller than our solar system, a quasar, which **is looked**
like an ordinary star, emits more light than an entire galaxy.

> 어구 quasar *n.* 준성(準星)   emit *v.* 발산하다   galaxy *n.* 은하계

091 Marine snails **are occurred** in all seas from the Arctic to the Antarctic, though they reach their greatest development in tropical waters.

> 어구 marine *a.* 바다의   Arctic *n.* 북극   Antarctic *n.* 남극   tropical *a.* 열
> 대의

타동사

Grammar Focus 11: 타동사

제3형식 (주어+타동사+목적어)

- We all **had** a good time.
  우리 모두 즐거운 시간을 보냈다.

- He's **agreed** to let the family know.
  그는 가족이 알도록 하는 것에 동의하였다.

- He **stopped** smoking.
  그는 담배를 끊었다.

- He **claimed** that he had been underpaid.
  그는 박봉이었다고 주장하였다.

  cf. He **complained** that he had been underpaid.
       그는 박봉이었다고 불평하였다.

- They **decided on** the boat.(자동사+전치사)
  그들은 배를 타기로 결정하였다.

  cf. The boat was decided on.

제4형식 (주어+동사+간접목적어+직접목적어)

- He **sold** me his old car.
  그는 나에게 그의 낡은 차를 팔았다.

  cf. He sold his old car **to** me.

- He **built** her a cabin.
  그는 그녀에게 오두막을 지어 주었다.

  cf. He built a cabin **for** her.

- He **promised** me to sell the car.
  그는 나한테 차를 팔겠다고 약속했다.

- I gave **it** a thought.
  나는 그것을 생각해 보았다.

- I **envy** you your fine garden.
  나는 너의 훌륭한 정원이 부럽다.

제5형식(주어+동사+목적어+목적보어)

- They **declared** Newton President of the Royal Society.
  그들은 Newton을 Royal Society의 회장으로 발표하였다.

- They **saw** the thief running away.
  그들은 그 도둑이 달아나는 것을 보았다.

- I've never **known** him sing so beautifully before.
  나는 그가 전에 그렇게 아름답게 노래를 부른다는 것을 전혀 알지 못했다.

Point 14

타동사는 서로 다른 유형의 목적어를 취하며, 전치사가 불필요하다.

---

092 The tough skin formed by dried linseed oil does not break or chip, and **resists to** changes in the weather.

> 어구 linseed *n.* 아마씨   chip *v.* 깨지다   resist *v.* 저항하다, 견디다

093 The experts offered their thoughts on how to bridge that gap and **discussed about** the diversity of businesses.

094 The Supreme Court **comprises of** the chief justice of the United States and eight associate justices.

> 어구 chief justice 대법원장   associate justice 대법원판사

095 This chapter **describes about** how to protect data against operating system crashes, file corruption, disk failures, and total machine failure.

Point 15

5형식 동사는 목적어와 목적보어를 취하며, 수동태에서는 목적보어가 나타나야 한다.

---

096 Steven Spielberg, whose highly successful films have given popular cinema a new appeal, is **considered by** one of the best movie directors in the United States.

097 Alaska's rough climate and terrain divide the state into isolated regions, making highway maintenance **difficulty**.

> 어구   terrain *n.* 지형

098 Stress suppresses the body's immune system, thus making people **are more** likely to become ill.

> 어구   suppress *v.* 억누르다, 막다   immune system 면역 체계

099 The giraffe's long neck and legs are the most obvious features that **make** different from all other animals.

> 어구   feature *n.* 특징

100 X-rays are able to pass through objects and thus make **them** visible details that are otherwise impossible to observe.

> 어구   visible *a.* 가시적인

101 Like other women who pioneered in the field of medicine, Sara Mayo _____.

    (A) found the beginning years difficult

    (B) found difficult the beginning years

    (C) found the beginning years difficultly

    (D) found that the beginning years difficult

> 어구   pioneer *v.* 개척하다

SECTION 3-3

도치

> **Grammar Focus 12: 도치**
>
> 부정어가 문두에 오면 주어와 조동사가 도치된다. 조동사가 없을 때는 do(es)나 did 를 쓴다.
>
> - **Neither** did he do his homework, nor took a shower.

그는 숙제도 안 하고, 샤워도 하지 않았다.

- **Scarcely** was she seated afresh when she heard the voice again.
  그녀가 자세를 고쳐 앉자마자 그 목소리가 다시 들렸다.

- **No sooner** had I arrived at the station than the train came in.
  역에 도착하자마자 기차가 들어왔다.

- **Not** until yesterday did he tell me something about the trip.
  그는 여행에 대해서 어제서야 나한테 말해 주었다.

부사나 형용사가 문두에 올 때 도치가 되는 경우가 있다. 이런 구문에 쓰이는 동사나 부사는 매우 제한되어 있다.

- Here comes the sun.
  여기에 태양이 떠오른다.

- There lived a king and a queen.
  어떤 왕과 왕비가 살았다.

- Happy are those whose hearts are pure, for they shall see God.
  마음이 순수한 자는 하느님을 볼 것이기 때문에 행복하다.

Point 16

간접의문문에서는 도치가 일어나지 않는다.

---

102 Could you tell me where **is Tim** so I can give him a message before I leave?

103 Our report was translated into English, so they should understand what **means it**.

104 She wanted to know when **was the last staff meeting** so that she could prepare for the next one.

105 In the field of acting theory, controversy arises over the question of whether **is acting** a behavioral or a mental process.

어구   acting *n.* 연기   mental *a.* 정신적인

106 Hardly ever **the two were** able to talk freely without being over-heard by their parents.

107 But hardly _____ when the sky became overcast and down came the rain again.

(A) he had started (B) he started

(C) had he started (D) he has started

> 어구 overcast *a.* 흐린, 구름으로 덮인

108 Not until his life was over _____ which he had sown bear fruit.

(A) the seed did (B) the seed that

(C) did the seed (D) that the seed

> 어구 sow *v.* (씨를) 뿌리다 bear *v.* (열매를) 맺다

109 A sneeze cannot be performed voluntarily, _____ be easily sup-pressed.

(A) nor can it (B) and cannot it

(C) nor it can (D) it cannot

> 어구 sneeze *n.* 재채기 suppress *v.* 억압하다, 참다

110 No only _____ the suppliers send the wrong components, but they also sent them to the wrong department.

(A) had (B) did

(C) were (D) have

> 어구 component *n.* 부품

병렬구조

Grammar Focus 13: 병렬구조

등위접속사로 연결된 단어는 품사가 동일해야 한다.

- **Poverty, crime and migration** are acute issues as Eastern European cities continue to grow.
  동유럽의 도시들이 성장함에 따라 가난, 범죄, 이주는 민감한 문제이다.

- They **talked and sang and read** together in a **wonderful and unspeakable** intimacy.
  그들은 놀랍고도 말할 수 없는 정도의 친밀감을 가지고 함께 말하고, 노래하고, 읽었다.

- She is **pretty, tall, and athletic**, with a direct personality.
  그녀는 직선적인 성격으로, 예쁘고, 크고, 발랄하다.

- He replied, speaking **slowly but clearly**.
  그는 천천히 그러나 분명하게 말하면서 대답했다.

등위접속사로 연결된 구는 동일한 형태의 구이어야 한다.

- The key should be left **in the room or in the locked postbox** next to the elevator on the 1st floor when you leave.
  떠날 때 열쇠는 방이나 1층의 엘리베이터 옆의 잠긴 우편함에 넣어 두어야 한다.

- You have been pressured **to smoke or to continue smoking**, but you didn't.
  여러분은 담배를 피우도록 압력을 받거나 계속해서 담배를 피우도록 압력을 받아왔지만 담배를 피우지 않았다.

- Exercise—even simple everyday exercise like **walking, swimming or dancing**—helps boost your general **health, strength and balance**.
  걷기, 수영, 춤과 같은 일상적인 간단한 운동은 당신의 전반적인 건강, 힘, 균형을 향상시킨다.

등위접속사로 연결되는 절은 동일한 종류의 절이어야 한다.

- Most people do not buy furniture or fancy goods **because they like them, but because the shopman persuades them that**

what they buy is the fashion.

많은 사람들은 가구나 장신구를 좋아해서 사는 것이 아니라, 자기가 사는 것이 유행이라고 점원이 설득하기 때문에 산다.

Point 18

등위접속사로 연결된 요소들은 동일한 품사를 가져야 한다.

---

111 Before constructing a bridge, the designers must consider the **deep** and width of the barrier.

112 Cobalt resembles iron and nickel in tensile strength, appearance, and **hard**.

> 어구 tensile *a.* 잡아 늘일 수 있는, 신장성 있는

113 The doctor's records must be kept **thorough** and neatly, so as to insure good book-keeping.

> 어구 book-keeping *n.* 부기

114 *Poor Richard Almanac*, a series of writing by Benjamin Franklin, expounds the merits of such homely virtues as diligence, **thrifty**, and hard work.

> 어구 expound *v.* 설명하다   merit *n.* 장점   homely *a.* 가정적인, 수수한   virtue *n.* 미덕   thrift *n.* 검소

115 The brochures are being rechecked by the professional writers for accuracy and overall _____.

(A) clearance   (B) clarify

(C) clarity   (D) clear

> 어구 brochure *n.* 소책자   overall *a.* 전반적인   clearance *n.* 정리   clarify *v.* 명료하게 하다   clarity *n.* 명료성

Point 19

등위접속사로 연결된 요소들은 동일한 형태를 가져야 한다.

---

116 When **slowly dried** and naturally, raisins are high in iron and other minerals.

117 In this examination we will have to pass tests on our ability to read, reason clearly, follow directions and **spelling** correctly.

118 It is not work, but **to overwork**, that is hurtful; and it is not hard work that is injurious so much as unwilling work.

> 어구 injurious *a.* 유해한　　unwilling *a.* 내키지 않는　　not *A* so much as *B* A라기 보다는 B

119 Squanto acted as an interpreter in the treaty negotiations between the Pilgrims and the Navajos, and he taught the Pilgrims how to fish and **cultivating** corn.

> 어구 interpreter *n.* 통역가　　treaty *n.* 조약　　Pilgrim *n.* 청교도

120 Cooperation is the mutual endeavor of two or more persons to perform a task or **reaching** a jointly cherished goal.

> 어구 mutual *a.* 상호의　　endeavor *n.* 노력　　jointly *adv.* 공동으로　　cherish *v.* 소중히 여기다

121 Worker bees labor for the good of the hive by collecting food, caring for the young, and **to expand** the nest.

> 어구 worker bee 일벌　　for the good of … 을 위하여

122 Since Atlanta is a chief transportation center, many leading firms have branches there for manufacturing, warehousing, and **distribute** their products.

> 어구 leading *a.* 일류의　　warehouse *v.* 창고에 넣다　　distribute *v.* 분배하다

123 Graying hair, **gain weight**, and greater difficulty in recuperating from physical exertion may be physiological indices of a person's advancing age.

> 어구 recuperate *v.* 회복하다　　exertion *v.* 노력, 힘든 작업　　physiological *a.* 생리적인

124 Some people prefer hotels to apartment buildings, but most like _____ the best of the three.

(A) a house

(B) the house

(C) houses

(D) the houses

125 The end of law is not to abolish or restrain, _____ and enlarge freedom.

    (A) but to preserve   (B) but preserve

    (C) but preserving   (D) but also to preserve

> 어구   abolish *v.* 철폐하다   restrain *v.* 구속하다   enlarge *v.* 확대하다

126 Americans can conserve gasoline by picking fuel-efficient autos, joining car pools, and _____.

    (A) mass transit use   (B) use of mass transit

    (C) using mass transit   (D) use mass transit

> 어구   transit *n.* 수송

PRACTICE TEST

127 The works of the author Herman Melville are literary creations of a high order, blending fact, fiction, adventure, and subtle symbolic.

> 어구   adventure *n.* 모험   subtle *a.* 미묘한

128 The mechanic studied electronics in night school so as to be promoted and transferring to another job.

129 The photoperiodic response of algae actually depends on the duration of darkness, but is not on light.

> 어구   photoperiodic *a.* 광주기의   algae *n.* 녹조

130 Natural adhesives are primarily of animals or vegetable origin.

> 어구   adhesive *n.* 접착제

131 Why is a man in civil life perpetually slandering and backbiting his fellow men, and is unable to see good even in his friends?

> 어구   slander *v.* 비방하다   backbite *v.* 험담하다

132 Ethics is the branch of philosophy that deals with the values of life in coherent, systematic, and science manner.

어구 ethics *n.* 윤리학   coherent *a.* 일관성 있는

133 Perhaps the most popular film in movie history, *Star Wars* was written and direction by George Lucas.

134 "Tom is going fishing tomorrow."

"_____."

(A) So am I (B) So Mary is

(C) So I am (D) So do I

135 Unlike hummingbirds, sunbirds tend to perch on the flower they are probing _____.

(A) rather than to hover around it

(B) than rather hover around it

(C) rather than their hovering around it

(D) to hover rather than around it

어구 hummingbird *n.* 벌새   sunbird *n.* 태양새   perch *v.* 앉다   probe *v.* 찾다   hover *v.* 맴돌다

136 Congress chartered the first Bank of the United States in 1791 to engage in general commercial banking and _____ as a fiscal agent of the federal government.

(A) to act (B) acting

(C) that has acted (D) having acted

어구 charter *v.* 인가하다   fiscal *a.* 국가재정의

137 The astronomical unit is the average distance of the Earth from the Sun _____ is the standard of distances in the Solar System.

(A) and (B) also

(C) in addition (D) because

어구 astronomical *a.* 천문학의

138 The function of Congress is to make laws, but nowhere in the Constitution _____ about the exact steps that must be taken in the law-making process.

(A) a statement is there
(B) it is a statement
(C) there a statement is
(D) is a statement

어구   Constitution *n.* 헌법

139 _____ allow it to reach the highest branches, but also it lets the animal see over long distances.

(A) Not only the giraffe's tall neck
(B) The giraffe's tall neck not only
(C) Not only does the giraffe's tall neck
(D) Only the giraffe's tall neck does not

140 It would be difficult for a man of his political affiliation, _____, to become a senator from the south.

(A) though charming and capable is he
(B) even with charm and so capable
(C) charming and having capability
(D) however charming and capable

어구   affiliation *n.* 소속, 제휴

Chapter 04

Tenses

동사는 시제(tense), 태(voice), 서법(mood)을 나타내는데, 특히 시제동사는 문장을 이루는 중요한 요소로 부정사, 동명사, 분사와 같은 준동사와 구별된다.

SECTION 4-1

현재시제

Grammar Focus 14: 현재시제

단순현재는 일반적 사실이나 습관을 나타낸다.

- At sea level water **boils** at 212 degrees Fahrenheit.
  해면에서 물은 화씨 212도에서 끓는다.

- School doors **open** for children eating breakfast at 7:45 AM.
  교문은 아침식사를 하는 어린이를 위해 오전 7시 45분에 연다.

- I **start** for school at 10 past 8 in the morning.
  나는 아침 8시 10분에 등교한다.

현재진행은 지금 일어 나고 있는 일, 최근에 일어 나고 있는 일을 나타낸다. always 나 usually와 같은 표현과 함께 쓰이면 짜증나는 일을 나타낸다.

- He **is studying** in the library right now.
  그는 지금 도서관에서 공부하고 있다.

- He **is writing** a book on the American novel since World War II.
  그는 2차 세계대전 이후의 미국소설에 관한 책을 쓰고 있다.

- She **is always talking** back to me, and I am not sure how to stop this.

  그녀는 항상 말대꾸를 하는데, 어떻게 이것을 그만두게 할지 모르겠다.

Point 20

일반적 사실이나 진리를 나타낼 때 단순현재를 쓴다.

141 The first tooth usually emerges when an infant **was** about six months old.

142 During the period of inflation, the value of money drops as prices **rose**.

143 Kiwi birds mainly eat insects, worms, and snails and **searched** for their food by probing the ground with their long bills.

> 어구 kiwi *n.* 뉴질랜드의 새   probe *v.* 찾다   bill *v.* 부리

Point 21

현재의 습관을 나타낼 때 단순현재를 쓴다.

144 He **commuted** by subway between Seoul and Incheon every day.

> 어구 commute *v.* 출퇴근하다

145 Buyers are responsible for supplying the goods and services that an organization **required** for its operations.

146 Everyone usually leaves the office as soon as the boss _____ home.

(A) will go   (B) goes to

(C) goes   (D) went

Point 22

말하는 시점에서 일어나고 있는 일을 나타낼 때 현재진행형을 쓴다.

147 One of the essential features of the modern skyscraper **is being** the elevator.

> 어구   skyscraper *n.* 고층건물

148 Battery-operated reading lamps _____ very well right now.

(A) sale   (B) are selling

(C) were sold   (D) sold

149 We are _____ David to arrive on the 3:30 flight from Boston.

(A) to expect   (B) expecting

(C) to expecting   (D) expected

> 어구   flight *n.* 항공편

SECTION 4-2

과거시제

Grammar Focus 15: 과거시제

과거에 일어난 일, 혹은 역사적 사실을 서술할 때는 단순과거를 쓰는데 ago나 last year와 같이 구체적으로 과거 시점을 나타내는 표현과 함께 쓰인다. 과거시점을 나타내는 표현이 없을 때는 used to와 would를 사용하여 과거의 습관을 나타내는데, 특히 과거의 상태는 used to를 쓴다.

- It doesn't make a difference where they **went** to school last year.
  그들이 지난해에 어디서 학교를 다녔든 차이가 없다.

- Columbus **discovered** the islands he thought to be the Indies on the twelfth of October, 1492.
  Columbus는 1492년 10월 12일 인도제국이라고 생각했던 섬을 발견하였다.

- They **used to** call me Snow White.
  그들은 나를 백설공주라고 부르곤 했다.

- I **used to** be very shy.
  나는 매우 수줍었다.

- They **would** often listen to their father read aloud to their mother.

  그들은 아버지가 어머니한테 책을 크게 읽어 주시는 것을 자주 듣곤 했다.

과거진행은 과거의 어떤 사건이 일어난 시점에 진행되고 있는 일을 나타내는 데 쓰인다. 즉, 단순과거로 표현된 사건은 짧은 순간에 일어난 일인 반면, 과거진행으로 표현된 사건은 일정한 시간동안 일어난 일이다.

- I thought a girl **was singing** when I heard voices through my speaker.

  나는 내 스피커를 통해 목소리를 들었을 때 그녀가 노래를 부르고 있다고 생각했다.

Point 23

과거 어떤 시점에 일어난 일은 과거를 쓴다.

---

150 During most of the last century, A. Philip Randolph struggled for Black rights in the United States and **becomes** an important figure in the labor movement.

> 어구 figure *n.* 인물   labor movement 노동운동

151 Louis Armstrong quickly won recognition as a trumpeter and vocalist and **has** a major influence on the development of jazz in the 1920's.

> 어구 recognition *n.* 인정

152 Once the scientist had figured out the precise path of comet, he **is finding** that he was able to predict its next appearance.

> 어구 figure out 이해하다   comet *n.* 혜성

153 The French explorers Marquette and Joliet were the first Europeans to explore the region that later **becomes** Illinois.

154 He _____ a few minutes ago.

  (A) goes out   (B) has gone out
  (C) went out   (D) will go out

155 I _____ my airline reservation last Monday.

(A) have made	(B) make
(C) made	(D) will make

> 어구   reservation *n.* 예약

156 Do you remember how many years ago _____ the corporation there?

(A) we visit	(B) we visited
(C) did you visit	(D) we have visited

> 어구   corporation *n.* 회사

157 The reception clerk _____ on the telephone when the phone went dead.

(A) talked	(B) is taking
(C) was talking	(D) would talk

> 어구   reception clerk 객실 접수원

SECTION 4-3
현재완료와 과거완료

Grammar Focus 16: 현재완료(진행)

과거의 어떤 시점에 일어난 일이 현재까지 일어나거나 금방 종료된 사건을 나타낼 때 현재완료를 쓴다. 흔히 for나 since와 같은 기간을 나타내는 표현과 함께 쓰인다. 어떤 사건이 종료되지 않고 계속되고 있다는 것을 명확히 하고자 할 때는 현재완료 진행을 쓴다.

- I **have just bought** a car from my neighbour.
  나는 내 이웃한테서 방금 차를 한 대 샀다.

- She **has been** happy doing what she does in Oxford.
  그녀는 옥스퍼드대학교에서 하고 있는 것에 만족해왔다.

- I **have been working** with computers for the last twelve years.
  나는 지난 12년간 컴퓨터로 일을 해왔다.

Point 24

현재완료는 have+V-en의 형태로 과거와 현재가 모두 포함된 것을 나타낸다.

158 Since he went to New York, we have not **hear** of him yet.

159 Baltimore claims to have **being** the first city in the U.S. to have streets illuminated by gas light.

> 어구   illuminate *v.* 비추다

160 The company **doesn't** decided yet where to locate the new branch office.

> 어구   locate *v.* 찾다

161 The job market _____ tight recently owing to the depression in business.

(A) is   (B) have been

(C) has been   (D) is become

> 어구   depression *n.* 불황

162 _____ the trumpet has played a leading role in the development of jazz.

(A) From this century

(B) Since this century has begun

(C) As this century began

(D) Since the beginning of this century

> 어구   leading *a.* 중요한

163 Our company _____ the Metro Messenger Center since 1990.

(A) use   (B) used

(C) has been using   (D) had used

164 He _____ several sessions of the Board of Directors since he was promoted to the post of director.

(A) attended   (B) has attended

(C) attends   (D) was attended

> 어구   board of directors 이사회   session *n.* 회의

165 Ten years _____ since he died of liver cancer.

(A) are   (B) have passed

(C) has passed   (D) passed

Grammar Focus 17: 과거완료

주어진 어떤 과거 시점보다 먼저 일어난 사건을 기술하고자 하거나, 과거의 어떤 시점에 종료된 사건을 기술하고자 할 때 과거완료를 쓴다.

- I thought she **had stopped** breathing.
  나는 그녀가 숨을 쉬지 않는다고 생각했다.

- I **had just finished** working a five hour shift of extremely physical labor.
  나는 아주 체력이 필요한 5시간의 근무를 금방 마쳤다.

Point 25

과거완료는 had+V-en의 형태로 과거 이전에 일어나 과거에 종료된 일이나, 과거보다 먼저 일어난 일을 나타낸다.

---

166 It was discovered where he had **was** all the while.

> 어구   all the while 그 동안 내내

167 Archaeologists recently unearthed artifacts indicating that the pre-Incan people of South America **developed** artistic and architectural skills as complex as those of the Incas.

> 어구   archaeologist *n.* 고고학자   unearth *v.* 발굴하다   artifact *n.* 인공
> 유물

168 By 1988 Gordon Parks had made two documentary films, **wrote** two bestselling books, and had accrued thirty years of experience in still photography.

> 어구   accrue *v.* 모으다, 생기다   still photography 정물사진

169 _____ received the message a week before he came.

    (A) I'm   (B) I've

    (C) I'd   (D) I

170 Hardly _____ I arrived at the branch office when I took measures to reform it.

    (A) did   (B) have

    (C) had   (D) am

> 어구   branch office 지점   measure *n.* 조치

171 Before 1892, the atom _____ a tiny, unsplittable particle, the smallest portion of matter.

    (A) has been considered   (B) were considering

    (C) had been considered   (D) had been considering

> 어구   atom *n.* 원자   unsplittable *a.* 쪼갤 수 없는   particle *n.* 분자

SECTION 4-4

미래시제

Grammar Focus 18: 단순미래

미래의 사건을 기술하고자 할 때 will이나 be going to를 쓴다.

- I don't think it **will rain** this afternoon.
  I don't think it**'s going to rain** this afternoon.
  오늘 오후에 비가 올 것 같지 않다.

둘 다 예측을 나타낼 때 쓸 수 있지만, 그 자리에서 결정되는 일을 나타낼 때는 will을 쓰며, 사전에 결정된 것을 나타낼 때는 be going to를 쓴다.

- I **will pick** up the phone.
  내가 전화를 받을게.

- I **am going to have** steak within the next few days.
  나는 며칠 내에 스테이크를 먹으려고 해.

미래를 나타내는 다양한 표현이 있는데, 현재진행, 현재가 미래를 나타내기도 한다.

- We **are leaving** tonight and won't be back for almost a month.
  우리는 오늘밤 떠나서 거의 한 달간 돌아오지 않을 거야.

- The plane **leaves** Chicago at 11:30 and **arrives** in Atlanta at 2:45.
  비행기가 11시 30분에 Chicago를 떠나서 2시 45분에 Atlanta에 도착한다.

- The sky was cloudy as if it **was about to** rain.
  곧 비가 올 것처럼 하늘이 흐렸다.

특히 시간이나 조건을 나타내는 부사절에서는 미래를 나타낼 때 반드시 단순현재를 쓴다.

- When I **leave** school I will go to University and then work with the endangered birds of New Zealand.
  학교를 졸업하면 대학에 가서 멸종위기에 처한 뉴질랜드의 조류를 연구할 것이다.

- Will you come for a walk in the afternoon if it **does not rain**?
  비가 오지 않으면 오후에 산보하려 오겠니?

Point 26

미래를 나타내는 표현이 있을 때는 미래시제를 쓴다.

---

172 It is reported that the railroad fare **is** raised by 30% next January.

어구   fare *n.* 요금

173 The girl _____ going to the movies with her boyfriend this Saturday.

  (A)   will   (B)   she always was

  (C)   she is   (D)   is

174 The spaceship _____ the earth for the moon next Saturday.

  (A)   leaving   (B)   left

  (C)   leave   (D)   leaves

175 As soon as the work **will be** done, we will have our dinner.

176 A desert area that has been without water for six years will still bloom when rain **will come**.

177 The paychecks are deposited in the employees' accounts unless the employees **will require** otherwise.

> 어구 paycheck *n.* 급여   deposit *v.* 예치하다   account *n.* 계좌   otherwise *adv.* 다른 방법으로

178 She is going to buy a hat after she _____ the check.

(A) will cash

(B) cashes

(C) cashed

(D) could cash

> 어구 cash a check 수표를 현금으로 바꾸다

Grammar Focus 20: 미래진행 및 완료

미래진행은 어떤 일이 미래에 자연스럽게 일어나게 되는 것을 나타낼 때 쓰인다. 미래완료는 미래의 특정 시간 이전에 일어나는 일을 나타낼 때 쓴다.

- I **will be staying** at a Disney World hotel in June.
  나는 6월에 디즈니월드의 한 호텔에 묵고 있을 거야.

- I **will have taught** English for 10 years by next March.
  나는 다음 3월이면 영어를 10년간 가르치게 된다.
---

179 By next year, the most of our staff will **be trained** to use the new computer system.

180 He _____ one-third of his military service by this time next year.

(A) is completing   (B) completes

(C) will complete   (D) will have completed

어구	military service 군복무

181 This time next month we _____ the result of the market research.

(A) will have received   (B) have received

(C) had received   (D) were receiving

SECTION 4-5

시제 일치

Grammar Focus 21: 시제 일치

주절의 시제가 과거일 때 주절과 같은 시간에 일어난 일은 과거, 주절보다 먼저 일어난 일은 과거완료를 쓴다.

- John **believes** that Mary **is** pregnant.
  → John **believed** that Mary **was** pregnant.

- John **believes** that Mary **was** in Egypt.
  → John **believed** that Mary **had been** in Egypt.

- They **believe** that John **was** in Egypt.
  → John **is believed** to **have been** in Egypt.

진리, 습관, 역사적 사실은 시제 일치의 예외이다.

- They **believed** that the earth **is** round.
  그들은 지구가 둥글다고 믿었다.

- Susie **said** she **rises** as early as 5 a.m. to work at the coffee shop.
  Susie는 커피숍에서 일하기 위해 새벽 5시에 일어난다고 말했다.

- I **learned** that Columbus **discovered** America in 1492.

나는 Columbus가 1492년에 미대륙을 발견했다고 배웠다.

Point 29

주절의 시제가 과거이면 종속절의 시제는 과거나 과거완료를 쓴다.

---

182 The officials said the leaders **confirm** their commitment to maintain close cooperation.

> 어구   commitment *n.* 약속, 헌신

183 Ms. Jenkins knew she **will** have to go as soon as possible if she wanted to catch the last flight.

PRACTICE TEST

184 We expect that he is promoted to the manager of the new workshop.

> 어구   promote *v.* 승진시키다

185 After his trips to the west between 1860 and 1872, Ralph Alber Bakelock would often painted American Indian encampments on brown-and-yellow-toned canvases.

> 어구   encampment *n.* 야영지

186 Over forty years ago, Helen Hall's outstanding contributions as a settlement organizer catch the attention of president Franklin Roosevelt, who appointed her to his advisory committee on economic security.

> 어구   advisory committee 자문위원회

187 Soil science begun with the formulation of the theory of humus in 1809.

> 어구   soil science 토양학   humus *n.* 부식

188 Coal and petroleum resulted when plants become buried in swamps and decayed.

> 어구   coal *n.* 석탄   petroleum *n.* 석유   swamp *n.* 늪, 습지

189 Delaware is known as the "First State" because on December 7, 1787, it was being the first state to approve the United States Constitution.

> 어구 constitution *n.* 헌법

190 In the New England colonies, Chippendale designs are adapted to local tastes, and beautiful furniture resulted.

> 어구 adapt *v.* 적응하다

191 Some art historians have say that too many artists have tried only to imitate previous painting styles.

192 _____, Antarctica was part of the giant continent that geologists call Gondwanaland.

(A) In about 175 million years ago

(B) About 175 million years ago

(C) Since about 175 million years ago

(D) For about 175 million years ago

> 어구 Antarctica *n.* 남극   geologist *n.* 지질학자

193 She is one of the few girls who _____ passed the examination.

(A) have   (B) has

(C) had   (D) was

194 Penicillin is perhaps the drug _____ more lives than any other in the history of medicine.

(A) what has saved   (B) which saved

(C) which has saved   (D) who saves

195 The corporation, which underwent a major restructuring seven years ago, has been growing steadily _____ five years.

(A) for   (B) on

(C) from   (D) since

어구 corporation *n.* 회사   undergo *v.* 겪다

196 The board meeting _____ going on since nine o'clock in the morning.

(A) is

(B) was

(C) has been

(D) will be

어구 board meeting 이사회

197 The people of that country _____ amicable to those of other countries so far.

(A) have not been

(B) are not

(C) has not been

(D) do not

어구 amicable *a.* 우호적인

Chapter 05

Conditional Sentences

사실을 있는 그대로 말하지 않고 반대의 가정을 하여 말하고자 할 때 가정법을 쓴다. 가정법의 종류는 조건절 동사의 시제에 따라 분류한 것으로, 가정법과거는 현재사실의 반대, 가정법과거완료는 과거사실의 반대를 나타낸다.

SECTION 5-1

가정법과거

Grammar Focus 22: 가정법과거

가정법과거는 현재 사실의 반대를 나타낸다. 조건절에 과거동사가 오며 귀결절에 would/could/might/should+V가 온다.

- If I **taught** a morning class, then I **would need** several bath-room runs.
  내가 오전반을 가르친다면 화장실에 수차례 가야 할 것이다.

- If he **were** your son, how **would** you **respond**?
  내가 당신의 아들이라면 당신은 어떤 반응을 보이실 겁니까?

가정법과거완료

Grammar Focus 23: 가정법과거완료

가정법과거완료는 과거사실의 반대를 나타낸다. 조건절에 had+V-en이 오며, 귀결절에 would/could/might/should+have+V-en이이 온다.

● If he **had been** able to read, as he once had been, he **would have read** something similar.
만약 그가 한 때 그랬던 것처럼 읽을 수 있었다면 비슷한 것을 읽었을 것이다.

● If he **had been playing** we **would have won**.
만약 그가 경기를 했었더라면 우리가 이겼을 것이다.

Point 30

현재 사실의 반대를 나타낼 때는 가정법과거를 쓴다. 특히 was 대신 were를 쓴다.

---

198 Ms. Furtado would help with the program testing if she **is not** supervising the inventory project.

어구 | supervise *v.* 감독하다   inventory *n.* 목록

199 He became, as it **was**, a hero as he managed to return home from the land where he had lived as a detainee for about forty years.

어구 | as it were 사실상   manage *v.* 간신히 ··· 하다   detainee *n.* 구류자, 억류자

200 If you _____ closer to the supermarket, you could walk there.

(A) lived   (B) had lived

(C) live   (D) have lived

201 If the penalties _____ tougher, fewer criminals would be on the street and more teenagers would be in school.

(A) are   (B) be

(C) was   (D) were

어구 | penalty *n.* 벌   criminal *n.* 범죄자

과거사실의 반대를 나타낼 때는 가정법과거완료를 쓴다.

202 If he **would have** lain quietly as instructed by the doctor, he might not have had a second heart attack.

어구 heart attack 심장마비

203 If he had not seen the storekeeper's scissors, he **will** have forgotten to buy a pair.

204 If Watergate **did** not occurred, Nixon would not have resigned from the presidency.

어구 resign *v.* 사임하다   presidency *n.* 대통령직

205 If you **haven't** noticed the smoke, the house would have burned down.

206 He _____ his business if he had advertised efficiently.

(A) will double   (B) would double

(C) doubled   (D) could have doubled

어구 efficiently *adv.* 효율적으로

207 The stranger said that if he _____ there yesterday, he might have been wounded.

(A) had been   (B) were

(C) has been   (D) was

┌─ **Grammar Focus 24: 혼합가정법** ─────────

조건절이 가정법과거완료이고, 귀결절이 가정법과거인 구문을 혼합가정법이라 한다. 일반적 사실이 조건절일 때는 조건절이 가정법과거이고, 귀결절이 가정법과거완료인 경우도 있다.

- If I **had not worked** hard with my studies, I **would** still **be** in that situation.
  만약 내가 공부를 열심히 하지 않았더라면, 난 지금도 그 상황에 놓여 있을 것이다.

- If I **had not worked** hard at English, I **would** not **have been** able to help John.
  만약 내가 영어 공부를 열심히 하지 않았더라면 John을 도와줄 수 없었을 것이다.

- If he **were** a good student, he **would have studied** for the test.
  만약 그가 훌륭한 학생이라면 시험 공부를 했을 것이다.

┌─ **Point 32** ─────────────────
│ 과거의 일이 현재에 영향을 미치는 것을 가정할 때 혼합가정법을 쓴다.
└

208 If he had studied the language before coming here, he _____ so much trouble adjusting to the culture now.

(A) wouldn't have　　　　(B) would have

(C) isn't having　　　　(D) wouldn't be having

> 어구 adjust v. 적응하다, 조절하다

209 If she _____ in this town, she would have come to see me by now.

(A) is　　　　(B) were

(C) has been　　　　(D) would be

가정법 구문

Grammar Focus 25: wish, as if 구문

wish나 as if가 주절에 오면 종속절에 과거나 과거완료가 와서 현재사실의 반대나 과거사실의 반대를 나타낸다.

- I *wish* you **were** here.
  네가 여기에 있으면 좋을 텐데.

- I *wish* I **had been** at Ken's party.
  내가 Ken의 파티에 있었더라면 좋을 텐데.

- I *wished* you **were** there with your arms around me.
  네가 나를 팔로 감싸고 함께 있었더라면 좋았을 텐데.

- I *wished* I **had been** able to sleep a little longer.
  내가 좀 더 잠을 잘 수 있었더라면 좋았을 텐데.

- He *looks* as if he **enjoyed** every moment of those bold scenes.
  그는 마치 배짱이 필요한 장면의 매 순간을 즐기는 것처럼 보인다.

- He *looks* as if he **had seen** a ghost.
  그는 마치 귀신을 보았던 것처럼 보인다.

- He *looked* as if he **were** about to cry.
  그는 마치 울려고 하는 것처럼 보였다.

- He *looked* as if he **had witnessed** the birth of everything.
  그는 모든 것의 탄생을 목격했던 것처럼 보였다.

- **But for** your help, I would be in trouble.
  Without your help, I would be in trouble.
  If it were not for your help, I would be in trouble.

- **But for** his help, we wouldn't have succeeded.
  Without his help, we wouldn't have succeeded.
  If it had not been for his help, we wouldn't have succeeded.

wish나 as if 다음에 가정법구문이 쓰인다.

210 The chairman must not have been in his right mind; otherwise he would not **make** such wild statements.

> 어구   in one's right mind 제정신으로, 본심으로

211 The secretary sometimes **wished** that she were not working in a big corporation.

212 She has a curious expression on her face as if she **was** smiling about something that amused her.

> 어구   expression *n.* 표정   amuse *v.* 즐겁게 하다

213 If they had not been for their wives' understanding, they would not have succeeded in the project.

214 He sometimes wishes he _____ better qualified for his job.

    (A) was   (B) would

    (C) were   (D) has been

215 I _____ sales volume would increase this month.

    (A) wish   (B) wish to

    (C) know   (D) think

216 If it had not _____ your help, I should have failed.

    (A) have been for   (B) been for

    (C) had been for   (D) for

Grammar Focus 26: 기타 구문

동사 insist, require, suggest와 형용사 imperative, important, necessary 다음
에 오는 that절은 원형동사를 쓴다.

- Since he was not keen on engineering, his father *insisted* that he **study** at least basic science.

그가 공학에 관심이 없었기 때문에 그의 아버지는 적어도 기초 과학은 공부해야 한다고 주장하였다.

- It is *imperative* that everyone **be** afforded the experience of respect and **be** given the chance to speak.
  모든 사람은 존경을 경험할 기회가 있어야 하며, 말할 기회가 제공되어야 한다.

단순한 가정을 나타낼 때는 조건절에 현재시제를 쓰며, 귀결절에는 현재나 미래가 쓰인다.

- If you **boil** water, it never **goes** above 100 degrees Celsius.
  물을 끓이면 섭씨 100도를 넘지 않는다.

- If it **doesn't rain**, we**'ll go** to the beach tomorrow.
  내일 비가 오지 않으면 해변에 갈 것이다.

미래의 불확실한 사실을 가정할 때 should를 쓰며, 가능성이 없거나 낮을 때는 were to를 쓴다.

- If you **should** meet an elephant on a summer's day, what would you say?
  만약 네가 어떤 여름날 코끼리를 만나면, 뭐라고 말하겠니?

- If you **were to** cancel, I would be very surprised indeed!
  만약 네가 취소한다면, 나는 매우 놀랄 것이다.

Point 34

suggest, insist, recommend 등과 같은 동사나, imperative, critical 등과 같은 형용사 다음의 that절에는 원형동사가 쓰인다.

☞ that절에 원형동사가 쓰이는 동사와 형용사

advise, demand, insist, propose, recommend, require, suggest

desirable, essential, imperative, natural, necessary, vital, urgent

217 Mr. Johnson insists that his secretary **is** responsible for writing all reports as well as for balancing the books.

어구   balance the book 결산하다

218 The prime minister's conviction for improper campaign practices is likely to result in increasing pressure that she **resigns**.

> 어구   conviction *n.* 유죄선고

Point 35

현재나 미래에 대한 불확실한 상상이나 가정을 할 때 가정법현재나 가정법미래를 쓴다.

---

219 If a severe earthquake **would occur**, survivors would have to be housed in temporary shelters and provided with emergency supplies of food and water.

> 어구   shelter *n.* 거처

220 If traffic problems are not solved soon, driving in cities **becomes** impossible.

221 I recommend you hire Andy Roth as your accountant. If Andy _____ a mistake, he won't charge you for his time.

(A) making   (B) should make

(C) have made   (D) is making

> 어구   accountant *n.* 회계사   charge *v.* 청구하다, 부담시키다

222 If any signer of the Constitution _____ return to life for a day, his opinion of our amendments would be interesting.

(A) was to   (B) were to

(C) should have   (D) had to

> 어구   amendment *n.* 수정안

Grammar Focus 27: 생략구문

가정법구문에서 if가 생략되고, 주어와 동사가 도치되기도 한다. if가 생략되면 가정법과거에서는 were가 주어와 도치되며, 가정법과거완료에서는 had가 주어와 도치된다. 그리고 조건절에 should가 올 때는 should가 주어와 도치된다.

- **Were** I a fish I would swim upstream.

내가 물고기라면 상류로 헤엄칠 것이다.

- I should grieve less **had** you been brought up in what was wrong.
  네가 잘못 양육되었더라면 내가 덜 슬펐을 것이다.

- **Should** you miss an exam, an excused absence must be presented upon your return to class.
  시험을 놓치면 수업에 다시 들어오자마자 결석 사유서를 제출해야 한다.

Point 36

조건절의 if가 생략되면 주어와 조동사가 도치된다. if가 생략된 구문이 가정법이라는 것에 유의해야 한다.

---

223 **The Board of Directors should** decide to hire him, we should advise the personnel office to prepare all the necessary papers.

> 어구 Board of Directors 이사회   personnel office 인사과

224 Had they known the snowstorm would be so treacherous, the hikers **did not venture** into it without proper equipment.

> 어구 snowstorm *n.* 눈보라   treacherous *a.* 배반하는, 위험한   venture *v.* 위험을 무릅쓰다

225 _____ so ruthlessly for food and ivory for many years, elephants nowadays would have much larger populations.

(A) Had they not been hunted   (B) If they had not hunted

(C) If they didn't hunt   (D) Have they not been hunted

226 Should the quality of your products decline, all our future orders _____.

(A) will cancel   (B) cancel

(C) shall be canceled   (D) will have canceled

> 어구 decline *v.* 쇠퇴하다

227 _____ of the proposals considered separately, there would not be enough time for discussion and voting before the end of the conference.

(A) Each

(B) If each

(C) Were each

(D) Since each

PRACTICE TEST

228 Mary told me that she would accept the invitation if she was in my place.

229 Had he told the boss he had a traffic accident the night before, he could had taken the day off.

230 If you will have friends, first learn to do without them.

231 If the organizers of the conference have spent a little more time preparing, half the problems probably wouldn't have occurred.

232 Since you had come on time, we would have been able to see the movie, but we just missed the last showing.

어구   on time 정각에

233 If they _____ themselves in the beginning, the volunteers would have helped finish the project.

(A) were not overworked

(B) was not overworked

(C) had not overworked

(D) have not overworked

234 Some historians say that if the South had not lacked essential industries, it _____ the American Civil War.

(A) won

(B) had won

(C) would win

(D) would have won

235 If the factory had not been damaged by the fire, it _____ by the end of the year.

(A) would finish
(B) will be completed
(C) would be completed
(D) would have been completed

236 _____ at you, I would give you my favorite book.

(A) Not she had smiled
(B) Had she have smiled
(C) That she would smile
(D) Should she smile

237 Had the damage been worse, the insurance company _____.

(A) would pay
(B) paid
(C) would have paid
(D) had paid

Chapter 06

Infinitives

부정사*(infinitive)*는 동사의 원형으로 시제나 일치에 따른 변화가 없는 동사형을 말한다. 부정사는 흔히 *to*와 함께 쓰여 명사적, 형용사적, 부사적 기능을 갖는다. *to*가 붙지 않는 원형부정사는 사역동사나 지각동사 같은 매우 제한된 동사와 함께 쓰인다.

SECTION 6-1
부정사의 용법

Grammar Focus 28: 명사적 용법

to 부정사는 문장의 필수 성분인 주어, 목적어, 보어 역할을 한다. to 부정사를 목적어로 취하는 동사로는 agree, decide, expect, hope, intend, plan, want, wish 등이 있다.

- For me **to win** the race is unbelievable.
  내가 경기에 이긴다는 것을 믿기 어렵다.

- Prince Harry says he hopes **to return** to combat as soon as possible.
  Harry 왕자는 가능한 한 빨리 전투하러 돌아가길 바란다고 말한다.

- Our mission was **to make** sure that the bad guys, basically, did not get nuclear weapons.
  우리의 임무는 나쁜 사람들이 근본적으로 핵무기를 소유하지 않도록 확실히 대책을 강구하는 것이었다.

to 부정사가 명사를 수식하는 데 쓰이기도 하는데, 이 경우에는 관계절과 유사하다.

- Neil Armstrong is the first man **to walk** on the moon.
  Neil Armstrong은 달에 발을 처음 내디딘 사람이다.

- Mr. Davis is the man **to talk** to.
  Davis씨가 말해야 할 상대이다.

be to 용법으로 쓰인 to 부정사는 보어 역할을 하며, 예정, 의무 등을 나타낸다.

- This is why you must have good body language if you **are to** attract women.
  여성에게 매력적으로 보이고자 한다면 훌륭한 몸짓언어를 가져야 하는 이유가 바로 이것이다.

to 부정사가 동사, 형용사, 부사를 수식하는 경우로, 주로 목적이나 이유를 나타낸다.

- I met her **to discuss** a role that I wanted her to do in my film.
  나는 그녀가 내 영화에서 하기를 원하는 역할을 논의하기 위해 그녀를 만났다.

- I was very relieved **to find** someone that was willing to help me.
  나는 나를 돕고자 하는 사람을 발견하고서 매우 안심이 되었다.

Point 37

어떤 동사/형용사/명사는 to 부정사를 취한다.

☞ to 부정사를 목적어로 취하는 동사

agree, ask, decide, expect, hope, manage, plan, promise, wish

238 Three months after they have been laid, crocodile eggs are ready **hatched**.

> 어구 hatch *v.* 부화하다

239 Those who had participated in the negotiation decided not **making** an offer until they looked over the contract.

> 어구 negotiation *n.* 교섭   look over 대충 훑어보다

240 The mechanics haven't been able _____ the problem with the car yet.

(A) to find　　　　　　　　　(B) find

(C) finding　　　　　　　　　(D) to found

어구 | mechanic *n.* 정비공

241 It is difficult _____ a foreign text literally.

(A) for translating　　　　　(B) that translating

(C) to translate　　　　　　(D) to be translated

어구 | literally *adv.* 문자 그대로

242 In both debate and discussion, opposing ideas are presented _____.

(A) an attempt in persuade people

(B) an attempt to persuade people

(C) in an attempt to persuade people

(D) when attempt persuade to people

어구 | opposing 반대되는

> **Point 38**
> 동사+목적어+to 부정사 구문으로 쓰이는 동사가 있다. help는 사역동사가 아니지만 원형부정사를 쓰는 경향이 있다.

☞ to 부정사를 목적보어로 취하는 동사

advise, allow, ask, believe, convince, expect, order, persuade

243 He advised me **sending** a verbal message to them before making an official complaint against them.

어구 | verbal *a.* 언어의　make a complaint against ... ···를 고소하다

244 I was **compelled pay** the bill because my boss did not have enough money to cover it after having dinner at a very fancy restaurant with some clients.

어구 client *n.* 고객

245 Acute hearing helps most animals **sensitive** the approach of thunderstorms long before people do.

어구 acute *a.* 민감한

246 The purpose of inductive logic is _____ from particular occurrences.

(A) general laws to infer   (B) to inferring general laws

(C) to general laws infer   (D) to infer general laws

어구 inductive *a.* 귀납적인   infer *v.* 추론하다

247 The function of language is to enable _____ to one another, primarily through audible speech, and secondarily through written words.

(A) people to communicate ideas

(B) people communicate ideas

(C) ideas to communicate people

(D) people's communication ideas

어구 audible *a.* 들을 수 있는

248 Although a biography is primarily intended to recount a person's life, many biographers examine the social forces _____.

(A) that was helped shape it   (B) that helped shape it

(C) that they helped shape it   (D) that helped shaping it

어구 recount *v.* 자세히 말하다   force *n.* 영향력

249 In 1852 Massachusetts passed a law requiring all children from four to eighteen years of age _____ school.

(A) attending   (B) attend

(C) to attend   (D) who attend

동사를 수식하여 목적, 결과 등을 나타내기 위해 to 부정사를 쓴다.

250 If you use a credit card **paying** for the meal, you may include the tip on the credit card slip or leave the tip in cash.

> 어구 card slip 카드전표

251 The practice of making excellent films based on rather obscure novels has been going on so long in the United States **as for** constitute a tradition.

> 어구 obscure *a.* 불명료한, 잘 알려지지 않은   constitute *v.* 이루다, 구성하다

252 A statue, a monument, a building, or a park may be dedicated to **commemoration** a distinguished individual.

> 어구 monument *n.* 기념비   commemorate *v.* 기념하다   distinguished *a.* 유명한

253 _____, we must apply the ultimate strength.

(A) If we overcame conflict

(B) To overcome conflict

(C) Though we overcame conflict

(D) Overcoming conflict

> 어구 ultimate *a.* 궁극적인

254 When Columbus discovered the New World he was not surprised _____; he thought he had landed in India or Japan.

(A) finding it inhabited   (B) to find it inhabited

(C) to find it inhabit   (D) to find inhabited it

> 어구 inhabited *a.* 거주하는

255 Because the arctic regions receive little sunlight, the air there is too cold _____.

(A) for hold much moisture

(B) that it cannot hold much moisture

(C) to hold much moisture

(D) of holding much moisture

> 어구   moisture *n.* 수분

Point 40

명사를 수식하여 목적을 나타내거나 관계절을 대신하여 to 부정사가 쓰인다.

---

256 Although Canada's Parliament can neither administer or enforce laws nor initiate policy, it does have the power **for making** laws and vote on the allocation of funds.

> 어구   allocation *n.* 배당   administer *v.* 집행하다   enforce *v.* 시행하다   initiate *v.* 발의하다

257 In 1924 Nellie Taylor Ross of Wyoming became the first woman _____ elected governor in the United States.

(A) was   (B) was to

(C) she was   (D) to be

> 어구   governor *n.* 주지사

SECTION 6-2

부정사의 의미상의 주어

Grammar Focus 31: 의미상의 주어

to 부정사의 의미상의 주어를 나타내기 위해서는 for/of + 명사를 형태를 쓰는데, 타동사의 경우에는 전치사가 불필요하여 목적어 + to 부정사의 형태를 취한다.

- It is not good **for the man** *to be* alone.
  그 사람이 혼자 있는 것은 좋지 않다.
  It is good **of you** *to invite* me.
  초대해 주셔서 고맙습니다.

- I expect (**the man**) *to leave* tomorrow.

나는 (그가) 내일 떠날 것이라고 예상한다.

The physician persuaded **the patient** *to lie* in bed.

내과 의사는 환자에게 침대에 누우라고 설득하였다.

- **The lady** promised the man *to meet* his family.

그 여자는 그 남자에게 그의 가족을 만나겠다고 약속했다.

Point 41

의미상의 주어를 나타내기 위해 for+명사가 쓰인다.

---

258 It takes several years _____ that can be used for commercial purposes.

(A) if bamboo seeds grow into plants

(B) of bamboo seeds to grow into plants

(C) for bamboo seeds to grow into plants

(D) for bamboo seeds while growing into plants

어구   commercial *a.* 상업의

259 _____ to design irregularly shaped buildings when their clients ask for something unique.

(A) Not unusually, architects

(B) It is not unusual that architects

(C) It is not unusual for architects

(D) Architects are not unusually

SECTION 6-3

원형부정사

Grammar Focus 32: 원형부정사

지각동사와 사역동사는 to부정사 대신 원형부정사를 취한다. 다만 수동태의 경우에는 to 부정사를 쓴다.

- We *watch* him **walk** into the kitchen without first taking off his muddy boots.

  우리는 그가 먼저 진흙투성이의 장화를 벗지 않고 부엌으로 걸어가는 것을 보았다.

- They were waiting for him to recover before they *made* him **talk**.

  그들은 그가 말하도록 하기 전에 그가 회복하기를 기다리고 있었다.

수동태에서는 원형부정사 대신 to부정사를 쓴다.

- After some hours he *was seen* **to wave** his hat for assistance.

  몇 시간 후에 그가 도움을 요청하기 위해 모자를 흔드는 것이 보였다.

- He *was made* **to** quickly **sign** papers he was not given the chance to read.

  그는 읽어보지도 못한 종이에 재빨리 서명하도록 강요당했다.

Point 42

사역동사 다음에는 원형부정사가 온다. 단, cause, lead는 사역의 의미를 갖지만 사역동사가 아니어서 to 부정사를 취한다.

---

260 All airlines have a policy of letting passengers in the lavatory **to move** back to their seats when the airplane is about to take off or land.

  어구 lavatory *n.* 화장실

261 The face of the Moon is changed by collisions with meteoroids, causing new craters **appear**.

  어구 collision *n.* 충돌   meteoroid *n.* 유성체   crater *n.* 분화구

262 Daylight saving time came into use in the United States in an effort to conserve electricity by having business hours **to correspond** to the hours of natural daylight.

263 I'll have my secretary _____ a copy of the fax.

    (A) to make   (B) to have made

    (C) make   (D) made

264 The company attempts to make all its employees _____ like family.

    (A) feel   (B) felt

    (C) feels   (D) feeling

265 Finally, the police _____ the suspect go.

    (A) allowed   (B) permitted

    (C) let   (D) wanted

> 어구   suspect *n.* 혐의자

266 Heating and cooling can cause matter _____.

    (A) expanding and contracting   (B) expansion and contract

    (C) to expand and contract   (D) expand and contract

> 어구   contract *v.* 수축하다

Point 43

지각동사 다음에는 원형부정사나 현재분사가 온다.

☞ 원형부정사를 목적보어로 취하는 지각동사

    see, watch, hear, notice

267 It's no longer important to have the flowers **to bloom** at the same time I have the baby.

268 The witness said he saw someone **was placing** the bag on the park bench.

269 The men in the mines stop work when they hear the whistle _____.

(A) blow   (B) to blow

(C) be blow   (D) to be blowing

어구   mine *n.* 탄광

SECTION 6-4

독립부정사

Grammar Focus 33: 독립부정사

문장을 수식하는 부정사로 주절의 주어와 다르지만 의미상의 주어가 나타나지 않는다. 대개 콤마로 분리되며, 관용적 표현이다.

- **Needless to say**, I ended the interview very quickly.
  =It is needless to say that I ended the interview very quickly.
  말할 것도 없이 나는 아주 빨리 인터뷰를 마쳤다.

- **To make the matter worse**, it began to rain, which made it impossible for us to see even a foot ahead.
  설상가상으로, 비가 오기 시작했으며, 심지어 바로 앞도 볼 수 없게 되었다.

Point 44

독립부정사는 관용적 표현으로 주절의 주어와 관계 없이 주어가 생략된다.

☞ 대표적인 독립부정사

strange to say, to sum up, to be honest, to begin with, to say nothing of, to be frank with

270 **To telling the truth**, so little care have I given to my library's well-being at normal times.

어구   well-being *n.* 행복, 복지

SECTION 6-5

부정사의 시제

Grammar Focus 34: 부정사의 시제

주절 동사가 기대나 의지를 나타내면 미래의 의미를 갖는다.

- I expect my daughter **to come** to see me.
  =I expect that my daughter will come to see me.
  나는 내 딸이 나를 만나러 오길 기대한다.

주절의 시제와 동일한 시제를 갖는다.

- He seems **to be** in trouble.
  =It seems that he is in trouble.
  그는 어려움에 처한 것처럼 보인다.

완료부정사는 주절의 시제보다 먼저 일어난 일은 나타낸다.

- He seems **to have been** in trouble.
  =It seems that he was in trouble.
  그는 어려움에 처했었던 것처럼 보인다.

- Tom was believed **to have been** rich.
  =It was believed that Tom had been rich.
  Tom은 부자였었던 것으로 믿어졌다.

Point 45

주절의 시제보다 먼저 일어난 일은 완료부정사를 쓴다.

---

271 The representative was announced **to be killed** in the car accident.

어구 representative *n.* 대표단

272 We are glad to _____ when you needed our help.

(A) help you　　　　　　　　(B) helping you

(C) have helped you　　　　(D) having helped you

PRACTICE TEST

273 The hormone insulin, which is produced by specialized cells in the pancreas, enables the body using and store glucose quickly.

어구   pancreas *n.* 췌장   glucose *n.* 포도당

274 You must warn your soldiers to not be tempted by street girls when your platoon marches through the city.

어구   platoon *n.* 소대

275 Margaret Mead studied many different cultures, and she was one of the first anthropologists _____ .

(A) and photograph her subjects

(B) to photograph her subjects

(C) that were photographed her subjects

(D) while photograph her subjects

어구   anthropologist *n.* 인류학자

276 Henry Ford's introduction of the assembly line vastly reduced the time it took _____ .

(A) to make a car   (B) for making a car

(C) making a car   (D) a car to make

어구   assembly line 조립라인   vastly *adv.* 대단히

277 A footnote is characteristically employed to give information _____ to be included in the body of a text.

(A) and that is too long or too detailed

(B) that is so long or so detailed as

(C) that is too long or too detailed

(D) is too long or too detailed

어구   footnote *n.* 각주   characteristically *adv.* 특질상   detailed *a.* 상세한

278 The greater an object's mass, the more difficult it is _____.

    (A) to speed it up or slow it down

    (B) it speeds up or slows down

    (C) than speeding it up or slowing it down

    (D) than speeding up or slowing down

279 Identical colors _____ when they are viewed against different backgrounds.

    (A) may appear to be quite different

    (B) may appear being quite different

    (C) may appear be quite different

    (D) may appear quite different to be

Chapter 07

Gerunds

동명사는 동사에 *-ing* 어미가 붙어 만들어진 형태로 명사적 특성과
동사적 특성을 동시에 가지고 있다. 기능상 명사의 역할을 하지만
내부적으로는 동사처럼 목적어를 가지며, 관사를 쓰지 않는다.

SECTION 7-1
동명사의 기능과 특성

> **Grammar Focus 35: 동명사의 기능**
>
> 동명사는 명사적 성격을 가지고 있어서 주어, 목적어, 보어 역할을 한다. 주어로
> 쓰였을 경우 단수 취급한다.
>
> - **Swimming** in a river is always going to be more dangerous
>   than swimming in a pool.
>   강에서 수영하는 것은 수영장에서 수영하는 것보다 항상 더 위험할 것이다.
>
> - He never regretted **smoking** until he was diagnosed with lung
>   cancer.
>   그는 폐암 진단을 받을 때까지 흡연을 후회한 적이 없다.
>
> - Seeing is **believing** when you want to change people's percep-
>   tions.
>   사람들의 인식을 바꾸기를 원한다면 백문이 불여일견이다.

동명사는 관사를 쓰지 않는다.

- **Camping** in a forest is a lot different.
  숲 속에서의 캠핑은 매우 다르다.

동명사는 의미상의 주어를 가질 수 있으며, 부사의 수식을 받을 수 있다.

- **His constant going** in and out of the house was really weird.
  그가 집을 끊임없이 드나드는 것은 참 이상했다.

- We were accustomed to **Uncle (his) eating** a big breakfast.
  우리는 삼촌이(그가) 아침 식사를 많이 하는 것에 익숙하다.

- While more women are opting to propose to their boyfriends, many men still believe in the traditional role of **the man proposing** to the woman.
  많은 여성들이 남자친구에게 청혼하기를 택하지만, 많은 남성들은 여전히 남자가 여성에게 청혼하는 전통적인 역할이 옳다고 생각한다.

동명사는 목적어를 취할 수 있다.

- **Composing music** isn't actually that hard, once you know the general idea how it works.
  작곡이 어떤 식으로 이루어지는지 전반적인 개념을 알게 되면 작곡이 실제로는 그렇게 어렵지 않다.

동명사는 동사처럼 완료형을 취할 수 있다.

- I will let you know after **having finished** talking to Mary.
  Mary에게 말을 마치고 나서 네게 알려줄게.

Point 46

동명사는 명사적 성격을 가지고 있어서 주어, 목적어, 보어로 쓰이며, 소유격 주어나 한정사를 취한다.

---

280 Unless an athlete is physically fit, there is not sense in **him** sacrificing himself for victory in any one game and, therefore, facing a lifetime injury.

281 The **land** of a spaceship requires the precise coordination of numerous intricate mechanisms.

> 어구　coordination *n.* 조합, 협력　intricate *a.* 복잡한　mechanism *n.* 장치

282 Do you mind _____ here?

(A) smoking

(B) smoke

(C) my smoking

(D) my smoke

283 My father's hobby is _____ roses.

(A) raise

(B) rise

(C) rising

(D) raising

284 Scientists think _____ helps some tree to conserve water in the winter.

(A) when losing leaves

(B) leaves are lost

(C) that losing leaves

(D) the leaves losing

285 Unlike the owl, bats cannot see very well, but they do have _____.

(A) it hears very well

(B) very good to hear

(C) hearing very well

(D) very good hearing

Point 47

동명사는 동사의 성격을 가지고 있으며, 부정형은 'not + 동명사'이다.

---

286 The dictionary functions primarily as a tool for **the definings** the meaning of words.

287 The primitive men were proud of their masks and laughed at the visitor for **wearing not** one.

288 A complete biography of a person's life is not written by merely _____ in chronological order.

(A) the pertinent facts are to be listed

(B) listing the pertinent facts

(C) list of the pertinent facts

(D) when the pertinent facts are listed

> 어구　pertinent *a.* 적절한, 관계있는　　chronological *a.* 연대순의

289 The participants are committed to dealing _____ with the opponents.

(A) fairly　　　　　　　(B) fair

(C) fairness　　　　　　(D) fairer

> 어구　participant *n.* 참가자　　commit *v.* 약속하다　　opponent *n.* 상대

Point 48

동격의 of 다음에는 동명사가 온다.

---

290 We are still in the process **to build** up the data base with a wide
range of information.

291 Translated into terms of psychological theory, association has been
thought of as the basis of **to learn**, conditioning, and creative thinking.

> 어구　association *n.* 연상

292 The main purpose of **classified** animals is to show the most probable
evolutionary relationship of the different species to each other.

> 어구　evolutionary *a.* 진화의　　species *n.* 종

동사/전치사+동명사

Grammar Focus 37: 동사+동명사

avoid, consider, deny, enjoy, finish, quit 등은 동명사 목적어를 취한다.

- He denied **having attended** a terrorism camp in Pakistan in 2003.
  그는 2003년에 파키스탄에서 테러리스트 캠프에 참여했다는 것을 부정하였다.

- I can't believe I have postponed **reading** it for so many days.
  그것을 읽는 것을 그렇게 오랫동안 내가 미루었다는 것을 믿을 수 없다.

begin, start, continue, plan, cease와 같은 동사는 동명사와 부정사를 모두 취한다.

- It began **to rain** five minutes ago.
  It began **raining** five minutes ago.
  5분 전부터 비가 오기 시작했다.

forget, remember, regret은 동명사와 부정사를 모두 취할 수 있지만 의미 차이가 있다.

- I remembered **to bring** a plastic bag for shopping.
  나는 쇼핑하기 위해 비닐봉투를 가지고 가는 것을 기억했다.

- I remembered **bringing** her to college last summer.
  나는 작년에 그녀를 대학에 데리고 간 것을 기억했다.

Grammar Focus 38: 전치사 + 동명사

동사나 형용사가 전치사를 수반하면 동명사 목적어를 취한다.

- I am looking forward to **meeting** you in person at the interview.
  인터뷰하면서 개인적으로 당신을 만나길 기대합니다.

- I am interested in **spending** time doing research in Germany.
  나는 독일에서 연구하면서 시간을 보내는 것에 관심이 있다.

Point 49

동명사 목적어만을 취하는 동사가 있다.

293 If you are considering **to buy** your house, take advantage of our low rates of interest.

> 어구   interest *n.* 이자

294 In England as early as the twelfth century, young boys enjoyed **to play** football.

295 You have to pay taxes by the end of the month in order to avoid **to pay** an overdue charge.

> 어구   overdue charge 연체료

296 I wish you would mind your own business and stop **interfere** in the matter.

297 The suspect denied _____ the money.

     (A)   stole   (B)   steal

     (C)   having stolen   (D)   to steal

> 어구   suspect *n.* 혐의자

Point 50

전치사 다음에는 동명사가 와야 한다.

---

298 In addition to **spend** time with her family, Pat enjoys knitting, walking, reading and spending time with her group of lady friends.

> 어구   knit *v.* 뜨개질을 하다

299 The woodwind section of an orchestra may enrich the melody by **provide** different tonal qualities.

> 어구   woodwind *n.* 목관악기   enrich *v.* 풍요롭게 하다

300 Doing a good deed is like _____ a good seed.

     (A)   sow   (B)   sowing

     (C)   to sow   (D)   to sowing

> 어구   sow *v.* 뿌리다

301 Our landlord insisted _____ additional cleaning expenses when we moved out of the rented house.

(A) that we paid   (B) us to pay

(C) on our paying   (D) in our paying

> 어구   landlord *n.* 주인, 임대주

302 We do not take up a book, either to pass time or for amusement, _____ from it more or less definite instruction.

(A) without get   (B) without to get

(C) without getting   (D) without have got

> 어구   instruction *n.* 지시

> **Point 51**
>
> (전치사가 생략되어) 관용적으로 동명사를 쓰는 표현이 있다.

---

303 People may have difficulty **to think** clearly when overcome by excitement.

> 어구   excitement *n.* 흥분

304 I had much trouble _____ the house.

(A) on finding   (B) finding

(C) find   (D) found

305 Mariam didn't go to the movies last night because she was so busy _____ for her trip to Guam.

(A) preparing   (B) that prepared

(C) by preparing   (D) to prepare

> **Point 52**
>
> 부정사와 동명사를 모두 취할 수 있지만 의미 차이가 있는 동사가 있다.

---

306 His name sounds familiar, but I don't remember _____ him before.

    (A) to meet   (B) of meeting

    (C) meeting   (D) that I meet

307 Her old house needs _____.

    (A) to paint   (B) being painted

    (C) painting   (D) paint

PRACTICE TEST

308 Engineers and scientists have had no trouble to find high-level, high-paying positions.

309 Technological innovation has affected our civilization by change the nature of technology.

> 어구   innovation *n.* 혁신

310 A telescope improves our view of the skies, partly by forming a large image that magnifies the detail in objects, but even more importantly by gather more light than the human eye can.

> 어구   telescope *n.* 망원경   magnify 확대하다

311 A commercial embargo may include the official seizure of merchandise or the detention of the persons involved in transportation cargo.

> 어구   embargo *n.* 출항금지   seizure *n.* 압수   merchandise *n.* 상품   detention *n.* 억류   cargo *n.* 화물

312 Friction can be reduced by smooth and polishing the surface of contact, by lubricating surfaces with grease or oil, or by rolling instead of sliding.

> 어구   friction *n.* 마찰   polish *v.* 윤을 내다, 다듬다   lubricate *v.* 윤활유를 바르다   grease *n.* 그리스, 기름

313 Historians believe that some forms of an advertising must be as old as barter and trade.

314 He should stop _____ and take a rest.

(A) work   (B) working

(C) to work   (D) to working

315 A previous engagement prevented him from _____ the party.

(A) attend   (B) to attend

(C) attending   (D) the attending

316 _____ is difficult because some of the corals are very fragile: even the touch of a diver's hand can kill them.

(A) The protection Florida's coral reefs

(B) Protecting Florida's coral reefs

(C) It is protecting Florida's coral reefs

(D) When protecting Florida's coral reefs

317 Although the many hours of summer sunshine in Canada's Klondike region produce good vegetable crops, the long winters rarely permit _____ .

(A) grain crops ripen   (B) grain crops are ripe

(C) the ripening of grain crops (D) to ripen grain crops

Chapter 08

Participles

분사(*participle*)에는 현재분사와 과거분사가 있는데, 모두 형용사처럼 수식어로 쓰이거나 보어로 쓰인다. 현재분사가 능동의 의미를 갖는 반면, 과거분사는 수동의 의미를 갖는다.

SECTION 8-1
현재분사와 과거분사

> **Grammar Focus 39: 현재분사**

현재분사가 동사적으로 쓰여 목적어나 수식어와 함께 쓰인다.

- As I was **clearing** the room, others were **looking** for more people.
  내가 방을 치우는 동안 다른 사람들은 더 많은 사람을 찾고 있었다.

- I remember talking with friends who were **reading** the book at the same time that I was.
  동시에 나와 똑같은 책을 읽고 있던 친구들과 이야기하던 기억이 난다.

현재분사가 형용사처럼 명사를 수식한다.

- Don't let **sleeping** babies lie in car seats.
  잠자는 아기들을 자동차 좌석에   히지 마라.

- I've attached a photo of the babies **sleeping** on the lounge.
  라운지에서 자고 있는 아기들의 사진을 첨부하였습니다.

현재분사가 주격보어나 목적보어로 쓰인다.

- He sat **reading** a novel.

그는 앉아서 소설을 읽고 있었다.

- A few days ago, I found him **reading** a difficult instruction manual.

  며칠 전에 나는 그가 어려운 안내 책자를 읽고 있는 것을 발견하였다.

Grammar Focus 40: 과거분사

be 동사와 함께 쓰여 수동태 구문을 만든다.

- As the room **was being cleared** of reporters, the President and the General Secretary shook hands across the table several times for photographers.

  방에서 기자들을 내 보낸 뒤 대통령과 총서기는 카메라맨들을 위해 탁자 너머로 몇 번씩 악수를 나누었다.

과거분사가 형용사처럼 명사를 수식한다.

- The writer cast doubt on the notion that the **Broken** Windows theory was wholly responsible for New York's drop in crime.

  그 저자는 뉴욕의 범죄율 하락이 전적으로 깨진 유리창 이론에 기인한다는 견해에 대해 의문을 제기했다.

- I was standing near him while the glass of the windows **broken** by missiles showered over him.

  미사일에 의해 부숴진 창문의 유리가 그에게 쏟아지는 동안에 나는 그 옆에 서 있었다.

과거분사가 주격보어나 목적격보어로 쓰인다.

- Had he remained **satisfied** with this secondary role he could have enjoyed a successful life.

  그가 2인자 역할에 만족하였더라면 성공적인 삶을 누릴 수 있었을 것이다.

- I found him **satisfied** with what he had done.

  나는 그가 했던 것에 만족한다는 것을 알고 있었다.

Point 53

현재분사는 능동의 의미/사물 주어일 때 쓰이며, 과거분사는 수동의 의미/사람 주어일 때 쓰인다.

318 The president became very **depressing** because his company couldn't get the bid.

> 어구   bid *n.* 입찰

319 He thought that it would be **excited** to see this tree fall with a crash to the ground.

320 As far as I am **concerning**, I have no objection to the bill laid before the House.

> 어구   objection *n.* 반대

Point 54

수식어로 쓰였을 때 현재분사는 능동, 과거분사는 수동의 의미를 갖는다.

---

321 The executive's **speaking** messages have always been much more powerful than his published reports.

> 어구   executive *n.* 간부

322 That was one of the most **interested** films I have ever seen.

323 During the Middle Ages, **handwriting** notices kept groups of nobles informed of important events.

> 어구   handwritten *a.* 손으로 쓴   noble *n.* 귀족

Point 55

후치수식하는 분사의 경우 관계대명사 + be동사를 보충하여 의미를 파악한다.

---

324 It is believed that people **referring** to as "Vikings" reached North America about the year A.D. 1,000.

325 A type of ocean fish _____ in warm and temperate seas, groupers are born as females and later change into males.

(A) is living   (B) while living

(C) living   (D) that is lived

> 어구   grouper *n.* 그루퍼(농어과(科)의 식용어)

326 The United States Constitution provides for a count of the population _____ a census, every ten years.

(A) that it is called
(B) when called
(C) called
(D) as called

어구 count *n.* 수치

327 The nine-banded armadillo of the southern United States is one of few mammals _____ to bear identical quadruplets.

(A) that known
(B) that is known
(C) which know it
(D) known

어구 armadillo *n.* 아르마딜로   quadruplets *n.* 네 쌍둥이

SECTION 8-2
분사구문

Grammar Focus 41: 분사구문 1

분사구문은 현재분사나 과거분사로 이루어진 구문으로 주절을 수식하는 부사적 역할을 한다. 분사구문은 시간, 이유, 원인, 조건, 양보, 부대상황을 나타낸다.

- **Walking** along the street she spotted a nice hill not far from the town.
  그녀는 길을 걷다가 마을에서 그리 멀리 떨어지지 않은 곳에 있던 좋은 산을 발견하였다.

- **Not knowing** what to do next, she began reading the second page.
  다음에 뭘 해야 할지 몰라서 그녀는 두 번째 페이지를 읽기 시작했다.

- **Written** in haste to brainwash the masses during time of war, propaganda plays tend to be simplistic in theme.
  전시에 군중을 세뇌시키기 위해 쓰여지기 때문에 선전용 연극은 주제가 단순한 경향이 있다.

- **Turning** to the right, you will find a path leading to his cottage.
  오른쪽으로 돌면, 그의 오두막으로 가는 길을 찾을 수 있을 것이다.

- **Seen** from the moon the earth appears several times larger than the sun.

  달에서 보면 지구는 태양보다 몇 배 크게 보인다.

- **Being** young he has a lot of experience in product development.

  그는 젊지만 제품개발 경력이 풍부하다.

- **Smiling** brightly, she went in and spread the paper out on her desk.

  밝은 미소를 지으면서, 그녀는 들어와서 그 종이를 책상에 펼쳤다.

Grammar Focus 42: 분사구문 2

주절보다 앞선 시제를 나타내고자 할 때는 완료분사를 쓴다.

- **Having finished** her speech, Mary suddenly slapped on my cheek, leaving an impression of her fingers on it.

  연설을 끝낸 뒤 Mary는 갑자기 내 뺨을 때렸고, 그녀의 손가락 자국이 뺨에 남았다.

- **Having read** the newspaper, and having no reason to disbelieve what it says, I replied 'Yes'.

  신문을 읽었으며, 그 내용을 믿지 않을 이유가 없어서, 나는 그렇다고 대답했다.

의미를 분명히 하기 위해 접속사를 쓰기도 한다.

- It wasn't clear whether the boy had been bitten **while swimming** in the river.

  그 소년이 강에서 수영하는 동안 맞았는지는 분명하지 않았다.

- **While walking** along the street, she was struck in the back by a young guy.

  길을 걷는 동안 그녀는 젊은이한테 등을 맞았다.

주절의 주어와 다를 때, 주어를 생략하지 못한다.

- **It being** fine, we went out for a walk.

  날씨가 화창하여 우리는 산보하러 나갔다.

- There will be a garden party Friday night, **weather permitting**.

  날씨가 허락하면 금요일 저녁에 가든 파티가 있을 것이다.

일반인 주어는 생략할 수 있는데, 이를 독립분사구문이라 한다.

- **Strictly speaking**, the rules of science require complete disclosure of all experimental methods, data, and analysis tools.
  엄격히 말하자면, 과학 규칙은 모든 실험 방법, 자료, 분석 도구의 완전한 공개를 요구한다.

- **Generally speaking**, is it possible to train a disobedient dog?
  일반적으로 말해, 순종적이지 않은 개를 훈련시킬 수 있나요?

with가 분사와 함께 쓰여 부대상황을 나타낸다.

- Jackson ran out of the house **with** *his dog barking and following* him.
  Jackson은 집을 나왔으며, 그의 개가 짖으면서 뒤를 따랐다.

- **With** *his eyes filled* with tears, he looked up at the sky and cried out.
  그는 눈물을 흘리면서 하늘을 바라보며 소리쳤다.

Point 56

주절의 주어와 부사절의 주어가 동일할 때, 분사구문을 쓴다. 주어가 서로 다를 경우 생략되지 않으며, 접속사도 의미상 필요할 경우 생략하지 않는다.

---

328 **Looking** back, the house seemed to have been engulfed by the snow, which fell faster and faster.

    어구 engulf *v.* 삼키다

329 _____ absent, I took the place of him.

　(A)　Being　　　　　　　　　　(B)　He being

　(C)　Having been　　　　　　　(D)　Been

330 Although _____, skin is often viewed as simply a barrier between the body and the outside world.

　(A)　a part of the immune system

　(B)　there is a part of the immune system

(C) it is the part of a immune system

(D) the immune system is a part of it

> 어구   barrier *n.* 장벽   immune *a.* 면역의

331 _____, manufacturers usually use additives to improve keeping qualities and ease of serving.

(A) When make ice cream

(B) When making of ice cream

(C) When they making ice cream

(D) When making ice cream

> 어구   additive *n.* 첨가제

332 It has not been determined how many years sea turtles can live in their natural environment, but they will reach a very old age _____.

(A) if they left undisturbed by humans

(B) if undisturbed left by humans

(C) if left them undisturbed by humans

(D) if left undisturbed by humans

> 어구   determine *v.* 알아내다   undisturbed *a.* 방해받지 않

333 Throughout her career Georgia O'Keeffe paid meticulous attention to her craft: her brushes were always clean, _____.

(A) her colors fresh and bright

(B) her colors were fresh and bright

(C) her fresh and bright colors

(D) because her colors fresh and bright

> 어구   career *n.* 일생, 직업   meticulous *a.* 소심한, 정확한

334 When thinking about living abroad, _____ in that country.

(A) it is different customs that we are concerned about

(B) we are concerned about different customs

(C) different customs are being concerned about

(D) different customs concern ourselves

Point 57

분사구문에서 분사와 주절의 주어가 능동의 관계이면 현재분사를 쓰며, 수동의
관계이면 과거분사를 쓴다.

---

335 **Facing** with dismissal, he decided to submit his resignation.

> 어구   dismissal *n.* 면직, 해고   resignation *n.* 사표

336 _____ the world's foremost linguistic theorist, Noam Chomsky
continues to create new theories about language and language learning.

(A) Regarded as   (B) As he regards as

(C) Regarding him as   (D) If regarded as

> 어구   foremost *a.* 일류의, 주요한   linguistic *a.* 언어학의   theoriest *n.* 이
> 론가

Point 58

주절의 동사보다 앞서 일어난 일은 완료분사구문을 쓴다.

---

337 **Struck** an iceberg, the British liner Titanic sank on its first voyage,
resulting in the deaths of some 1,500 passengers.

> 어구   iceberg *n.* 빙산   voyage *n.* 항해

338 _____ steadily for two weeks, the roads were impassable.

(A) It having snowed   (B) Having snowed

(C) Snowing   (D) Being snowed

> 어구   impassable *a.* 통행할 수 없는

339 _____ of the vote, Jane M. Byrne became the first woman to be elected mayor of Chicago.

(A) Having been received over eighty percent

(B) After had received over eighty percent

(C) Having received over eighty percent

(D) Have received over eighty percent

어구 mayor *n.* 시장

PRACTICE TEST

340 As has been the case with many artistic geniuses, Edgar Allan Poe was not adequate appreciated in his own time: many of his contemporaries criticized him as morbid and excessive.

어구 morbid *a.* 병적인, 끔찍한

341 It is always silly of you to get on the bus with your rain coat _____.

(A) in   (B) on

(C) over   (D) off

342 _____ what to do, he applied to me for advice.

(A) Knowing not   (B) Not knowing

(C) Not know   (D) Not to know

어구 apply to … 에게 묻다

343 Monkeys and apes are extraordinarily communicative, _____ to tell one another how they feel.

(A) they use body language and facial gestures

(B) use body language and facial gestures

(C) used body language and facial gestures

(D) using body language and facial gestures

344 Many people living on the North American frontier in the mid-1800's _____ the bowie knife.

(A) were carried a weapon called

(B) carried a weapon was called

(C) were carried a weapon which called

(D) carried a weapon called

345 One of the great engineering feats of the world, the 44-mile Panama Canal bisects the continents of North and South America, _____ to sail between the Atlantic and Pacific Oceans.

(A) making it possible for ships

(B) made it possible for ships

(C) it made it possible for ships

(D) making possibility for ships

346 Many writers in the eighteenth century were inspired by the educational and scientific ideas of the Enlightenment, _____ of literature to reach a wide readership.

(A) seeing the potential

(B) saw the potential

(C) which was seen the potential

(D) they saw the potential

347 Economics as a science is a small subsystem, _____ the economic behavior of people.

(A) dealing with   (B) in dealt with

(C) which deal with   (D) with which are dealt

348 While staying in Florence, Italy, in 1894, _____ that she had a talent for sculpture and began taking lessons.

(A) philanthropist Winifred Holt discovered

(B) that the philanthropist Winifred Holt discovered

(C) discovered by philanthropist Winifred Holt

(D) there philanthropist Winifred Holt discovered

> 어구   philanthropist *n.* 박애주의자   sculpture *n.* 조각

349 _____, Native Americans made beads that they strung together and used as money.

(A) Using northern quahog clam shells

(B) Northern quahog clam shells using

(C) Northern quahog clam shells are used

(D) When using northern quahog clam shells

> 어구   quahog *n.* 대합의 일종   clam *n.* 대합   bead *n.* 구슬, 목걸이

350 Chain reactions _____ thermal or fast neutrons can be controlled in a reactor.

(A) involve   (B) involved

(C) involving   (D) are involved

> 어구   thermal *a.* 열의   neutron *n.* 중성자   reactor *n.* 원자로

Chapter 09

Nouns and Articles

명사는 성, 수, 격, 인칭을 갖는데, 문법적으로는 수가 가장 중요하다. 가산명사는 단수와 복수의 구별이 있는 반면, 비가산명사는 단수형만을 갖는다. 부정관사는 가산명사에만 쓰이며, 정관사는 가산명사와 비가산명사의 구별과 관계 없이 쓰인다.

SECTION 9-1

가산명사와 비가산명사

Grammar Focus 44: 가산명사와 비가산명사

보통명사와 집합명사는 가산명사로 단·복수의 구별이 있으며, 단수에는 부정관사, 복수에는 -(e)s가 붙는다.

- I read **a book** yesterday.
  나는 어제 한 권의 책을 읽었다.

- He bought **two books** three days ago.
  그는 3일 전에 두 권의 책을 샀다.

- He got married and started **a family**.
  그는 결혼해서 가정을 꾸렸다.

- Healthy **families** tend to return to normal functioning after the crisis passes.
  건강한 가정은 위기가 지나가면 정상적인 기능을 회복하는 경향이 있다.

- **The police** are the officers of the state who have the task of the investigation of crime.

경찰은 범죄를 조사할 임무를 가진 주정부 관료이다.

고유명사, 물질명사, 추상명사는 비가산명사로 단수에서 부정관사를 쓰지 않으며, 복수형이 없다.

- He used to live in **Seoul**.
  그는 서울에 살았었다.

- When you go deep diving, you breathe **air** under pressure.
  깊이 다이빙을 하면 압력 하에서 숨을 쉰다.

- For more **information** on getting a new passport, please visit our website.
  새로운 여권을 얻는 것에 관한 더 많은 정보를 얻으려면 우리 홈페이지를 방문하세요.

비가산명사를 세려면 a piece of와 같은 표현을 쓰며, 비가산명사가 가산명사화되기도 한다.

- We received **a piece of** information on the new product last week.
  우리는 지난주에 새로운 제품에 관한 정보를 얻었다.

- It's scary to think about **a fire** happening at your house.
  너의 집에 화재가 발생하는 것은 생각만 해도 끔찍하다.

Point 59

주어 자리와 목적어 자리에는 명사가 온다.

---

351 Your great **intelligent** and energy will help you solve any problem you encounter if you use these strengths wisely.

어구 | encounter *v.* 마주치다

352 The energy needed for animal **grow** is derived primarily from carbohydrates and fats.

어구 | carbohydrate *n.* 탄수화물

353 The **directing** of the wind is indicated by a weather vane.

어구 | weather vane 풍향계

354 Don't forget to note that these pamphlets have minor **revising** from the original pamphlets.

> 어구   minor *a.* 사소한   revision *n.* 수정, 개정

355 In the early twentieth century, there was considerable **interesting** among sociologists in the fact that in the United States the family was losing its traditional roles.

356 In these circumstances, you may only have a partial discount for the _____ of the month or no discount at all.

(A) remain   (B) remaining

(C) remained   (D) remainder

Point 60

비가산명사는 복수를 사용하지 못한다.

☞ 대표적인 비가산명사

baggage, bread, equipment, furniture, hair, homework, information, mail

357 He was kind enough to carry the **baggages** all the way to the train station.

> 어구   baggage *n.* 수화물

358 Peas require rich soil, constant **moistures**, and a cool growing season to develop well.

> 어구   pea *n.* 완두콩   moisture *n.* 습도

359 Encyclopedias may be used to answer questions, to solve problems, or to obtain **informations** on a particular topic.

> 어구   encyclopedia *n.* 백과사전

360 Langston Hughes always seemed to know exactly who he was, and **those knowledges** helped make him one of the most respected writers in the United States.

361 Yesterday we saw **the Millet** at the exhibition, but it was not a genuine painting.

> 어구 | exhibition *n.* 전시회   genuine *a.* 진짜의, 진실한

362 This school has produced many **Einstein** since it was founded.

> 어구 | found *v.* 설립하다

363 Every year Colorado is visited by millions of tourists who come for a variety of **reason**.

364 The importance of mythology within a culture is reflected in the status of **storyteller**.

> 어구 | mythology *n.* 신화   status *n.* 지위

365 Numerous professional associations have educational **program** for their members.

> 어구 | numerous *a.* 많은

366 Sprinkler **system** have proven to be the most effective means of fighting hotel fires.

> 어구 | effective *a.* 효과적인   means *n.* 수단

367 Most mammals maintain a relatively constant body **temperatures**, regardless of what the air temperature might be.

> 어구 | mammal *n.* 포유류   relatively *adv.* 비교적

368 Fish are the most ancient form of vertebrate life, and from them evolved all other **vertebrate**.

> 어구 | vertebrate *n.* 척추동물   evolve *v.* 진화하다

Point 63

어떤 명사는 관습적으로 복수형을 주로 쓰거나, 단수와 복수가 의미가 다르다.

369 The importance of mythology within a culture is reflected in the status of **storyteller**.

> 어구 mythology *n.* 신화   status *n.* 지위

370 Numerous professional associations have educational **program** for their members.

> 어구 numerous *a.* 많은

371 Baseball and other popular **sport** have provided a number of new words for the English language.

Point 64

of + 추상명사는 형용사의 역할을 하여 주어를 서술하는 보어로 쓰인다.

☞ 대표적인 of+추상명사

of importance, of significance, of no use

372 The measures being taken to renovate the company are of great **significant** to the shareholders.

> 어구 measure *n.* 조치, 법안   renovate *v.* 개조하다   shareholder *n.* 주주

373 This information is _____ to us.

(A) much used   (B) able to use
(C) of not use   (D) of no use

374 Capital and labor are of equal _____ in the modern corporation.

(A) import   (B) importantly
(C) important   (D) importance

> 어구 capital *n* 자본

375 Because the equipment is delicate, it must be handled with _____.

(A) caring	(B) careful
(C) care	(D) carefully

어구   delicate *a.* 정교한   with care 조심스럽게

Section 9-2

수량사

Grammar Focus 45: 수량사

가산명사에는 many를 쓰며, 비가산명사에는 much를 쓴다. many 다음에는 복수명사가 온다.

- I have no idea how **many books** I read last year, but it was a lot.
  작년에 얼마나 많은 책을 읽었는지 알 수 없지만, 많은 책을 읽었다.

- How **much water** you need depends on many factors, including your body size and your age.
  얼마나 많은 수분이 필요할지는 체격, 연령과 같은 많은 요소에 의존한다.

가산명사에는 (a) few를 쓰며, 비가산명사에는 (a) little을 쓴다. (a) few 다음에는 복수명사가 온다.

- Not only are there **a few** good men, but there are a few good women as well.
  좋은 남자가 좀 있을 뿐만 아니라 좋은 여자도 좀 있다.

- Because there are **few** good movies which can substitute the Da Vinchi Code, I agreed to see it tonight.
  다빈치코드를 대신할 좋은 영화가 없어서 오늘밤 그것을 보기로 합의했다.

- My suggestion is that most houses still look better with **a little** furniture than nothing at all.
  내 생각으론 대부분의 집은 가구가 전혀 없는 것보다는 조금 있는 것이 훨씬 낫다.

- Like many country houses, city homes have very **little** furniture.
  많은 시골집처럼 도시의 집도 가구가 거의 없다.

a lot of와 lots of는 모두 가산명사와 비가산명사에 쓰인다.

- I saw **a lot of** museums and churches and ate **a lot of** chocolate.

나는 많은 박물관과 교회를 보았으며, 많은 초콜릿을 먹었다.

- The film industry says Wisconsin is losing **lots of** movies and **lots of** money.
  영화업계는 Wisconsin주가 많은 영화와 많은 돈을 잃고 있다고 말한다.

Point 65

many는 복수 가산명사와 함께 쓰이며, much는 (단수) 비가산명사와 함께 쓰인다.

---

376 Among Thomas Jefferson's many **accomplishment** was his work to establish the University of Virginia.

> 어구   accomplishment *n.* 성취, 업적   establish *v.* 설립하다

377 **Much** nutritionists argue that people's intake of fat should be reduced.

> 어구   nutritionist *n.* 영양학자   intake *n.* 섭취

378 I got a letter from that company yesterday, but there wasn't **many** news in it.

379 **Much** unknown plants and animals are disappearing as the tropical forests are destroyed.

380 It was not so much the **much** blows he received as a lack of spirit that led to his losing the fight.

> 어구   not so much *A* as *B*   A라기 보다는 B

381 Data received from two spacecraft indicate that there is **many evidence** that huge thunderstorms are occurring around the equator of the planet Saturn.

> 어구   thunderstorm *n.* 뇌우   equator *n.* 적도   Saturn *n.* 토성

382 **Many of** companies have to pay millions of dollars to establish their trademarks as symbols of reliability and value.

> 어구   trademark *n.* 상표   reliability *n.* 신뢰할 수 있음

383 As a rule, the police don't have _____ power in a situation like this.

(A) many	(B) much
(C) some	(D) big

384 You should try to have _____ to speak English with native speakers.

(A) many times	(B) many chances
(C) much chances	(D) any chance

385 She likes to buy _____ furniture.

(A) few	(B) many
(C) much	(D) several

386 Flowers make a lot of _____ to a room.

(A) differences	(B) difference
(C) different	(D) the difference

Point 66

비가산명사를 세고자 할 때는 특정 표현을 사용한다.

☞ 수량표시어

a drop/cup of water, a cake of soap, a stick of chalk, a piece of advice

387 When a human being walks, he or she exerts a certain **number** of
force on the gland.

어구 | exert *v.* 쓰다, 노력하다   gland *n.* 선, 분비기관

388 _____ mail travels faster when the zip code is indicated on the

envelope.

(A) A	(B) A piece of
(C) A pack of	(D) A pair of

어구 | zip code 우편번호

389 The writer smokes _____ of cigarettes a day at work.

(A)	20 sticks	(B)	40 pieces
(C)	two boxes	(D)	two packs

390 I'd like a steak, a salad, and _____ with butter.

(A)	a few corns	(B)	ears of corns
(C)	an ear of corns	(D)	an ear of corn

SECTION 9-3

부정관사

Grammar Focus 46: 부정관사

총칭적 표현으로 쓰인다.

- **A** tiger is a ferocious animal.
  호랑이는 사나운 동물이다.

하나를 뜻한다.

- Rome was not built in **a** day.
  로마는 하루에 이루어진 것이 아니다.

same

- Birds of **a** feather flock together.
  똑 같은 깃털을 가진 새는 함께 모인다(유유상종).

a certain

- **A** man came to see us.
  어떤 사람이 우리를 찾아 왔다.

모음 앞에는 an을 쓰는데, 특히 약자에 유의해야 한다.

- **a** cat, **a** university; **an** apple, **an** hour; **an** IBM computer, **an** MP

Point 67

단수가산명사에는 부정관사를 쓰는데, 부정관사 다음에 자음이 오면 a를, 모음이 오면 an을 쓴다.

391 Drying food by means of solar energy is **a** ancient process applied wherever food and climatic conditions make it possible.

> 어구　by means of ... …에 의한　　solar *a.* 태양의　　process *n.* 가공　　climatic *a.* 기후상의

392 Last year **a** honor which is rarely conferred was awarded to this scientist, one of the greatest men of our age.

> 어구　honor *n.* 명예, 훈장　　confer *v.* 수여하다

393 Fiber is **a** important element in nutrition, and it aids in protecting the digestive tract as well.

> 어구　fiber *n.* 섬유질　　digestive tract 소화기관

394 Francis Hopkinson, a New Jersey signer of the Declaration of Independence, was an American statesman, artist, writer, lawyer, and **a judge**.

395 Between the ages of nine and fifteen, almost all young people undergo **rapid** series of physiological changes.

> 어구　physiological *a.* 생리적

396 There is **rumor** that the workers are discussing establishing a labor union.

> 어구　labor union 노동조합

397 The political party took **the** announcement a week ahead of schedule.

> 어구　political party 정당

398 His decision to retire came as **surprise** to everyone in the department.

> 어구　retire *v.* 은퇴하다

399 The snowy egret is about the size **of large crow**.

> 어구　snowy *a.* 새하얀　　egret *n.* 왜가리

Point 68

가산명사가 총칭적으로 쓰일 때는 부정관사를 쓰거나 복수형을 쓴다.

---

400 **Ruler** is mainly used to measure and to draw straight lines on flat surfaces.

401 **Grass-eating**, river-dwelling mammal, the hippopotamus is related to the pig.

> 어구 dwell *v.* 거주하다   hippopotamus *n.* 하마

┌───┐
SECTION 9-4

정관사
└───┘

Grammar Focus 47: 정관사

총칭적 표현으로 쓰인다.

- **The** tiger is a ferocious animal.
  호랑이는 사나운 동물이다.

문맥에 의해 알 수 있을 때

- Shut **the** door.
  문을 닫아라.

앞에 나온 명사를 가리킬 때

- Once upon a time there lived a king. **The** king had a beautiful daughter.
  옛날 한 임금이 살았는데, 그 왕은 아름다운 딸이 있었다.

유일한 대상을 가리킬 때

- **The** earth revolves **the** sun.
  지구는 태양 주위를 돈다.

악기

- He plays **the** violin.
  그는 바이올린을 연주한다.

  cf. He likes to play golf.
       그는 골프 치기를 좋아한다.

단위

- We buy them by **the** hundred.
  우리는 그것을 백 개씩 산다.

신체의 일부

- Newton was sitting under a tree when an apple fell and hit him on **the** head.
  뉴튼이 나무 아래에 앉아 있었는데, 그때 사과가 떨어져 머리를 맞았다.

고유명사

- **the** Netherlands, **the** Alps, **the** Thames

수식을 받을 때

- **the** man in the moon
  달에 있는 남자

- **The** man who walked on the moon
  달을 걸었던 남자

Point 69

문맥에서 특정한 것을 가리키는 것이 분명하면 정관사를 쓴다.

---

402 The victim of the traffic accident sued the bus company for **damage**.

   어구   victim *n.* 희생자 · traffic accident 교통사고   sue *v.* 고소하다

403 The sugar the cook left **on shelf** was eaten by a mouse as large as a rat.

404 Part of the sunlight that strikes the Earth is reflected into the sky, and **a rest** is absorbed by the ground.

405 American manufacturers depend on ocean shipping for most **of trade** with other countries.

Point 70

총칭표현은 가산명사의 경우 무관사+복수명사, 부정관사+단수명사, the+단수명사가 쓰이며, 비가산명사는 무관사+단수명사를 쓴다.

406 Lack of animal protein in the human diet is a serious cause of **the malnutrition**.

> 어구   protein *n.* 단백질   malnutrition *n.* 영양 결핍

407 **The clay** is a material that has the fundamental characteristic of becoming plastic when moist.

> 어구   fundamental *a.* 기본적인   plastic *a.* 유연한

408 When used for studies of learning and memory, the octopus is a more interesting subject than **squid**.

> 어구   octopus *n.* 문어   squid *n.* 오징어

409 _____ relies more on its sense of smell than on any other sense.

     (A)   The elephants   (B)   Elephants

     (C)   Elephant   (D)   The elephant

Point 71

후치수식을 받아 특정한 대상을 가리키면 정관사를 쓴다.

410 Agriculture is defined as **science** and art of cultivating the soil, growing crops, and raising livestock.

> 어구   agriculture *n.* 농업   art *n.* 예술, 기술   cultivate *v.* 경작하다, 기르다   livestock *n.* 가축

411 **First** European settlers of Australia left the city of Portsmouth in May 1787.

> 어구   settler *n.* 정착민

412 Computers that are not accessed remotely should be turned off **at end of** the business day and on weekends.

> 어구   remotely *adv.* 원격으로

413 I want _____ that is on the desk.

(A) document

(B) a document

(C) the document

(D) a piece of document

Point 72

최상급에는 the를 쓴다.

---

414 One of **most** impressive collections of nineteenth-century European paintings in the United States can be found in the Philadelphia Museum of Art.

> 어구 collection *n.* 소장품

415 Of all the Native American in the United States, the Navajos form **largest** group.

Point 73

단위를 나타낼 때 전치사+the 명사, 혹은 부정관사+명사를 쓴다.

---

416 A number of doctors believe that taking an aspirin **the day** can reduce a person's chances of having a heart attack.

> 어구 heart attack 심장병

417 As a rule, the factory workers get paid _____.

(A) by an hour

(B) by the hour

(C) by a hour

(D) by hours

> 어구 as a rule 대체로

Point 74

신체의 일부를 나타낼 때 the를 쓴다.

---

418 In an exchange of gunfire, one police officer was wounded in _____ and another was hit in the shoulder.

(A) a foot

(B) the foot

(C) his foot

(D) his feet

> 어구 gunfire *n.* 총격, 발포

관사의 생략

Grammar Focus 48: 관사의 생략

식사, 질병, 운동, 계절

- **Breakfast** is at seven.
  아침 식사는 7시이다.
  cf. **The dinner** I ate yesterday was Chinese noodles.
  어제 저녁에 먹었던 식사는 중국 국수였다.

- allergy, asthma, cancer, cholera, consumption, pneumonia

  cf. a toothache, a headache, a cold, the flu

- If **winter** comes, can **spring** be far behind.
  겨울이 오면 봄은 머지 않으리.

원래의 용도로 쓰인 기관(institution)

- **School** is over.
  수업이 끝났다.

  ex. in school, go to church/hospital/bed/prison, at church, at table

교통수단

- Others traveled 1,000 miles across the country by **horse** or on **foot**.
  다른 사람들은 말을 타거나 도보로 전국을 1천마일 여행했다.

  ex. by train, by car, by bus, by steamer, by subway, by taxi
  cf. go on a bus, in a car, go on a plane

숙어

- arm in arm, face to face, day and night, hand in hand, step by step, day after day

등위접속사로 연결되었을 때

- the Korean and Japanese **languages**
  한국어와 일본어

관직명이 보어로 쓰일 때

- Greene was appointed Principal of La Paloma High School.
  Greene은 La Paloma 고등학교의 교장으로 임명되었다.

양보절에서 도치되었을 때

- Tom is more sensible than Mary, **child** though he is.
  Tom은 어리지만 Mary보다 분별력이 있다.

Point 75

식사, 질병, 악기, 관직의 이름은 관사를 생략한다.

---

419 After **the church** the men stood together in the churchyard saying he must be crazy.

420 **The baseball** has been approved as an extracurricular activity.

> 어구 extracurricular *a.* 과외의

421 The doctor told me that the major's wife had died _____.

  (A) of the pneumonia   (B) of a pneumonia
  (C) of pneumonia   (D) with pneumonia

> 어구 major *n.* 소령   die of ···로 죽다   pneumonia *n.* 폐렴

422 Dr. Brown was _____ of Foreign Affairs from 1991 till 1996.

  (A) a Minister   (B) Minister
  (C) the Minister   (D) Ministerial

PRACTICE TEST

423 Moonquakes originating at deep of some 800 kilometers indicate the Moon has considerable rigidity and is not molten at such levels.

> 어구 moonquake *n.* 월진, 달의 지진   considerable *a.* 상당한

424 The wide range of elevations in the southern Appalachian Mountains allows for the great diverse of plant life found there.

> 어구 elevation *n* 고도

425 The 1897 discover of gold in the Klondike hastened the commercial development of Washington State, as did the increasing trade with Pacific Islands.

426 Even though they do not have webbed foot, gallinules are excellent swimmers.

> 어구 webbed *a.* 물갈퀴가 있는   gallinule *n.* 쇠물닭

427 Fossils of plant that have been extinct for fifty million years have been found in large deposits of amber near the Baltic Sea.

> 어구 extinct *a.* 멸종된   deposit *n.* 매장층   amber *n.* 호박

428 Approximately one-third of all persons involved in adult education programs in 1970 were enrolled in occupational education course.

> 어구 occupational *a.* 직업의

429 You could prove my identity by seeing my driver license or my passport.

> 어구 identity *n.* 신분

430 The city of Boston was settled in 1630 on a hilly, wooded peninsula where the Charles River flows into a natural harbors.

431 Philosophers are concerned with the truth, the good, and the beautiful.

432 Hickories are medium to large trees common in eastern and the central areas of North America.

> 어구 hickory *n.* 히코리 (북미산의 단단한 나무)

433 The cultures early of the genus Homo were generally distinguished by regular use of stone tools and by a hunting and gathering economy.

> 어구   genus Homo   사람속

434 Nowadays, every virtually kind of organization throughout the world conducts business with computers.

> 어구   virtually *adv.* 거의, 사실상

435 Maryland's economy is based largely on service industries, which account for more than four-fifth of Maryland's gross state product.

> 어구   account for 차지하다

436 We made a three weeks business trip through America and Europe last fall.

437 There are several way to become an office worker without having to take the examination.

> 어구   office worker 사무직 근로자

438 After Holmes's departure for the concert, I lay down upon the sofa and endeavored to get _____ sleep.

    (A) a couple of hours   (B) a couple of hours'

    (C) a couple of hour   (D) a couple of hour's

> 어구   endeavor *v.* 노력하다

439 _____ began in ancient Greece thousands of years ago.

    (A) The study of mathematics   (B) Study of the mathematics

    (C) A study of mathematics   (D) A study of the mathematics

440 _____ of our office furniture is uncomfortable.

    (A) Much   (B) Many

    (C) Several   (D) One

Chapter 10

Determiners and Pronouns

명사 앞에 오는 요소 가운데 형용사를 제외한 요소를 한정사라 한다. 대명사는 가리키는 대상이 일정하지 않고 문맥에 의해 가리키는 대상이 정해지는 표현이다. 특히 한정사가 흔히 부정대명사로 쓰이기도 하는데, 부정대명사는 대명사와 달리 막연한 대상을 가리킨다.

SECTION 10-1
한정사의 종류

Grammar Focus 49: 한정사의 종류

정관사, 부정관사

- **a** boy, **the** boy, **the** music

수량사

- **some**/**any** boys, **some**/**any** music

- **each** student, **every** student

- **no** book/books

지시형용사

- **this** boy, **these** boys, **this** music

의문형용사

- **what** color, **which** information

소유격(대)명사

- **John's** book, **my** books

Grammar Focus 50: 전치한정사

all, both, half

- **all** (the) students, **half** an hour, **half** the furniture

double, twice, three times

- **double** the price, **twice** my age

분수

- The total site will be **two-thirds** the area of the National Mall in Washington, DC.

such, what, quite, rather

- **such** a pretty girl, **rather** a shock

Grammar Focus 51: 후치한정사

기수와 서수

- my **three** books, the **first** visit, my **last three** lovers

수량

- the **few** people, the **many** faces of Santa, **several** mistakes

---

Point 76

such, so 형용사, quite는 전치한정사로 관사보다 앞에 온다.

441 It is **a such lovely day** that I'd like to go on a picnic.

442 Our manager is a man of character, and yet he is well known as
_____ strict manager.

(A) quite a   (B) a quite

(C) the quite   (D) quite the

어구 manager *n.* 지배인   a man of character 인격자

443 An ultrasonic wave has _____ high frequency that it is inaudible.

(A) this a   (B) so a

(C) a such   (D) such a

어구 ultrasonic wave 초음파   frequency *n.* 주파수   inaudible *a.* 들을
수 없는

Point 77

all, both, half, 배수사 등은 전치한정사로 한정사 앞에 오며, 수사는 후치한정사로
한정사 뒤에 온다.

---

444 The best known of **the all** Arctic birds, ptarmigans are a favorite of
birdwatchers.

어구 ptarmigan *n.* 뇌조

445 **The all three** people in the car were seriously injured in the car
crash.

446 In 1992, Albert Gore, Jr., the son of a former United States senator,
became the **forty-five** Vice President of the Unites States.

447 The bank is the **two** largest bank in the country, according to the
monthly magazine.

448 _____ migrating water birds in North America visit the Gulf of
Mexico's winter wetlands.

(A) Four of three every   (B) Three every four

(C) Three of every four   (D) Every four of three

어구 migrating *a.* 이주하는   water bird 물새   wetland *n.* 습지대

한정사는 형용사 보다 앞에 온다.

449 Thomas Jefferson's **the** achievements as an architect rival his contributions as a politician.

> 어구 rival *v.* …와 맞먹다   architect *n.* 건축가   contribution *n.* 공헌

450 The swamp maple tree grows well in virtually **every** kinds of soil.

> 어구 swamp *n.* 습지   maple tree 단풍나무

451 The decimal numeral system is one of the _____ ways of expressing numbers.

(A) useful most world's

(B) world's most useful

(C) useful world's most

(D) most world's useful

> 어구 decimal *a.* 십진법의

SECTION 10-2

인칭대명사

Grammar Focus 52: 인칭대명사

인칭대명사는 인칭, 성, 수, 격에 따라 형태가 달라진다.

- When **I** saw **her**, **she** was looking at **me**.
  내가 그녀를 보았을 때 그녀는 나를 보고 있었다.

- When **you** came home with **us**, **you** met **your** new sister Daisy.
  네가 우리와 함께 집에 갔을 때, 너는 너의 새로운 누이인 Daisy를 만났다.

소유격 대명사는 앞의 소유격+명사를 대신하며, 한정사를 둘 쓰고자 할 때 of+ 소유격 대명사 구조를 쓴다.

- Students do not want to present if they think the quality of the preceding presentation is better than **theirs**.
  학생들은 앞선 발표의 질이 자기 것보다 낮다고 생각하면 발표를 원하지 않는다.

- He achieved his first success in Hamburg where an opera of **his** was presented.

  그는 자기 오페라를 발표한 함부르크에서 첫 번째 성공을 거두었다.

Grammar Focus 53: 비인칭의 it

시간, 거리, 날씨, 무게 등을 나타낼 때 비인칭주어 it을 쓴다.

- **It** is early spring and the land is just now beginning to show new signs of life.

  때는 초봄이며, 대지는 이제 막 새로운 생명의 징표를 보이기 시작한다.

- How far is **it** from San Francisco to Los Angeles?

  San Francisco에서 Los Angeles까지는 거리가 얼마나 됩니까?

Point 79

(대)명사는 격에 따라 형태가 달라진다.

---

452 When you've finished with his proposals, could you write some comments on **it**?

453 **That dog of Tom** barks more ferociously when it sees a stranger than my neighbor's.

> 어구 ferociously *adv.* 사납게

454 Mark joined a health club, but _____ works out irregularly.

(A) he   (B) his

(C) him   (D) himself

> 어구 work out *v.* 운동하다

455 If you need my help, just dial the number written in _____ phone book.

(A) me   (B) my

(C) mine   (D) myself

456 As Jack was leaving the house, his wife chased after _____ with an important document he left behind.

(A) he

(B) his

(C) himself

(D) him

457 If you compare _____ with the best of French wines, we are definitely not there. But if you compare it to the worst of French wines, we are definitely better.

(A) us

(B) ours

(C) ourselves

(D) we

458 In spite of his aged appearance, his movements were as spirited as _____ .

(A) a young man's

(B) young man's

(C) a young man

(D) young men

| 어구 | spirited a. 활기찬 |

Point 80

대명사는 지시하는 명사의 성, 수, 인칭을 따라야 한다.

---

459 The greatest natural resource of the state of North Dakota is **their** fertile farmland.

| 어구 | natural resource 천연자원   fertile a. 비옥한 |

460 Countries tend to specialize in the production and export of those goods and services that **it** can produce relatively cheaply.

| 어구 | relatively adv. 비교적 |

461 A varnish leaves a hard, glossy film when **they** dries.

| 어구 | varnish n. 광택제, 니스   glossy a. 윤이 나는 |

462 Our urge to classify different life forms and give **it** names seems to be as old as the human race.

| 어구 | urge n. 자극, 충동 |

463 Robert Frost was not well known as a poet until he reached **the** forties.

464 In Africa, the feeding habits of migratory locusts make **it** one of the most feared of pests.

> 어구   locust *n.* 메뚜기

465 **That** always seems to be raining harder than it really is when you look through the window.

466 The odd thing about truth is that **one** keeps changing its clothes.

467 All cashiers should remember to have _____ daily transaction sheets approved by the shift supervisor.

     (A)   they   (B)   them

     (C)   their   (D)   theirs

> 어구   cashier *n.* 회계원   transaction *n.* 거래   approve *v.* 승인하다   shift *n.* 교대   supervisor *n.* 감독관

SECTION 10-3

지시대명사

Grammar Focus 54: 지시대명사

앞선 단수명사를 대신할 때는 that을 쓰며, 복수명사를 대신할 때는 those를 쓴다. that과 those 다음에 흔히 of + 명사가 따른다.

- There can be no greater *issue* than **that** of economy in this country.
  이 나라에서 경제보다 더 큰 문제가 있을 수 없다.

- *Governments* in the region, including **those** of Korea and China, have sought to prevent the issue coming to the surface.
  한국과 중국을 포함하여 그 지역의 정부는 그 문제가 표면에 부상하는 것을 막으려 해왔다.

앞선 명사를 대신할 때 one이나 ones를 쓰는데 흔히 형용사나 관계절의 수식을 받는다.

- We have light pink *paint* on our walls and so chose the red **one**.
  우리는 벽에 밝은 분홍색 페인트가 칠해져 있어서 빨강색 페인트를 선택했다.

- When I was presented with a choice of *shoes* last night, I chose the red **ones**.
  지난밤에 신발 선택권이 주어졌을 때 빨강색 신발을 선택했다.

- For financially healthy *companies* we chose the **ones** which were in business for a longer period of time.
  재정적으로 건전한 회사로 우리는 오랫동안 사업을 한 회사를 선택했다.

- Few *poets* can be so obscure as this **one**.
  이 시인만큼 이해하기 힘든 시인은 얼마 되지 않는다.

Point 81

of의 수식을 받는 대명사는 that/those이며, 형용사나 관계절의 수식을 받는 대명사는 one(s)이다 .

---

468 The American standard of living is still higher than **those** of the other countries of the world.

> 어구   still *adv.* 더욱

469 Even though San Francisco's harbor is a splendid one, few harbors in the world are as fine and large **as Rio de Janeiro**.

> 어구   splendid *a.* 훌륭한

470 The dialects of America are not so widely apart as **that** of England.

> 어구   dialect *n.* 방언   widely *adv.* 대단히

471 As we have finished the first lesson, now we will read the second **ones**.

472 Martha tried to find a good book on astronomy, but the bookstore she went to did not have **none**.

> 어구   astronomy *n.* 천문학

473 Walt Whitman originated a distinctive form of free verse that sets his work apart from _____ of all other poets.

(A) what   (B) that

(C) how   (D) it

SECTION 10-4

재귀대명사와 상호대명사

Grammar Focus 55: 재귀대명사와 상호대명사

주어와 목적어가 동일할 때 혹은 강조할 때 재귀대명사를 쓴다.

- *A South Korean truck driver* killed **himself** on Saturday by set-ting **himself** on fire.
  한국의 한 트럭 운전수는 토요일에 불에 몸을 던져 자살했다.

- *He* **himself** was always in frail health.
  그 자신이 항상 건강이 허약했다.

- An English nobleman was abandoned and grew up all **by him-self** in the jungle.
  한 영국 귀족이 정글에 버려져서 홀로 자랐다.

상호대명사 each other와 one another

- When the couple chased **each other** upstairs, Michael entered the house, walked into the kitchen and opened a drawer full of wine bottles.
  그 두 사람이 윗층에서 서로 잡으려고 뛰어 다닐 때, Michael은 집에 들어와 부엌으로 가서 포도주병이 가득한 서랍을 열었다.

- As *the girls* chased **each other** in the grass, he and I talked in whispers.
  소녀들이 풀밭에서 서로 뒤쫓을 때 그와 나는 속삭이며 말했다.

- For the first few days *they* chased **one another** back and forth from one end of the tank to the other.
  처음 며칠간 그들은 한 탱크에서 다른 탱크로 서로 뒤쫓았다.

주어와 목적어가 동일한 사람이나 사물을 가리킬 때 재귀대명사를 쓴다.

474 To appreciate what the hybrid corn breeder does, it is necessary to understand how corn reproduces **it**.

> 어구 | appreciate *v.* 이해하다, 감사하다   hybrid *n.* 잡종   breeder *n.* 사육자   reproduce *v.* 재생하다, 생식하다

475 As the current society is being globalized rapidly, people living today have to adapt **himself** to such a circumstance.

> 어구 | globalize *v.* 세계화하다   adapt *v.* 적응하다   circumstance *n.* 환경

476 To stay warm in cold weather, cold-blooded animals must expose **itself** to a source of warmth such as direct sunlight.

> 어구 | cold-blooded *a.* 냉혈의

477 The president announced that he himself would act upon the evidence as presented to **himself** by the Congressional Committee.

> 어구 | act upon ··· 에 따라 행동하다

478 People out of work organized and operated their own group by _____ in oder to overcome unemployment.

    (A) himself   (B) oneself

    (C) theirs   (D) themselves

479 The senator found the secret, but he has kept it to _____.

    (A) his own   (B) his

    (C) himself   (D) him

480 An oven that cleans _____ is very handy.

    (A) itself   (B) it

    (C) in itself   (D) them

481 Plants _____ of excess water through transpiration.

    (A) rid them   (B) rid themselves

    (C) rid itself   (D) rid of themselves

> 어구 | rid oneself of ··· 을 버리다   transpiration *n.* 증발, 발산

부정대명사

Grammar Focus 56: 부정대명사

막연한 다른 하나는 another를 쓴다.

- This computer isn't good for my job; I need **another** one.
  이 컴퓨터는 내 일에 적합하지 않으므로 다른 것이 필요하다.

- We have to provide children with an opportunity to learn to get along with one **another**.
  우리는 아이들이 서로 잘 지낼 수 있는 방법을 배울 수 있는 기회를 제공해야 한다.

문맥에 의해 정해지는 나머지를 가리킬 때 the other(s)를 쓴다.

- There are two forms of precipitation, of which rain is one and snow is **the other**.
  두 종류의 강수가 있는데, 그 하나는 비이며, 다른 하나는 눈이다.

- The only way to influence **others** is to talk about what they want and show them how to get it.
  다른 사람에게 영향을 미치는 유일한 방법은 그 사람들이 필요한 것이 무엇인지 말해주고, 그것을 어떻게 얻을 수 있는지를 보여주는 것이다.

- One of them is a physicist while **the others** are novices.
  그들 가운데 한 명은 물리학자이며, 다른 사람들은 초보자이다.

Point 83

another는 막연한 하나, the other(s) 는 정해진 나머지, others는 막연한 나머지를 가리킨다.

---

482 To help policymakers and **another**, the U.S. government spends as much as 4 billion a year in collecting statistics.

　어구　policymaker *n.* 정책입안자　　statistics *n.* 통계

483 Lizards lack the built-in body temperature control many **another** creatures possess.

　어구　lizard *n.* 도마뱀　　built-in *a.* 붙박이의, 내장된

484 Though Artist Tatun was totally blind in one eye and had only slight vision in **another**, he became an internationally renowned jazz musician.

> 어구   renowned *a.* 유명한, 명성 있는

485 Some people argue that atomic bombs should not have been used in the second world war, but **other** maintain using them was inevitable so as to put a quick end to the war.

> 어구   maintain *v.* 주장하다   inevitable *a.* 불가피한   so as to ... ··· 하기 위하여

486 Lightning is the transfer of electrical current from a cloud to the ground or from one cloud to **the other**.

> 어구   lightning *n.* 번개

487 Unlike the carnivores of their era, sauropods did not need to take the lives of **another** animals to find sustenance.

> 어구   carnivore *n.* 육식동물   sauropod *n.* 초식 공룡   sustenance *n.* 생계, 음식

Point 84

another는 단수명사와 함께 쓰이며, other는 복수명사와 함께 쓰인다.

---

488 Copper is a metal which is easily worked and which mixes well with **others** metals to form alloys.

> 어구   copper *n.* 구리   alloy *n.* 합금

489 Was it another **men** who had been lost in the middle of the ocean?

490 Electric lamps came into widespread use during the early 1900's and have replaced other **type** of fat, gas, or oil lamps for almost every purpose.

491 The ancient Hopewell people of North America probably cultivated corn and _____ crops, but hunting and gathering were still of critical importance in their economy.

(A) another   (B) the other's

(C) other   (D) other than

Point 85

every와 each는 단수명사와 함께 쓰이며, all은 복수명사와 함께 쓰인다.

---

492 Everyone in the delegation had _____ reasons for opposing the measure.

(A) his   (B) their

(C) your   (D) its

493 All are thought to have done _____ best to make the project a success.

(A) his   (B) her

(C) our   (D) their

Point 86

some은 긍정문에, any는 부정문 또는 의문문에 쓰인다.

---

494 _____ bag was left here all night. Do you think there is an address written inside?

(A) Anybody's   (B) Somebody's

(C) Everybody's   (D) Some people's

495 There are always _____ people who will disregard company regulations.

(A) any   (B) some

(C) every   (D) few

PRACTICE TEST

496 Even though a lot of people offered to help, he decided to do it by itself.

497 He was stopped each dozen yards by friends who wanted to congratulate him.

498 On the one hand, he always does his work on time; on the second hand, he is very untidy and dirty in his appearance.

어구   on time 제 시간에   untidy a. 지저분한

499 Some scientists predict that, despite greater material output, the people in the year 2,000 will be poorer in many ways than it is today.

500 Yesterday I met an old friend of _____.

(A) me   (B) my

(C) mine   (D) them

501 This computer isn't good for my job. I need _____ one.

(A) some   (B) another

(C) other's   (D) any other

502 To take pride in what deserves boasting is one thing, and to take good care of it is quite _____.

(A) others   (B) thing

(C) another   (D) the other

503 Most household appliances emit electromagnetic fields that are basically equivalent to _____ high-voltage lines.

(A) those emitted by   (B) what emitted by

(C) they are emitted by   (D) which are emitted by

어구   household appliance 가전제품   electromagnetic field 전자기장

504 The advisory board had implemented all of his ideas except
_____ would cause painful cutbacks.

(A) these which   (B) those what

(C) these that   (D) those that

어구   advisory board 자문위원단   implement *v.* 시행하다   cutback *n.* 삭
감, 감축

505 Health is more valuable than wealth; _____ cannot give such
true happiness as that.

(A) this   (B) that

(C) it   (D) one

506 His salary as a bus driver is much higher _____.

(A) in comparison with the salary of a teacher

(B) than a teacher

(C) than that of a teacher

(D) to compare as a teacher

Chapter 11

Number Agreement

시제동사는 주어의 수와 일치해야 하는데, 형태만으로 단·복수를 구별하기 어려운 경우가 있으며, 주의해야 할 구문이 있다.

SECTION 11-1

명사의 수

Grammar Focus 57: 복수형 단수

시간, 거리, 무게, 가격을 나타내는 주어는 형태가 복수이더라도 단수 취급한다.

- **Five years is** a short time in which to measure development.
  5년은 발전을 평가하기에는 짧은 시간이다.

- **Ten miles is** a long way to walk.
  10마일은 걷기에 먼 거리이다.

- For him, **two thousand dollars is** a small price to pay for it.
  그에게 2천 달러는 그것에 대한 값으로는 적다.

학문, 질병, 국가명은 복수형이더라도 단수 취급한다.

- While **economics is** a kind of theory-centered study, applied **statistics is** a skill-centered study.
  경제학이 이론 중심의 학문인 반면, 응용통계학은 기술 중심의 학문이다.

- **Measles is** among the most contagious diseases in the world.
  홍역은 세계에서 가장 전염성이 강한 질병 중의 하나이다.

- **The Philippines** is a country where democracy has not fully developed.

필리핀은 민주주의가 완전히 발달하지는 못한 나라이다.

Grammar Focus 58: 집합명사

집합명사는 집합 전체를 말할 때는 단수 취급하지만, 개체를 하나하나를 말할 때는 복수 취급한다.

- **My family are** gathering in Philadelphia, and I'm preparing a Thanksgiving feast for them.
  우리 가족이 필라델피아에서 모이므로, 그들을 위해 추수감사절을 준비하고 있다.

- **My family is** a lot smaller than it used to be.
  우리 가족은 예전에 비해 훨씬 작다.

Grammar Focus 59: the + 형용사

the + 형용사가 사람을 나타낼 때는 복수 취급한다. 다만 사람을 나타내더라도 문맥상 혹은 관습상 단수 취급하는 경우도 있다.

- **The rich** are not always happy.
  부자라고 항상 행복하진 않다.

- **The absent is** always in the wrong.
  부재자가 항상 잘못이다.

사물을 나타낼 때는 단수 취급한다.

- You'll see that **the inevitable** is finally about to happen.
  너는 불가피한 일이 마침내 일어나는 것을 볼 것이다.

Point 87
주어가 복잡할 때는 중심이 되는 명사를 찾아야 한다.

507 The growth of such international organization as the United Nations **have** changed the meaning of political neutrality.

508 In the past, the rulers of the country **has** been selfish, but the present king has great respect and concern for his people.

509 It is red blood cells in the bone that **produces** hemoglobin.

> 어구 red blood cell 적혈구   hemoglobin *n.* 혈색소, 헤모글로빈

510 Hurricanes are severe cyclones with winds over seventy-five miles an hour which **originates** over tropical ocean waters.

> 어구 originate *v.* 발생하다, 유래하다   cyclone *n.* 회오리 바람

511 One of the first results of the police investigation **were** a redesigning of the whole security system.

> 어구 investigation *n.* 조사

512 The applications of mathematics **has** undergone a tremendous growth over the past decade.

513 Cars, like any machine, **requires** regular maintenance and care in order to run well.

514 The number of people who own a computer _____ increasing with rapidity.

(A) are   (B) have been

(C) has been   (D) has

Point 88

부정사나 동명사가 주어로 쓰이면 단수 동사를 쓴다.

---

515 Ensuring an adequate water supply **have** been a concern ever since people began to live in towns and cities.

516 Making all the national convention arrangements **were** Mr. Huge's responsibility.

> 어구 convention *n.* 관습, 대회, 협약

517 Using many symbols **make** it difficult to put a large amount of information on a single map.

Point 89

the + 형용사가 사람을 나타낼 때는 복수 취급하며, 그렇지 않으면 단수 취급한다.

☞ the+형용사가 사람을 나타낼 때 단수 취급하는 것들이 있다.

the accused, the deceased, the Almighty

518 _____ more to be pitied than blamed.

(A) Uneducated are (B) The uneducated are

(C) The uneducated is (D) The uneducated people

519 _____ has been found guilty.

(A) Accused (B) Accused people

(C) An accused (D) The accused

Point 90

집합명사는 전체를 나타낼 때는 단수 취급하나, 구성원을 나타낼 때는 복수취급한다.

520 The planning committee **have** finalized the advertising and market-ing strategies for next fiscal year.

> 어구 strategy *n.* 전략 fiscal *a.* 재정의

Point 91

학문, 국가명, 질병 등은 형태가 복수더라도 단수취급한다.

☞ 다음 명사는 복수형만을 쓰며, 복수동사를 취한다.

belongings, clothes, goods, customs(세관), arms, surroundings, trousers, pants, scissors, glasses

☞ 다음 명사는 복수형만을 가지나 문맥에 따라 단수동사를 취하기도 하고, 복수동사를 취하기도 한다.

means, series, species, headquarters

521 The United States **celebrate** the birth of its independence every Forth of July.

522 Measles **spread** easily among individuals who haven't been vaccinated.

523 Whether we like it or not, it is true that mathematics **are** the language of science and the universe.

524 The bad **news** about the new contract have finally been confirmed.

SECTION 11-2

수량사와 분수

> **Grammar Focus 60: 수량사 및 분수**
>
> every와 each 다음에는 단수 명사가 오며, 단수 취급한다.
>
> - **Every student is** required to attend punctually at the hours notified.
>   모든 학생은 공지된 시간에 정확히 출석해야 한다.
>
> - **Each student is** required to pass a written comprehensive examination in the major field.
>   모든 학생은 전공분야에서 필기 종합시험을 합격해야 한다.
>
> 분수 + 명사의 경우 분수와 관계 없이 명사의 수에 의해 수가 결정된다.
>
> - About **one-third of the greenhouse gases** produced in New Zealand **come** from animals such as sheep and cows.
>   뉴질랜드에서 발생되는 온실 가스의 약 3분의 1이 양과 소 같은 동물에 의한 것이다.
>
> - **One-third of the food** we buy **ends** up in the bin.
>   우리가 사는 음식물의 3분의 1은 쓰레기통으로 사라진다.

접속사

Grammar Focus 61: 접속사

두 개의 명사가 and로 결합되어 마치 한 단위처럼 나타나는 경우에 단수 취급한다.

- **Time and tide waits** for no man.
  세월은 사람을 기다려 주지 않는다.

- **Bread and butter is** available in Korea but most people prefer rice.
  한국에서 버터 바른 빵을 먹을 수 있지만, 대부분 밥을 좋아한다.

두 개의 명사가 접속사로 연결될 때 수의 일치에 주의해야 한다.

- **Neither he nor I am** sure that this will happen.
  그도 나도 이 일이 일어날지 확신하지 못한다.

- **Not only he but also I have** been to the Great Wall.
  그 뿐만 아니라 나도 만리장성에 가본 적이 있다.

- **I, as well as he, am** in the wrong.
  그 뿐만 아니라 나도 과실이 있다.

Point 92

each와 every는 단수 명사와 함께 쓰이며 단수 취급한다.

---

525 Each student may leave the room whenever **they** may desire to do so.

526 The electronics company along with ELSS **are** having trouble preparing its employees for the new millenium.

527 _____ great chef prepares his or her food in a different way.

(A) Every (B) Any

(C) All (D) Some

528 Every boy and girl in our class _____ a camera.

(A) have   (B) has

(C) is having   (D) have had

Point 93 ─────────────────────

all은 복수 명사와 함께 쓰인다.

529 All the people who **is** interested in the problem should be invited to tomorrow's meeting.

530 _____ ballet dancers learn five basic positions for the arms and feet.

(A) All of   (B) Of every

(C) All   (D) Every

Point 94 ─────────────────────

neither of + 명사는 단수 취급한다.

531 Neither of them **have** turned in the report to the person in charge yet.

532 Neither of the two candidates having applied for admission to the department **were** eligible for it.

어구 eligible *a.* 적격의

533 Neither of them _____ satisfactory work.

(A) done   (B) hasn't done

(C) have done   (D) has done

Point 95 ─────────────────────

분수+명사의 수는 명사의 수를 따른다.

534 One-fourth of a worker's income **are paid** in taxes to the government.

535 Two thirds of women prisoners **has** dependent children under the age of 18.

536 It has been estimated that only 21 percent of the world's land surface **are** cultivatable and that only 7.6 percent is actually under cultivation.

537 Two-thirds of my project _____ finished.

    (A) are   (B) is

    (C) am   (D) be

Point 96

접속사에 따라 일치가 달라진다.

---

538 My nose as well as my ears **were** bleeding when the doctor was brought in.

539 Not only the plant workers but the manager _____ on strike.

    (A) are   (B) is

    (C) being   (D) have been

540 Neither you nor he _____ likely to be present at the meeting.

    (A) are   (B) is

    (C) were   (D) have

PRACTICE TEST

541 It is the interaction between people, rather than the events that occur in their lives that are the main focus of social psychology.

542 The group of people have been waiting some two hours in front of the theater before the movie started.

543 The National Cowboy Hall of Fame in Oklahoma City pay tribute to everyone associated with what Americans call the "Old West."

> 어구　tribute *n.* 찬사

544 Many people who live in New York City thinks that life in a large city offers special advantages.

545 Many American novelists, such as Gore Vidal, resides in other countries.

> 어구　reside *v.* 거주하다

546 The information presented were too technical for any beginning analyst.

547 The first libraries in the North American colonies was established in Massachusetts in the year 1638.

Chapter 12

Relatives

관계사에는 관계대명사, 관계부사, 유사관계대명사가 있는데, 관계사는 접속사＋대명사 또는 지시부사의 역할을 한다. 관계사의 선택은 선행사의 종류와 대명사/지시부사의 위치에 따라 결정된다.

SECTION 12-1

관계대명사

Grammar Focus 62: 관계대명사 who(m)

선행사가 사람이면 who(m)를 쓰는데, 주어이면 who, 목적어이면 whom을 쓴다. 흔히 목적어나 보어도 who를 쓴다. 계속적 용법으로 쓰일 경우에는 그 앞에 콤마가 온다.

- The police are looking for *a man* **who** attempted to disguise himself as a tree and rob a bank in Manchester.
  경찰은 Manchester에서 나무처럼 가장하고 은행을 털려던 사람을 찾고 있다.

- He must be considerate and well-behaved in the classroom of *the teacher* **whom** he so dislikes.
  그는 자기가 그렇게 싫어하는 선생님의 수업시간에 사려 깊고 품행이 단정해야 한다.

- I am next to *the teacher*, **who** I believe was Miss Taylor.
  나는 그 선생님 옆에 있는데, Taylor 선생님이라고 생각했던 분이다.

Grammar Focus 63: 관계대명사 which

선행사가 사물일 때 주어, 목적어, 보어 모두 which를 쓴다. 선행사가 문장의 일부나 전체일 때도 which를 쓴다.

- *The book* **which** is on the table is mine.
  책상 위에 있는 책은 내 것이다.

- You will come to hear about the good and bad about *the car* **which** you are planning to own.
  너는 소유하려고 계획하고 있는 차의 장단점을 듣게 될 것이다.

- We have to completely *rebuild the car*, **which** will take considerable time.
  우리는 차를 완전히 개조해야 하는데, 상당한 시간이 걸릴 것이다.

- To buy land you have to be very *rich*, **which** I'm not.
  네가 토지를 구입하기 위해서는 부자라야 하는데, 나는 그렇지 못하다.

- Tom is always late for school, which makes his teacher very angry.
  Tom이 항상 학교에 지각을 하는데, 이 때문에 선생님은 매우 화가 난다.

Grammar Focus 64: 소유격 관계대명사 whose

선행사의 종류와 관계 없이 소유격에는 whose를 쓴다.

- Sometimes we come across *celebrities* **whose** names we do not know.
  때로는 우리가 이름을 알지 못하는 유명 인사를 우연히 만나게 된다.

- *The table* **whose** leg was broken was removed from the room.
  다리가 망가진 책상이 그 방에서 치워졌다.

Grammar Focus 65: 관계대명사 that

선행사의 종류에 관계 없이 that을 쓸 수 있으며, 특히 선행사가 최상급, 서수, only 등의 수식을 받거나 사람 + 사물인 경우, 혹은 의문사인 경우는 that을 쓴다. 단, 계속적 용법에는 that을 쓰지 못한다.

- These are *the people* **that** keep my life running smoothly.
  이 분들은 내 삶이 평온하게 유지되도록 하는 사람들이다.

- The *only* thing **that** makes me happy anymore is helping people with their own problems.

  이제 내가 행복을 느끼게 만드는 유일한 것은 다른 사람들의 문제를 도와주는 것이다.

- *Who* **that** has common sense will believe such a story?

  상식이 있는 사람이라면 누가 그런 이야기를 믿겠는가?

Point 97

선행사가 사람이면 who를 쓰며, 사물이면 which를 쓴다.

---

548 Paulina Wright Davis was an American social reformer **which** worked for the right of women to own property and to vote.

　　어구　reformer *n.* 개혁가　　property *n.* 재산

549 Anne Elizabeth McDowell is best remembered for a weekly journal, *the Woman's Advocate*, **who** she launched in January 1855.

　　어구　launch *v.* 착수하다, 출판하다　　advocate *v.* 지지하다, 옹호자

550 Plant cuttings **who** are placed in water will develop roots and can then be planted in soil.

　　어구　cutting *n.* 꺾꽂이용으로 자른 나뭇가지

551 The job requires an expert _____ is capable of making the complex program needed for the software.

(A) whom　　　　　　　　(B) whose

(C) which　　　　　　　　(D) who

　　어구　expert *n.* 전문가

552 Anthony Burgess, _____ as a novelist, was originally a student of music.

(A) because of being famous

(B) who has achieved fame

(C) who because he was famous

(D) achieved fame

어구 novelist *n.* 소설가

553 Jane Addams, an American social reformer in Chicago, _____ for poor people, won the Nobel Peace Prize in 1931.

(A) she established a community center

(B) established a community center

(C) who was established a community center

(D) who established a community center

어구 community center 시민 문화 회관

554 Malvin Gray Johnson is noted especially for the pictures _____ in Brightwood, Virginia, in the late summer of 1934.

(A) which he was painted   (B) in which painted

(C) in which he painted   (D) which he painted

어구 noted *a.* 유명한

555 Rice, _____ of much of the world's population, grows best in hot, wet lands.

(A) still forms the staple diet

(B) which it still forms the staple diet

(C) which still forms the staple diet

(D) which is still formed the staple diet

어구 staple diet 기본 식료품

Point 98

관계사의 위치에 따른 형태에 유의해야 한다.
---

556 The director announced the names of those **whom** were to be named to the key posts.

어구 director *n.* 감독, 국장   key *a.* 주요한

557 Ripe fruit is often stored in a place **at which** contains much carbon dioxide so that the fruit will not decay too rapidly.

> 어구 carbon dioxide 이산화탄소

558 Mahalia Jackson, **who** singing combined powerful vitality with great dignity, was one of the best-known gospel singers in the United States.

> 어구 vitality *n.* 활력 dignity *n.* 위엄, 품위 gospel *n.* 복음

559 A web admin is a system administrator _____ job focus is primarily on web technologies such as web hosting on any given platform.

(A) what

(B) whose

(C) whom

(D) when

Point 99

관계대명사는 접속사+대명사 역할을 한다.

---

560 The earth is the sole planet in the solar system that **it** has appreciable amounts of oxygen gas in its atmosphere.

> 어구 planet *n.* 행성 solar system 태양계 appreciable *a.* 상당한 oxygen *n.* 산소 atmosphere *n.* 대기

561 The counselor Ms. Mary talked to **her** was very helpful in her new project because he had been in the business before.

562 Only the female and the worker wasps are equipped with a sting, which they use **it** to attack their prey or to protect themselves against enemies.

> 어구 wasp *n.* 말벌 prey *n.* 먹이, 희생자

563 Our understanding of the past is based on written records, oral traditions, and physical evidence, **all of them** must be interpreted.

> 어구 oral tradition 구비 interpret *v.* 해석하다

564 The city of Kalamazoo, Michigan, derives its name from a Native American word **means** "bubbling springs."

> 어구 derive *v.* 유래하다 bubbling *a.* 끓는

Grammar Focus 66: 관계대명사 what

관계대명사 what은 선행사를 포함하는 관계대명사로 주절의 문장 성분의 역할을 하면서 동시에 관계절의 문장 성분이 된다.

- **What** is done out of love always takes place beyond good and evil.
  사랑으로 행해진 것은 항상 선악을 넘어서 일어난다.

- They seem to be satisfied with **what** we are proposing.
  그들은 우리가 제안하고 있는 것에 만족하는 것처럼 보인다.

Point 100

관계대명사 what은 선행사를 포함한다.

565 **That** people consider a luxury at one time frequently becomes a necessity; many families find that ownership of two cars is indispensable.

어구 necessity *n.* 필수품   indispensable *a.* 필수 불가결한

566 Most of the food **what** elephants eat is brought to their mouths by their trunks.

어구 trunk *n.* 코끼리 코

567 **That** is most touching in P. Henry's stories is the gallantry with which ordinary people struggle to maintain their dignity.

어구 touching *a.* 감동적인   gallantry *n.* 용맹

568 _____ would be a fairly long speech in a play is often presented as a reductive in opera.

(A) That
(B) There
(C) It
(D) What

어구 fairly *adv.* 꽤   reductive *a.* 감소시키는 것

569 As _____ is now known in physics and chemistry, scientists have been able to make important discoveries in biology and medicine.

(A) a result of what (B) what a result of

(C) a result what of (D) a what result of

어구 physics *n.* 물리학 chemistry *n.* 화학 biology *n.* 생물학

> **Point 101**
>
> 목적격 관계대명사는 생략이 가능하며, 주격관계대명사는 be동사와 함께 생략된다.

570 The earthworm is a worm **that found** in moist, warm soil in many geographical areas.

어구 earthworm *n.* 지렁이 geographical *a.* 지리학의

571 As many as 50 percent of the income from motion pictures _____ comes from marketing the films abroad.

(A) produced in the United States

(B) are produced in the United States

(C) that produced in the United States

(D) and produced in the United States

어구 motion picture 영화

572 Before starting on a sea voyage, prudent navigators learn the sea charts, study the sailing directions, and memorize lighthouse locations to prepare themselves for any conditions _____.

(A) they might encounter

(B) or they might encounter

(C) when they might encounter

(D) and they might encounter

어구 prudent *a.* 신중한 navigator *n.* 항해사 lighthouse *n.* 등대

573 John F. Kennedy was only forty two when he was inaugurated as president of the United States—the youngest person _____ the presidency.

(A) ever electing to   (B) ever been elected to

(C) who ever elected to   (D) ever elected to

어구   inaugurate *v.* 취임식을 거행하다   presidency *n.* 대통령직

SECTION 12-2
관계부사

Grammar Focus 67: 관계부사

전치사+관계대명사는 관계부사로 바꿔 쓸 수 있다. 선행사가 장소이면 where, 시간이면 when을 쓰는데, 선행사의 종류 뿐만 아니라 문장에서의 역할도 살펴야 한다. 관계부사를 쓰려면 관계절에서의 역할이 주어나 목적어가 아닌 부사어라야 한다.

- If you live far away from *the store* **where** your family buys fruit, you might use a car to get there.
  네 가족이 과일을 사는 가게에서 멀리 산다면 그곳에 가려면 자동차를 이용해야 할 것이다.

- After the economy hit the bottom in *1998*, **when** GDP shrank 10.5%, growth has picked up.
  GDP가 10.5% 줄어든 1998년 경기가 바닥을 친 후, 경제가 성장하였다.

Point 102
관계부사는 부사를 대신하기 때문에 부사 자리가 비어 있어야 한다.

---

574 On the 1st floor there is the main hall **which** most entrance cere-monies, graduations, official events and parties take place.

575 Last spring, we visited Florida **where** is noted for its beautiful beach.

576 The day will come _____ my words will come true.

    (A) where   (B) when

    (C) why   (D) how

577 Dams can be very beneficial to the areas _____.

(A) in which they are built   (B) building them where

(C) which they are built   (D) where are they built

어구   beneficial *a.* 이로운

578 There are very few areas in the world _____ be grown successfully.

(A) where apricots can   (B) which apricots can

(C) apricots that can   (D) where can apricots

어구   apricot *n.* 살구

579 Chemistry is concerned with _____ interact with one another.

(A) the way of substances   (B) the way substances

(C) the substances way   (D) way substances

어구   substance *n.* 물질

580 Eastern meadowlarks abound in places _____, but eat harmful
insects rather than grain.

(A) land is cultivated there   (B) there is land cultivated

(C) where land is cultivated   (D) where is cultivated land

어구   meadowlark *n.* 들종다리   abound *v.* 풍부하다   grain *n.* 곡식,
알갱이

SECTION 12-3

복합관계사

Grammar Focus 68: 복합관계사

관계사+ever의 형태를 복합관계사라 하는데, 선행사를 포함하므로 선행사가 필요
없다. 선행사를 포함한다는 점에서는 what과 유사하지만 all의 뜻이 포함되어 있다.

• **Whoever** wins moves on to face the next winner in the next
round.

승리한 자는 다음 경기에서 다음 승자를 계속하여 만난다.

- He became fully immersed in achieving his best in **whatever** he chose to do.
  그는 그가 하고자 선택한 것이라면 무엇이든 최선을 얻는 데 전적으로 몰입하게 되었다.

- When you meet someone, remember, **however** hard you try to impress others, you cannot control their thought processes.
  다른 사람을 만날 때 네가 아무리 인상을 심어 주려고 하더라도 그들의 사고 과정을 조절할 수 없다는 것을 기억해라.

Point 103

복합관계사는 선행사를 포함하는 관계사이다.

---

581 The columnist feels sure that **who** wins the election will have the support of both parties.

582 A wise administrator will assign a job to **whomever** is best qualified.

> 어구 administrator *n.* 행정가

583 The teacher tells the same story to **whomever** participates in the class.

584 _____ gets home first starts cooking.

(A) Anyone (B) Whoever

(C) Who (D) Those

585 Send the invitation card _____ you think is likely to come to the party.

(A) whoever (B) to whoever

(C) whomever (D) to whomever

> 어구 invitation card 초대장

586 Please feel free to distribute this program to _____ you like.

(A) whom	(B) whoever
(C) whomever	(D) people

어구 distribute *v.* 분배하다

SECTION 12-4

유사관계대명사

Grammar Focus 69: 유사관계대명사

as, but, than이 관계사로 쓰이는 경우가 있다. 선행사에 as/so/such가 포함되어 있으면 as, 부정어가 포함되어 있으면 but, 그리고 비교급이 포함되어 있으면 than 을 쓴다.

- He was *as* good and decent a man **as** ever walked this earth.
  그는 지구상에 살았던 어떤 사람만큼이나 훌륭하고 고상하였다.

- I used to scold her for packing *more* books **than** are needed at school.
  나는 학교에서 필요한 이상의 책을 챙겨 넣는다고 그녀를 꾸짖곤 하였다.

- There is *no* man **but** has his faults.
  흠이 없는 사람은 없다.

Point 104

유사관계대명사는 선행사에 특정 표현이 포함되었을 때 쓴다.

---

587 The organization asked for more donation **which** was necessary.

어구 donation *n.* 기부

588 We are given just as much food _____ will keep the breath in our bodies.

(A) as	(B) that
(C) what	(D) but

589 There is no one _____ loves his mother.

(A) who   (B) as

(C) whom   (D) but

PRACTICE TEST

590 The decade of the 1920's was significant in Georgia's history because of the rapidity with what agriculture declined in the state.

어구 | decline *v.* 쇠퇴하다

591 Tenant farmers are those they either rent a farm and work it for themselves or work the farm for the owner and receive payment.

어구 | tenant farmer 소작농

592 Butterflies and moths undergo complete metamorphosis, then changing from caterpillar to adult via one intermediate stage, the pupa.

어구 | moth *n.* 나방   metamorphosis *n.* 변태   caterpillar *n.* 애벌레   pupa *n.* 번데기

593 A symbol of freedom, the Statue of Liberty represents a woman has just escaped from the chains of slavery, which lie at her feet.

어구 | represent *v.* 나타내다

594 Mathematics is an indispensable tool for anyone which desires to do graduate work in the sciences.

어구 | indispensable *a.* 필수의   graduate work 대학원 과정

595 These guns shoot large shells, any one of whom would blow up a house or sink a ship.

어구 | shell *n.* 포탄

596 Antonio Stradivari, whose generally acknowledged to be the greatest violin maker of all time, worked in the Italian town of Cremona and made over 1,000 instruments during the course of his career.

어구 | of all time 전무후무한   instrument *n.* 도구, 악기

597 Before every presidential election in the United States, the statisticians try to guess the proportion of the population that _____ for each candidate.

(A) are voted
(B) voting
(C) to be voted
(D) will vote

> 어구 presidential election 대통령 선거   statistician *n.* 통계전문가, 통계학자   proportion *n.* 비율   candidate *n.* 후보

598 By 1872 the United States had 70 engineering colleges, _____ astonishing expansion credited largely to the Morrill Act of 1862.

(A) because
(B) an
(C) to which
(D) was

> 어구 engineering college 공과대학   credit *B* to *A* B를 A의 공으로 믿다   act *n.* 법률

599 Since New York City is one of the world's most important centers of business, culture, and trade, _____ in the city affects what happens throughout the United States and around the world.

(A) much of happens
(B) much of what happens
(C) much of that happens
(D) much happenings

600 New Jersey and Delaware are separated by Delaware Bay, _____ connects with the Delaware River and thus enables oceangoing vessels to reach the ports of Wilmington, Del., and Philadelphia.

(A) which deep channel
(B) deep channel of it
(C) that is a deep channel
(D) whose deep channel

> 어구 bay *n.* 만   oceangoing *a.* 원양 항해의   vessel *n.* 선박

Solutions

001 [Sit up → Sitting up] late is not good for the health.

> 번역　늦게까지 자지 않으면 건강에 좋지 않다.

> 해설　동사를 주어자리에 쓰고자 할 때는 to부정사나 동명사를 쓴다.

002 In effect, [learn → learning] the meaning of things is better than learning the meaning of words.

> 번역　사실상 사물의 의미를 학습하는 것은 단어의 의미를 학습하는 것보다 낫다.

> 해설　시제동사 is 앞에는 주어로 쓰일 수 있는 표현이 와야 한다. learn이 the meaning of things를 목적어로 취하면서 is의 주어 역할을 하려면 동명사가 되어야 한다.

003 (C) The rarely found four-leaf clover is considered a lucky sign.

(A) It is rarely 　　　　　　(B) Rarely

(C) The rarely 　　　　　　(D) Despite its being rarely

> 번역　잘 발견되지 않는 네 잎 클로버는 행운의 징표로 여겨진다.

> 해설　is가 시제동사이므로 그 앞에는 명사 표현이 와야 한다. clover는 가산명사이므로 단수일 경우 정관사나 부정관사가 필요하다.

004 (A) Fossils of sea creatures have been discovered on top of peaks in the Rockies and the Appalachians, as far as a thousand miles from the nearest ocean.

(A) Fossils of sea creatures

(B) There are fossils of sea creatures

(C) Fossils of sea creatures that

(D) For fossils of sea creatures

> 번역　바다 생명체의 화석은 가장 가까운 바다로부터 천 마일이나 떨어진 로키산맥이나 애팔레치아산맥의 정상에서 발견되었다.

> 해설　시제동사 앞에는 주어가 온다. (B)의 경우 시제동사가 두 개이므로 접속사가 있어야 한다. (C)의 경우 시제동사가 that절에 속하게 되어 또 하나의 시제동사가 필요하다. (D)의 경우 전치사구는 주어가 될 수 없다.

005 (B) The game of tennis is of comparatively modern development.

(A) It is the game of tennis

(B) The game of tennis

(C) Though the game of tennis

(D) Like the game of tennis

> 번역 테니스 경기는 비교적 현대에 발달된 것이다.

> 해설 시제동사 is 앞에 주어가 와야 한다. (B)만이 명사 표현이다.

006 (B) Rocky shores that lack beaches are eventually destroyed by the sea.

(A) Rocky shores lack beaches

(B) Rocky shores that lack beaches

(C) Rocky shores that are lack beaches

(D) Rocky shores that lacks beaches

> 번역 해변이 없는 바위 해안은 결국 바닷물에 의해 침식된다.

> 해설 시제동사 are 앞에는 주어가 필요하다. are destroyed로 보아 의미상 destroy의 목적어가 주어자리에 온다. lack은 타동사로 목적어가 필요하며, 선행사 rocky shores가 복수라는 점에 유의해야 한다.

007 (D) That the dog was the first animal to be domesticated is generally agreed upon by authorities in the field.

(A) Until the   (B) It was the

(C) The   (D) That the

> 번역 개가 길들여진 첫번째 동물이라는 것은 일반적으로 그 분야의 권위자들이 동의한다.

> 해설 is의 주어로 쓰이려면 그 앞에 명사, 명사구, 명사절이 와야 한다. was가 있으므로 명사절이 되어야 하는데, that이 명사절을 이끄는 접속사이다.

008 Government library collections [they are → are] geared chiefly toward serving the need of government officials.

> 번역 정부 도서관의 장서는 주로 공무원의 요구에 부응하도록 구성되어 있다.

> 해설 Government library collections가 주어이므로 they가 불필요하다.

009 [My professor he → My professor] says that the history of philosophy is simply a series of footnotes to Plato's works.

> 번역 철학의 역사는 플라톤 저작에 대한 각주에 불과하다고 우리 교수님은 말씀하신다.

> 해설 동사인 says 앞에는 주어가 필요한데 My professor가 주어이며, he는 불필요하다.

010 Dancer Isadora Duncan [who rebelled → rebelled] against the rigid, formal training of classical ballet and created an individualistic form of expression.

> 번역 | 댄서인 Isadora Duncan은 고전 발레의 딱딱하고 격식을 차린 교육에 반대하였으며, 개성있는 형태의 표현법을 창조하였다.

> 해설 | and created로 보아 Dancer Isadora Duncan이 주어이다. who를 삭제 해야 Duncan이 rebelled and created의 공통 주어가 될 수 있다. 만약 who를 그대로 두고자 한다면 and를 삭제해야 한다.

011 James Farmer, an American civil rights leader, [he → φ] helped establish the Congress of Racial Equality, an organization that is dedicated to the principle of nonviolence.

> 번역 | 미국시민권 지도자인 James Farmer는 비폭력주의에 헌신하는 조직인 인종평등회를 조직하는 것을 도왔다.

> 해설 | James Farmer가 help의 주어로 쓰였으므로 he가 불필요하다. an American civil rights leader는 James Farmer와 동격이다.

012 [It → That it] took only 60 days to complete the merger is an extraordinary feat.

> 번역 | 합병하는 데 단지 60일이 걸린 것은 놀라운 업적이다.

> 해설 | 절이 주어 역할을 하기 위해서는 접속사가 필요하다. 명사절이 평서문인 경우 that을 쓰며, 의문문인 경우 whether나 의문사를 쓴다.

013 [What → That] both astrology and alchemy may be regarded as fundamental aspects of thought is indicated by their apparent universality.

> 번역 | 점성술과 연금술이 사고의 근본적 양상으로 간주된다는 것은 분명한 보편성으로 드러난다.

> 해설 | both astrology and alchemy may be regarded as fundamental aspects of thought가 완전한 문장을 이루며 is의 주어 역할을 하므로 접속사 that이 필요하다. what은 선행사를 포함하는 관계대명사로 그 뒤에 주어나 목적어가 빠진 자리가 있어야 한다.

014 (B) Whether an object floats on water depends on the density of both the object and the water.

(A) An object floats   (B) Whether an object floats
(C) Does an object float   (D) So an object floats

> 번역 | 물체가 물 위에 뜨는지는 물체와 물의 밀도에 달려 있다.

> 해설 | 시제동사 depends의 주어가 필요한데 그 앞에 주어-동사가 있으므로 주어가 절이 되어야 한다. 절이 주어가 되려면 명사절을 이끄는 접속사가 필요하며, whether가 명사절을 이끄는 접속사이다.

015 (A) Why the Mayan civilization declined is still a mystery but as with all mysteries there are a lot of theories.

(A) Why	(B) Since
(C) Because	(D) That

번역 마야 문명이 쇠퇴한 이유가 아직까지 수수께끼이지만, 모든 수수께끼가 그러하듯이 많은 이론이 있다.

해설 시제동사인 is 앞에는 주어가 와야 한다. 주어-동사가 이미 있으므로 명사절을 이끄는 접속사가 나타나야 한다. 보어가 a mystery로 의문과 관련이 있으므로 의문사 why를 쓴다. why가 이끄는 절은 명사절로 주어가 될 수 있다.

016 (B) That Betsy Ross made the first United States flag is widely believed.

(A) When Betsy Ross	(B) That Betsy Ross
(C) Betsy Ross	(D) Whether Betsy Ross

번역 Betsy Ross가 성조기를 처음 만들었다는 것은 널리 인정되고 있다.

해설 이 문장에는 두 개의 시제동사가 있다. flag까지가 is의 주어 역할을 해야 하는데 동사 made가 있으므로 명사절을 이끄는 접속사가 필요하며, 또한 made의 주어도 필요하다.

017 (A) Navigation is often considered both a science and an art.

(A) Navigation is	(B) It is navigation
(C) Navigation, which is	(D) Navigation that is

번역 항해술은 흔히 과학이자 기술로 간주된다.

해설 consider는 5형식동사로 다음에 목적어와 목적보어가 나타난다. considered 다음에 명사가 하나 나타나므로 목적어가 주어자리로 이동한 수동태이다. 빈칸에는 주어와 be 동사가 필요하다.

018 (B) There is an increasing international exchange of educational films.

(A) It is	(B) There is
(C) Though there is	(D) Although it is

번역 교육적인 영화의 국제적인 교류가 점차 늘어가고 있다.

해설 an 이하가 명사구이므로 그 앞에 주어-동사가 필요하다. It is도 주어-동사를 이루지만 의미상 적절하지 않다.

019 (A) Canada has a bicameral, or two-chamber, parliament.

(A) Canada has	(B) Having Canada
(C) Because Canada	(D) That Canada is having

번역 Canada는 양원제 의회를 가지고 있다.

주어진 표현이 명사구이므로 그 앞에는 주어-동사가 필요하다. or는 여기서 '즉'의 뜻으로 쓰였다.

020 The mediator in the labor dispute was replaced when her (A) neutrality was called into question.

(A) neutrality   (B) neuter

(C) neutral   (D) neutron

번역 노동분쟁에서 그 중재자는 중립성이 의심되자 교체되었다.

해설 시제동사 was 앞에 주어가 필요하다. her는 소유격이므로 명사와 결합하여 주어가 된다.

021 In the second half of the nineteenth century, textiles from the southwestern United States, particularly fabrics woven by the Navajo people, (A) began to be used as rugs.

(A) began to be used as rugs   (B) rugs began to be used

(C) as rugs began to be used   (D) began to use them as rugs

번역 19세기 후반에, 미국남서부의 직물, 특히 나바호족이 짠 천이 깔개로 사용되기 시작하였다.

해설 textiles가 주어이며, from the southwestern United States는 주어를 수식하며, fabrics woven by the Navajo people은 앞 부분을 부연 설명하는 표현이다. 따라서 textiles를 주어로 하는 동사가 와야 한다. 의미상 use의 목적어인 textiles가 주어자리에 있으므로 use는 수동형이 되어야 한다.

022 (B) The early gold prospector often lived a lonely and rugged life, far from home and family.

(A) However the early gold prospector often lived

(B) The early gold prospector often lived

(C) Not only did the early gold prospector often live

(D) The early gold prospector often living

번역 초기의 황금 탐사자는 종종 집과 가족으로부터 멀리 떨어져 외롭고 누추한 삶을 살았다.

해설 a lonly and rugged life가 명사이므로 문장을 이루기 위해서는 그 앞에 주어-동사가 와야 한다.

023 (B) The history of twentieth-century architecture is rooted in experiments in iron and steel conducted in the nineteenth century.

(A) While the history of twentieth-century architecture

(B) The history of twentieth-century architecture

(C) That the history of twentieth-century architecture

(D) Both twentieth-century architecture and its history

> 번역   20세기의 건축 역사는 19세기에 이루어진 철강 실험에 근거하고 있다.

> 해설   in iron and steel은 의미상 experiments의 목적어 역할을 하며, con-ducted in the nineteenth century는 experiments를 수식한다. 시제동사 is 앞에는 주어가 필요하다. (A)의 경우 while 다음의 명사가 주어 역할을 할 수 있으나 while이 이끄는 절은 종속절이 되어야 한다. (C)의 경우에도 that이 종속접속사이므로 종속절을 이끌게 되어 주절이 필요하게 된다. (D)의 경우 주어가 and로 연결되어 있으므로 복수동사가 필요하다.

024 (C) Economists gauge economic change by investigating the fluctuations in the relationship between workers' wages and their buying power.

(A) Economists gauging

(B) Economists gauge how

(C) Economists gauge

(D) Whenever economists gauge

> 번역   경제학자들은 노동자의 임금과 구매력 사이의 관계 변동을 조사함으로써 경제 변화를 측정한다.

> 해설   by 이하는 부사구이다. 따라서 economic change는 명사구로 목적어 역할을 하므로 주어-동사가 필요하다.

025 Although Emily Dickinson is now a well-known American poet, only seven of her poems were published while she [alive → was alive].

> 번역   Emily Dickinson이 지금은 유명한 미국 시인이지만, 생전에 그녀의 시 몇 편만이 출판되었다.

> 해설   while she alive에서 while은 접속사, she는 주어, alive는 형용사로 시제동사가 필요하다.

026 [It necessary → It is necessary] to contact the firm within a week or the contract will become ineffective.

> 번역   일주일 이내에 회사에 연락해야 합니다. 그렇지 않으면 계약은 무효가 될 것 입니다.

> 해설   It이 가주어, to가 진주어이다. necessary는 형용사로 보어 역할을 해야 하므로 시제동사가 필요하다. 주어와 보어를 연결하는 be 동사가 필요하다.

027 Margaret Fuller was not active in the women's rights movement, but she [asking → asked] for a fair chance for women in her book, *Woman in the Nineteenth Century*.

> 번역   Margaret Fuller는 여권운동에 활동적이지 않았지만, Woman in the Nineteenth Century라는 책에서 여성의 공평한 기회를 요구하였다.

but은 등위접속사인데 앞 부분이 절을 이루고 있으므로 뒷 부분도 절을 이루어야 한다. she asking이 절을 이루지 못하므로 asking을 시제동사로 바꾸어야 한다.

028 [Being → Be] sure to complete the evaluation form before you leave the seminar.

번역 세미나를 떠나기 전에 반드시 평가지를 완성하세요.

해설 before 이하는 부사절이며, 따라서 앞 부분에 시제동사가 와야 한다.

029 The grasslands of all continents [supporting → support] populations of grazing animals feeding on the grasses.

번역 모든 대륙의 목초지는 풀을 먹고 자라는 방목 동물 집단을 먹여 살린다.

해설 the grasslands of all continents가 주어이며, 따라서 다음에 오는 supporting이 시제동사가 되어야 한다. feeding on the grassess는 분사구로서 animals를 수식한다.

030 Marilyn Monroe, a US film actress widely known as a sex symbol, [starring → starred] in many adroit comedies.

번역 섹스심벌로 널리 알려진 미국 영화배우 Marilyn Monroe는 많은 재치 있는 코미디에 출연하였다.

해설 a US film actress widely known as a sex symbol은 Marilyn Monroe와 동격이며, widely known as a sex symbol은 a US film actress를 수식하는 분사구이다. 주어 Marilyn Monroe의 술어가 필요하므로 starring이 시제동사가 되어야 한다.

031 The nineteenth-century historian Harriet Maxwell Converse [having been → was] a tireless and effective lobbyist on behalf of American Indians.

번역 19세기 역사가인 Harriet Maxwell은 미국인디언을 대신한 지칠 줄 모르고 효과적인 로비스트였다.

해설 The nineteenth-century historian Harriet Maxwell Converse가 주어이므로 having been이 시제동사로 바뀌어야 한다.

032 The mission of the museum is to display objects and highlight significant events that [reflecting → reflect] the city's cultural and industrial history.

번역 박물관의 임무는 물건을 전시하고 그 도시의 문화와 산업 역사를 반영하는 중요한 사건을 집중조명하는 것이다.

해설 that이 주격관계대명사이므로 다음에 시제동사가 와야 한다.

033 The office manager (C) purchases supplies through a Web site that offers a wide range of products.

(A) purchase   (B) purchasing

(C) purchases   (D) to purchase

번역	사무실 관리자는 다양한 제품을 제공하는 웹사이트를 통해 물품을 구입한다.
해설	The office manager와 supplies 모두 명사구이다. 주어와 목적어를 연결하기 위해서는 시제동사가 필요하다.

034 With affection and humor, poet Phyllis McGinley (B) praised the virtues of ordinary life.

(A) the virtues were praised 　　(B) praised the virtues

(C) she praised the virtues 　　(D) her praise of the virtues

번역	애정과 유머로써 시인 Phyllis McGinley는 일상생활의 미덕을 칭송하였다.
해설	with affection and humor는 전치사구로서 부사 역할을 하며, poet Phillis McGinley가 주어 역할을 하므로 뒤에 시제동사가 와야 한다.

035 The large compound eyes of the dragonfly (D) enable it to see moving objects almost eighteen feet away.

(A) to enable it 　　(B) enabling it

(C) it enables 　　(D) enable it

번역	잠자리의 겹눈은 거의 18피트 떨어진 움직이는 물체를 볼 수 있게 한다.
해설	the large compound eyes of the dragonfly가 명사구이므로, 빈칸에 시제동사가 와야 한다. enable+목적어+to V 구문이다. it은 the dragonfly를 가리킨다.

036 Some economists maintain that fluctuations in the economy (D) result from political events.

(A) resulting 　　(B) which result

(C) these result 　　(D) result

번역	어떤 경제학자들은 경제의 변동이 정치적 사건에 기인한다고 주장한다.
해설	that절은 maintain의 목적어 역할을 하는 명사절이다. 종속절에서 fluctuations in the economy가 주어 역할을 해야 하므로 빈칸에 시제동사가 필요하다.

037 A paragraph is a portion of a text [consists → consisting] of one or more sentences related to the same idea.

번역	문단은 동일한 주제에 연결된 하나 이상의 문장으로 이루어진 글의 일부이다.
해설	A paragraphs is a portion of a text가 하나의 절을 이루고 있으므로 뒷부분은 수식어 역할을 해야 한다. consists는 시제동사로 주어가 필요하므로 현재분사인 consisting으로 바꾸면 주어가 불필요하다. consisting 이하가 분사구로서 a text를 수식한다.

038 People [return → returning] home after extended periods abroad often experience a number of problems connected with cultural gap.

> 번역 오랜 해외 체류 후에 돌아온 사람들은 종종 문화적 차이와 관련된 많은 문제를 겪는다.

> 해설 주어 People이 return과 experience 두 개의 시제동사를 가질 수 없다. 앞의 시제동사를 분사로 바꾸어 수식어로 바꾸어야 한다.

039 Ducks have been domesticated for many centuries (B) and are raised commercially for their meat and eggs.

(A) raised   (B) and are raised

(C) raised as   (D) are raised

> 번역 오리는 오랫동안 집에서 길러 왔으며, 고기와 알 때문에 상업적으로 사육한다.

> 해설 빈칸 앞까지 완전한 절을 이루므로 시제동사를 쓰려면 접속사가 필요하다. (A)의 경우 선행사인 ducks가 멀리 있어서 which are가 생략된 구문으로 볼 수 없다.

040 William Walker's mural, "Wall of Respect," (C) which covers an outdoor wall in Chicago, deals with social issues.

(A) covers   (B) covers it

(C) which covers   (D) which it covers

> 번역 시카고의 한 야외 벽을 덮고 있는 William Walker의 벽화 Wall of Respect는 사회 문제를 다루고 있다.

> 해설 William Walker's mural과 Wall of Respect는 동격이며, 시제동사 deals의 주어 역할을 하고 있다. 따라서 빈칸에 관계사+주어를 삽입하면 형용사절이 주어를 수식하게 된다. which covers 대신 covering을 쓸 수 있다.

041 Responsibilities of this position include [achieve → achieving] sales goals and promoting cooperation between the regional bureaus.

> 번역 이 자리의 임무에는 판매 목표를 달성하고 지부 사이의 협조를 활성화시키는 것이 포함된다.

> 해설 include는 타동사로 동사 achieve를 목적어로 쓰려면 동명사를 쓴다.

042 One of the tenets of New Criticism is that a critic need not tell readers [how to → what to] think about a story.

> 번역 신비평의 주장 가운데 하나는 비평가가 독자에게 이야기를 어떻게 생각할지를 이야기 할 필요가 없다는 것이다.

> 해설 think는 타동사로 목적어가 필요하므로 what을 써야 한다.

043 Pele, a Brazilian athlete, won [famous → fame] as the greatest soccer player of his time and the most recognized athlete in world sports.

> **번역** 브라질의 운동선수인 Pele는 그 당시의 가장 훌륭한 축구선수이자 세계 스포츠에서 가장 인정받는 선수로서 명성을 얻었다.

> **해설** win이 타동사이므로 그 다음에는 명사가 와야 한다.

044 Oliver Ellsworth, the third chief justice of the United States Supreme Court, was the author of the bill that [was established → established] the federal court system.

> **번역** 제 3대 미국 대법원장이였던 Oliver Ellsworth는 연방법원을 설립하는 법안을 제출한 사람이다.

> **해설** establish는 3형식동사로 수동태가 되면 뒤에 명사가 나타날 수 없다. 목적어를 취하기 위해서는 능동형을 써야 한다.

045 During adolescence many young people begin to question (A) the values held by their families.

(A) the values　　　　　　　(B) of the values

(C) the values are　　　　　(D) are the values

> **번역** 청소년기에는 많은 젊은이들이 가정의 가치관에 의심을 품기 시작한다.

> **해설** question은 타동사로 다음에 명사 목적어가 필요하다. held 앞에는 which are가 생략되어 있다.

046 Animals obtain their energy from (C) the food they eat.

(A) eat their food　　　　　(B) their food to eat

(C) the food they eat　　　 (D) they eat the food

> **번역** 동물들은 섭취하는 음식으로부터 에너지를 얻는다.

> **해설** 전치사 from 다음에 명사가 와야 한다. 명사 다음의 to 부정사는 목적을 나타내므로 의미상 적절하지 않다.

047 We often ask (B) whether pleasure is the proper standard for making our decisions.

(A) that pleasure is　　　　(B) whether pleasure is

(C) what is pleasure　　　　(D) which is pleasure

> **번역** 우리는 종종 의사 결정을 하는 데 있어 쾌락이 적절한 기준인지를 묻는다.

> **해설** ask는 간접의문문을 취하는 동사이다. the proper standard가 보어로 쓰일 수 있으므로 그 앞에 be 동사가 나타나야 한다.

048 The combination of two lenses makes [it → φ] possible greater magnification than can be achieved with a single lens.

두 개의 렌즈의 결합은 하나의 렌즈로 얻을 수 있는 것보다 훨씬 커다란 확대가 가능하게 한다.

해설 make+목적어+possible 구문에서 목적어가 부정사나 절일 경우 make it possible 구문을 쓸 수 있으나 목적어가 명사나 동명사일 경우 가목적어 구문을 쓰지 못한다.

049 Frederick Jones invented a refrigerator unit that [make it possible → made possible] the transportation of frozen foods by truck.

번역 Frederick은 트럭에 의한 냉동식품 운반을 가능하게 하는 냉장고를 발명하였다.

해설 make+목적어+possible 구문에서 목적어가 명사구이므로 가목적어 구문을 쓰지 못한다.

050 You need about forty different nutrients to stay [healthily → healthy].

번역 건강을 유지하려면 약 40 종류의 영양소가 필요하다.

해설 stay가 여기서 불완전자동사로 쓰여 보어가 필요한데, 보어는 대개 형용사이다.

051 The Red Wagon on Main Street is known for its impressive array of learning materials that encourage children to be [creativity → creative].

번역 Main Street의 Red Wagon은 아이들이 창의력을 갖도록 학습 자료를 인상적으로 배열하여 유명하다.

해설 be 다음에는 보어가 오는데 일반적으로 보어는 형용사이다.

052 Traders became [more caution → more cautious] as the finance department began to review the rules governing bond sales.

번역 무역업자들은 재무부가 공채 판매에 관한 법률을 재검토하자 조심스러워졌다.

해설 become이 불완전자동사로 보어가 필요하며, 보어는 일반적으로 형용사이다.

053 Coffee mixed with chicory is likely to taste (B) bitter to a person not used to it.

(A) sweetly   (B) bitter

(C) bitterly   (D) well

번역 치커리와 혼합된 커피는 익숙하지 않은 사람에게는 쓴 맛이 날 것이다.

해설 smell, taste, feel과 같은 감각동사는 사람이 주어일 때는 타동사로 쓰이며 (John smells the fish), 사물이 주어일 때는 불완전자동사로 쓰여 보어를 취한다(The fish smells bad).

054 A politician can make a legislative proposal more (C) understandable by giving specific examples of what its effect will be.

(A) to understand

(B) understandably

(C) understandable

(D) when understood

> 번역 | 정치인은 법률안의 효과에 대한 구체적인 예를 들어서 더욱 당연한 것으로 만들 수 있다.

> 해설 | make가 여기서는 불완전타동사로 쓰여 목적어 다음에 형용사 보어가 와야 한다.

055 The chief objectives of American Federation of Teachers (D) are to promote professionalism in teaching and to secure appropriate wages, better working conditions, and job security for its members.

(A) to promote

(B) are promote

(C) are promoting

(D) are to promote

> 번역 | 미국교사연합회의 주요 목적은 교수의 전문성을 향상시키고, 회원의 적절한 임금, 더 나은 근무 조건, 직업의 안전성을 확보하기 위한 것이다.

> 해설 | The chief objectives are to V and to V 형태로, 주어가 objectives이므로 보어로 to V를 쓴다.

056 Ken Demino is such a [well → good] professor that his class has very little withdrawal.

> 번역 | Ken Demino는 아주 훌륭한 교수여서 그의 수업은 취소가 매우 적다.

> 해설 | well은 부사로 명사를 수식할 수 없다. 명사를 수식하려면 형용사가 필요하다.

057 Mr. Hazel analyzed his [personally → personal] income to see if he could afford to rent a bigger house.

> 번역 | Hazel씨는 더 큰 집을 살 여력이 있는지 알아 보기 위해 개인 소득을 분석하였다.

> 해설 | 명사를 수식할 수 있는 것은 부사가 아니라 형용사이다.

058 Seldom has the mathematical theory of games been of [practically → practical] use in playing real games.

> 번역 | 게임의 수학이론은 실재의 게임을 하는 데 쓸모가 거의 없었다.

> 해설 | 명사는 형용사가 수식한다.

059 When the focus of a pair of binoculars is adjusted, [distance → distant] objects can be brought into view.

> 번역 | 쌍안경의 촛점이 조절되면 먼 물체가 시야에 들어올 수 있다.

> 해설 | 재료인 경우에는 명사+명사의 형태를 쓰지만, 일반적으로 명사는 형용사가 수식한다.

060 The only flaw to her otherwise (C) perfect travel was a little airsickness on the plane.

(A) perfection   (B) perfecting

(C) perfect   (D) perfected

| 번역 | 그 외에는 완벽했던 그녀의 여행의 유일한 단점은 약간의 비행기 멀미였다. |
| 해설 | travel이 명사로 형용사가 수식할 수 있다. |

061 Staff (B) remaining in the building after 10 PM are requested to use the rear exit when leaving.

(A) will remain   (B) remaining

(C) remain   (D) have remained

| 번역 | 저녁 10시 이후에 건물에 남아있는 직원들은 퇴근할 때 뒷문을 사용해야 한다. |
| 해설 | when leaving은 when they are leaving의 분사구문이다. staff는 단복 동형 명사로 여기서는 복수로 쓰였다. 명사 staff를 수식하려면 형용사가 와야 하는데 현재분사는 형용사 역할을 한다. Staff who remain in the building을 분사구문으로 바꾸면 Staff remaining이 되는데, 상태동사는 진행형을 쓰지 못하나 분사구문으로 바꿀 수는 있다. |

062 The maintenance shop has confirmed that (A) frequent assessments of the engine, brakes and tires are done for all delivery trucks.

(A) frequent   (B) frequently

(C) frequents   (D) frequency

| 번역 | 정비공장은 모든 배달 화물차의 엔진, 브레이크, 타이어에 대해 자주 점검을 한다는 것을 확인시켜 주었다. |
| 해설 | 명사 assessments는 형용사로 수식한다. |

063 The company's travel budget has been reduced [substantial → substantially], so our executives will not be attending as many conferences as in the past.

| 번역 | 회사의 여행 예산이 크게 삭감되어서 우리 간부는 과거처럼 많은 회의에 참석할 수 없을 것이다. |
| 해설 | reduced가 동사이므로 부사로 수식해야 한다. |

064 We are [regrettable → regrettably] unable to forward the document you asked for about the project the other day.

| 번역 | 안타깝게도 얼마 전에 그 프로젝트와 관련하여 요청한 문서를 보내 드릴 수 없습니다. |

의미상 문장 부사가 필요하다. about the project는 the document를 수식한다.

065 Obsidian, an uncommon volcanic rock, [polishes good → polishes well] and makes an attractive semiprecious stone.

번역 흔치 않은 화산석인 흑요석은 잘 닦이며, 매력적인 준보석이다.

해설 동사 polish는 부사로 수식해야 한다.

066 If it were too far from the Sun, the Earth would be [too much → much too] cold to support any living thing.

번역 지구가 태양과 너무 멀리 떨어져 있다면 너무 추워서 어떤 생명체도 살 수 없을 것이다.

해설 형용사 cold는 부사로 수식해야 하는데 much는 부사를 수식한다. too가 cold를 수식하고, much가 too를 수식한다.

067 A liter is [scientific → scientifically] defined as the volume of one kilogram of water at its maximum density.

번역 리터는 최대밀도 상태의 물 1kg의 양으로 정의된다.

해설 defined가 동사이므로 부사의 수식을 받는다.

068 He is (B) still working in the same department after 20 years.

(A) already   (B) still

(C) before   (D) after

번역 그는 20년 후에도 여전히 같은 부서에서 일하고 있다.

해설 조동사와 본동사 사이에 올 수 있는 부사를 찾아야 한다. already는 완료와 함께 쓰이며, before와 after는 문미에 나타난다.

069 The security expert recommended that closed-circuit cameras hang (C) low from the celling behind the store's cash registers.

(A) lowers   (B) lowly

(C) low   (D) lowest

번역 그 보안전문가는 폐쇄회로 카메라를 가게의 금전등록기 뒤에 천장에 낮게 달 것을 권장하였다.

해설 동사 hang을 수식하려면 부사가 필요한데, low는 형용사와 부사가 동형이다. lowly는 형용사로 '하찮은'을 뜻한다.

070 Springwater is (B) generally fairly clean, since it has been filtered through permeable rocks, but all spring water contains some dissolved minerals.

(A) generally fair   (B) generally fairly

(C) in general fair   (D) general and fair

> **번역** 스며들 수 있는 바위를 통해 여과되기 때문에 샘물은 일반적으로 매우 깨끗하지만, 모든 샘물은 용해된 미네랄을 함유하고 있다.
>
> **해설** clean이 형용사이므로 부사가 수식해야 한다.

071

If the computer system had been shutdown (B) correctly, the loss of data could have been avoided.

(A) correct   (B) correctly

(C) correction   (D) correctness

> **번역** 만약 컴퓨터를 제대로 껐었더라면 자료의 손실은 피할 수 있었을 것이다.
>
> **해설** 동사를 수식하려면 부사가 필요하다. 가정법과거완료 구문으로 조건절은 had+V-en이며, 주절은 could+have+V-en이다.

072

Ms. Agrawala, the representative who went to the trade show, was instructed to report all new orders (C) directly to headquarters.

(A) direction   (B) directing

(C) directly   (D) directive

> **번역** 무역전시회에 갔던 대표단원인 Ms. Agrawala는 본부에 직접 새로운 주문을 모두 보고하도록 지시를 받았다.
>
> **해설** to headquarters가 부사 역할을 하므로 부사의 수식을 받는다.

073

Geysers are found near rivers and lakes, where water drains through the soil (B) deep below the surface.

(A) surface below the deep   (B) deep below the surface

(C) the deep below surface   (D) the deep surface below

> **번역** 간헐온천은 강이나 호수 가까이서 발견되는데, 그곳에서 물이 지표보다 한참 아래에서 흐른다.
>
> **해설** soil이 명사이므로 다음에는 후치 수식어가 와야 한다. deep below the surface에서 deep은 부사적으로 쓰인 전치사구를 수식하는 부사이다.

074

Seaweed nurtures numerous communities of living things, which are protected under the wet coverings of the weeds while the [tide out → tide is out].

> **번역** 해초는 많은 생명체에 영양분을 공급하는데, 이 생명체들은 썰물일 때 해초의 축축한 덮개 아래서 보호를 받는다.
>
> **해설** while the tide out에서 while이 접속사, the tide가 주어, out이 부사구이므로 the tide와 out 사이에 연결동사 be가 필요하다.

075 After only five years in Hollywood, the man [able to → was able to] buy a house in the Beverly Hills and retired for life.

> 번역 │ 그 사람은 Hollywood에서 불과 5년을 활동한 뒤에 Berverly Hills에 집을 사서 평생 은퇴 생활을 할 수 있었다.

> 해설 │ the man이 주어이므로 그 다음에 시제동사가 필요하다.

076 The crocuses which bloom as the winter snow recedes [and are → are] harbingers of approaching spring.

> 번역 │ 겨울눈이 사라질 때 피는 크로커스는 다가오는 봄의 전령이다.

> 해설 │ as the winter snow recedes가 부사절로서 which bloom을 수식하며, which bloom은 형용사절로서 the crocuses를 수식한다. the crocuses가 주어이고 harbingers of approaching spring이 명사구 보어이므로 그 앞에는 시제동사가 와야 한다. 즉, 수식어를 제외하면 The crocuses are harbingers이다.

077 Sociology, the study of humans in their collective aspect, (B) examines all group activities: economic, social, political, and religious.

(A) and examines all group activities

(B) examines all group activities

(C) which examines all group activities

(D) examining all group activities

> 번역 │ 인간의 집단적 양상에 관한 학문인 사회학은 경제적, 사회적, 정치적, 종교적 집단 활동을 연구한다.

> 해설 │ Sociology와 the study of humans in their collective aspect는 동격이다. Sociology가 주어이므로 다음에는 시제동사와 목적어가 와야 한다.

078 Fairs that were held to improve farming methods have been (B) very important in the agricultural history of the United States.

(A) much importance   (B) very important

(C) very importantly   (D) very importance

> 번역 │ 경작법을 개선하기 위해 열린 품평회는 미국의 농업사에서 매우 중요한 역할을 해왔다.

> 해설 │ 동사 be는 불완전자동사로 쓰여 보어가 필요하다.

079 The (B) final result of the negotiation will be announced sometime next week.

(A) finalize   (B) final

(C) finally   (D) finalist

번역	교섭의 마지막 결과는 다음 주 중에 발표될 것이다.
해설	명사인 result는 형용사가 수식해야 한다.

080 According to researchers Katharine Payne and Linda Guinee, the long, complex songs of the humpback whale (D) contain sounds that appear to be similar to rhymes.

(A) containing sounds   (B) sounds contain

(C) which contain sounds   (D) contain sounds

번역	Katharine Payne과 Linda Guinee라는 연구자에 따르면, 혹등고래의 길고 복잡한 노래는 각운과 유사하게 들리는 소리를 포함하고 있다.
해설	that절에 주어가 없으므로 관계절이다. 관계절은 명사를 수식하는 형용사절로 그 앞에 선행사인 명사가 와야 한다. 이 문장에서 주어는 the long, complex songs of the humpback whale이므로 빈칸에 시제동사와 (관계절 때문에) 명사가 와야 한다.

081 Potential dehydration is (C) often the greatest hazard that a land animal faces.

(A) the often greatest hazard   (B) the greatest often hazard

(C) often the greatest hazard   (D) often the hazard greatest

번역	잠재적인 탈수증은 종종 육지 동물이 직면한 가장 커다란 위험이다.
해설	is 다음에는 보어로 쓰일 수 있는 형용사나 명사가 와야 하는데 that절이 형용사절이므로 명사가 와야 한다. often은 부사이므로 명사구 안에 포함되어서는 안 된다.

082 "Do you think that the labor bill will be passed?"

"Oh, yes. It's (B) very likely that it will."

(A) almost surely   (B) very likely

(C) near positive   (D) quite certainly

번역	노동법이 통과되리라고 생각합니까? 그렇습니다. 그럴 가능성이 매우 높습니다.
해설	it이 가주어, that절이 진주어이다. 빈칸에는 보어가 와야 한다.

083 Mr. Kobayashi spoke quite (D) excitedly while he was making sales presentation.

(A) exciting   (B) excitable

(C) excitement   (D) excitedly

번역	판매 발표회를 하면서 Kobayashi씨는 매우 흥분되어 말했다.

해설 speak는 완전자동사이므로 뒤에 수식어인 부사가 올 수 있다.

084 With the start for the penny papers in the 1830's, the number of people (A) regularly reading a newspaper rose considerably.

   (A) regularly reading   (B) were reading regularly
   (C) regularly reading what   (D) who reading regularly

   번역 1830년대에 값싼 신문이 나타나서 정기적으로 신문을 읽는 독자의 수가 상당히 증가하였다.
   해설 the number of people이 rose의 주어이므로 빈칸에는 명사를 취하여 people을 수식할 수 있는 요소가 와야 한다. 분사는 앞의 명사를 수식하면서 뒤의 명사를 목적어로 취하여 형용사의 역할과 동사의 역할을 동시에 할 수 있다.

085 At present production levels, (A) known deposits of bauxite can provide the world with aluminum for hundreds of years.

   (A) known   (B) known are
   (C) they are known   (D) what is known

   번역 현재의 생산 수준으로, 보크사이트의 알려진 매장량이 수백년간 알루미늄을 세계에 공급할 수 있다.
   해설 can provide가 동사이므로 그 앞에는 주어가 와야 한다. deposits가 명사이므로 그 앞에는 수식어가 와야 한다.

086 The most explosive issue which the government must [deal → deal with] is deregulation of the aviation industry.

   번역 정부가 다루어야 할 가장 까다로운 문제는 항공산업의 규제 철폐이다.
   해설 deal은 자동사로 전치사 with와 결합하여 타동사를 이룬다.

087 In general, prawns [live shallow → live in shallow] coastal waters or in streams.

   번역 일반적으로 참새우는 얕은 바다나 냇물에 산다.
   해설 live가 자동사이므로 뒷 부분이 부사구가 되어야 한다.

088 Her untiring energy (D) resulted in her obvious success.

   (A) resulted   (B) have resulted
   (C) resulted from   (D) resulted in

   번역 그녀의 지치지 않는 에너지가 확실한 성공을 가져다 주었다.
   해설 result는 자동사로 전치사 in 또는 from과 결합하여 타동사를 이룬다.

089 A lunar eclipse (D) occurs when the earth passes between the sun and the moon, causing the moon to become dark.

(A) occurs   (B) that occurs

(C) which occurs   (D) occurs when

| 번역 | 월식은 지구가 태양과 달 사이를 통과할 때 나타난다. |

| 해설 | occur는 자동사이다. A lunar eclipse가 주어이므로 다음에 시제동사가 와야 하며, occur가 자동사이므로 뒷 부분을 부사절로 만들어야 한다. |

090 Though smaller than our solar system, a quasar, which [is looked → looks] like an ordinary star, emits more light than an entire galaxy.

| 번역 | 일반적인 별처럼 보이는 준성은 태양계보다 작지만, 은하계 전체보다 더 많은 빛을 발산한다. |

| 해설 | look은 타동사로 쓰이기도 하지만 look like는 자동사이므로 수동태를 쓰지 못한다. |

091 Marine snails [are occurred → occur] in all seas from the Arctic to the Antarctic, though they reach their greatest development in tropical waters.

| 번역 | 바다 달팽이는 비록 열대 바다에 가장 많지만, 북극에서 남극에 이르기까지 모든 바다에 나타난다. |

| 해설 | occur는 자동사로 수동태를 쓰지 못한다. |

092 The tough skin formed by dried linseed oil does not break or chip, and [resists to → resists] changes in the weather.

| 번역 | 말린 아마씨 기름으로 생겨난 튼튼한 껍질은 깨지지 않으며, 날씨의 변화를 견딘다. |

| 해설 | resist는 타동사로 전치사가 필요 없다. |

093 The experts offered their thoughts on how to bridge that gap and [discussed about → discussed] the diversity of businesses.

| 번역 | 전문가들은 차이를 매꾸는 방법에 대한 견해를 제시했으며, 사업의 다양성에 대해 토의하였다. |

| 해설 | discuss는 타동사로 전치사가 따를 필요가 없다. |

094 The Supreme Court [comprises of → comprises] the chief justice of the United States and eight associate justices.

| 번역 | 미국 대법원은 대법원장과 8명의 대법원판사로 구성된다. |

| 해설 | comprise는 타동사이므로 전치사가 필요 없다. 다만 be comprised of 처럼 쓰는 데 유의해야 한다. |

095 This chapter [describes about → describes] how to protect data against operating system crashes, file corruption, disk failures, and total machine failure.

> 번역 본장은 운영체제의 충돌, 파일 손상, 디스크 손상, 전체적인 기계 고장으로부터 어떻게 자료를 보호할 것인지에 대해 기술한다.

> 해설 describe는 타동사이므로 전치사가 필요 없다.

096 Steven Spielberg, whose highly successful films have given popular cinema a new appeal, is [considered by → considered] one of the best movie directors in the United States.

> 번역 Steven Spielberg는 미국에서 가장 훌륭한 감독으로 여겨지며, 그의 아주 성공적인 영화는 대중 영화에 새로운 호소력을 부여하였다.

> 해설 consider는 5형식동사로 그 다음에 목적어와 목적보어가 온다. 따라서 수동태가 되더라도 목적보어가 남아 있어야 한다.

097 Alaska's rough climate and terrain divide the state into isolated regions, making highway maintenance [difficulty → difficult].

> 번역 Alaska의 혹독한 기후와 지형 때문에 주와 고립된 지역으로 나뉘어, 고속도로의 유지가 힘들다.

> 해설 여기서 make가 5형식동사로 쓰였는데, 목적보어자리에는 형용사가 온다. 여기서 making은 and it makes로 바꿔 쓸 수 있다.

098 Stress suppresses the body's immune system, thus making people [are more → more] likely to become ill.

> 번역 스트레스는 인체의 면역 체계를 억제하여, 사람들이 더 쉽게 병을 앓게 만든다.

> 해설 make는 5형식동사로 목적어 다음에 형용사 목적보어가 와야 한다.

099 The giraffe's long neck and legs are the most obvious features that [make → make it] different from all other animals.

> 번역 기린의 긴 목과 다리는 다른 모든 동물과 구별되는 가장 뚜렷한 특징이다.

> 해설 make가 여기서 5형식동사로 쓰여 목적어가 필요하다. different from all other animals가 목적보어로 쓰였으며, it은 the giraffe를 가리킨다.

100 X-rays are able to pass through objects and thus make [them → φ] visible details that are otherwise impossible to observe.

> 번역 X-ray는 사물을 통과할 수 있으며, 따라서 달리 관찰할 수 없는 부분을 볼 수 있게 한다.

> 해설 make+목적어+보어 구문에서 목적어가 to V이거나 that절일 때 가목적어-진목적어 구문을 쓰는데, 목적어가 긴 명사구나 동명사일 때는 make+보어+명사구의 구문을 취한다.

101 Like other women who pioneered in the field of medicine, Sara Mayo (A) found the beginning years difficult.

    (A) found the beginning years difficult

    (B) found difficult the beginning years

    (C) found the beginning years difficultly

    (D) found that the beginning years difficult

> **번역** 의학의 다른 선구자들과 마찬가지로 Sara Mayo도 처음 몇 해 동안 어려웠다.
>
> **해설** find는 5형식동사로 명사 목적어 다음에 형용사 보어가 나타난다.

102 Could you tell me where [is Tim → Tim is] so I can give him a message before I leave?

> **번역** 내가 떠나기 전에 그에게 메시지를 전달할 수 있도록 Tim이 어디에 있는지 말씀해 주시겠습니까?
>
> **해설** 간접의문문에서는 도치가 일어나지 않는다.

103 Our report was translated into English, so they should understand what [means it → it means].

> **번역** 우리의 보고서는 영어로 번역되어서 그들이 그 의미를 이해할 수 있다.
>
> **해설** mean은 타동사로 의미상 what이 목적어이다. 따라서 의문사 목적어+ 주어+동사의 어순을 가져야 한다.

104 She wanted to know when [was the last staff meeting → the last staff meeting was] so that she could prepare for the next one.

> **번역** 그녀는 다음 회의를 준비할 수 있도록 마지막 임원회의가 언제인지 알고자 했다.
>
> **해설** 간접의문문에서는 도치가 일어나지 않는다.

105 In the field of acting theory, controversy arises over the question of whether [is acting → acting is] a behavioral or a mental process.

> **번역** 연기이론에서 연기가 행위적 과정인지, 아니면 정신적 과정인지에 대한 논란이 생긴다.
>
> **해설** whether는 의문문을 이끄는 접속사인데, 특히 간접의문문에서만 쓰인다는 점에 유의해야 한다.

106 Hardly ever [the two were → were the two] able to talk freely without being overheard by their parents.

> **번역** 그 두 사람이 자유롭게 이야기할 때마다 부모님이 엿들었다.
>
> **해설** 부정어인 Hardly가 문두에 있으므로 주어와 동사가 도치되어야 한다.

107 But hardly (C) had he started when the sky became overcast and down came the rain again.

    (A) he had started   (B) he started

    (C) had he started   (D) he has started

> **번역** 그가 출발하자마자 하늘이 구름으로 덮이고, 비가 다시 왔다.

> **해설** hardly A when B 구문으로 A하자마자 B하다의 뜻을 갖는다. 이때 A 는 과거완료형이며, B는 과거형을 갖는데, 부정어 hardly 때문에 도치가 일어난다. down came the rain도 도치구문인데, 몇몇 자동사의 경우 주어＋동사＋부사 구문이 부사＋동사＋주어의 순서로 도치되기도 한다.

108 Not until his life was over (C) did the seed which he had sown bear fruit.

    (A) the seed did   (B) the seed that

    (C) did the seed   (D) that the seed

> **번역** 그가 죽어서야 그가 뿌린 씨앗이 열매를 맺었다.

> **해설** 도치구문으로 부정어인 Not until his life was over가 문두에 있으므로 도치가 일어났으며, which he had sown은 the seed를 수식하는 형용사 절이다. 따라서 주어는 the seed이며, 동사는 bear이다.

109 A sneeze cannot be performed voluntarily, (A) nor can it be easily sup-pressed.

    (A) nor can it   (B) and cannot it

    (C) nor it can   (D) it cannot

> **번역** 재채기는 의도적으로 할 수 없으며, 또한 쉽게 참을 수도 없다.

> **해설** nor는 접속사로 부정의 의미를 가지며, 따라서 주어와 동사가 도치된다.

110 No only (B) did the suppliers send the wrong components, but they also sent them to the wrong department.

    (A) had   (B) did

    (C) were   (D) have

> **번역** 공급자들이 부품을 잘못 보냈 뿐만 아니라, 부품을 다른 부서에 보내기도 했다.

> **해설** Not only A but also B 구문으로 부정어 not 때문에 도치가 일어난다.

111 Before constructing a bridge, the designers must consider the [deep → depth] and width of the barrier.

> **번역** 교량을 건설하기 전에 설계자는 방벽의 깊이와 넓이를 고려해야 한다.

해설 width가 명사로 등위접속사 and로 연결되려면 deep의 명사형을 써야 한다.

112 Cobalt resembles iron and nickel in tensile strength, appearance, and [hard → hardness].

번역 코발트는 신장성, 외관, 경도에서 철과 니켈을 닮았다.

해설 함께 and로 연결된 strength와 appearance가 명사이기 때문에 다음의 hard도 명사형을 써야 한다.

113 The doctor's records must be kept [thorough → thoroughly] and neatly, so as to insure good book-keeping.

번역 의사의 기록이 훌륭한 부기가 되려면 철저하고 반듯하게 보존되어야 한다..

해설 kept를 수식하기 위해서는 부사가 필요하다. 특히 and neatly로 보아 그 앞에는 부사가 와야 한다.

114 Poor Richard Almanac, a series of writing by Benjamin Franklin, expounds the merits of such homely virtues as diligence, [thrifty → thrift], and hard work.

번역 Benjamin Franklin의 시리즈 저작인 Poor Richard Almanac은 근면, 검소, 노력과 같은 가정적인 미덕의 장점을 설명하고 있다.

해설 virtue와 hard work이 and로 연결되어 있으므로 thrifty도 명사형을 써야 한다.

115 The brochures are being rechecked by the professional writers for accuracy and overall (C) clarity.

(A) clearance   (B) clarify

(C) clarity   (D) clear

번역 정확성과 전반적인 명확성을 위해 소책자를 전문 작가가 재확인하고 있다.

해설 accuracy가 명사이므로 and 다음에 명사가 와야 한다. clearance도 명사이지만 의미상 부적절하다.

116 When [slowly dried → dried slowly] and naturally, raisins are high in iron and other minerals.

번역 천천히 자연 상태에서 말릴 때 건포도는 철분 외에 다른 미네랄이 많다.

해설 등위접속사 and 다음에 slowly가 있으므로 그 앞에 역시 부사가 와야 한다. 수식어인 부사가 동사 뒤에 오면 된다.

117 In this examination we will have to pass tests on our ability to read, reason clearly, follow directions and [spelling → spell] correctly.

번역 이 시험에서 우리는 읽고, 명확하게 생각하고, 지시를 따르고, 정확하게 철자하는 능력에 대한 평가를 통과해야 할 것이다.

해설 and 앞에 동사인 read, reason, follow가 있으므로 동명사 spelling 대신 동사형인 spell을 써야 한다.

118 It is not work, but [to overwork → overwork], that is hurtful; and it is not hard work that is injurious so much as unwilling work.

번역 해로운 것은 일이 아니라 과로이다. 해로운 것은 힘든 일이 아니라 하기 싫은 일이다.

해설 not A but B의 구조이므로 명사가 필요하다.

119 Squanto acted as an interpreter in the treaty negotiations between the Pilgrims and the Navajos, and he taught the Pilgrims how to fish and [cultivating → cultivate] corn.

번역 Sqanto는 청교도와 나바호족 사이의 조약 협상에서 통역가 역할을 했으며, 그는 청교도들에게 고기를 낚는 방법과 옥수수 재배하는 방법을 가르쳤다.

해설 등위접속사 and 앞에 동사가 있으므로 그 다음에 동사가 와야 한다. how to (fish and cultivate)의 구조이다.

120 Cooperation is the mutual endeavor of two or more persons to perform a task or [reaching → to reach] a jointly cherished goal.

번역 협동은 어떤 일을 하거나 공동으로 소중하게 생각하는 목표에 도달하기 위한 두 사람 이상의 상호 노력이다.

해설 (to perform ...) or (to reach ...)의 구조이다.

121 Worker bees labor for the good of the hive by collecting food, caring for the young, and [to expand → expanding] the nest.

번역 일벌은 식량을 모으고, 새끼를 보살피고, 집을 확장함으로써 벌집을 위해 노동을 한다.

해설 by (collecting ...), (caring ...) and (expanding ...)의 구조이다. 전치사 by 다음에는 동명사가 와야 하며, 또한 등위접속사 and 다음에는 앞의 형태와 동일한 것이 와야 한다.

122 Since Atlanta is a chief transportation center, many leading firms have branches there for manufacturing, warehousing, and [distribute → distributing] their products.

번역 Atlanta가 주요한 수송의 중심지이기 때문에 많은 주요 회사들이 제품의 생산, 보관, 분배를 위해 지점을 두고 있다.

해설 등위접속사 and 앞에 동명사인 manufacturing과 warehousing이 있으므로 distribute도 동명사형으로 바꾸어야 한다.

123 Graying hair, [gain weight → gaining weight], and greater difficulty in recuperating from physical exertion may be physiological indices of a person's advancing age.

번역 흰머리, 늘어나는 체중, 육체노동으로부터 회복의 어려움은 나이가 들어 간다는 생리적 지표이다.

해설 graying, advancing은 현재분사로 다음에 오는 명사를 수식한다. 현재 분사는 능동의 의미를 가지므로 자동사에 해당한다. recuperating은 in 의 목적어로 쓰인 동명사이다. gain은 동사로 다음의 명사를 수식하기 위해서는 분사형으로 바뀌어야 한다.

124 Some people prefer hotels to apartment buildings, but most like (C) houses the best of the three.

(A) a house
(B) the house
(C) houses
(D) the houses

번역 어떤 사람들은 아파트보다는 호텔을 좋아하지만, 대부분 셋 가운데 주택을 제일 좋아한다.

해설 hotels와 apartment buildings가 무관사 복수형이므로 동일한 형태인 houses가 와야 한다.

125 The end of law is not to abolish or restrain, (A) but to preserve and enlarge freedom.

(A) but to preserve
(B) but preserve
(C) but preserving
(D) but also to preserve

번역 법의 목적이 자유를 없애거나 제한하는 것이 아니라 자유를 보존하고 확대하는 것이다.

해설 not A but B 구문으로 A와 B가 같은 형태여야 한다. not (to abolish or restrain) but (to preserve and enlarge) freedom의 구조이다. 즉, not to V but to V의 형태이며, freedom은 preserve와 enlarge의 공통 목적어이다. 또한 abolish와 restrain이 동일한 형태이며, preserve와 enlarge가 동일한 형태를 취하고 있다.

126 Americans can conserve gasoline by picking fuel-efficient autos, joining car pools, and (C) using mass trasit.

(A) mass transit use
(B) use of mass transit
(C) using mass transit
(D) use mass transit

번역 미국인들은 고효율 자동차를 선택하고, 카풀을 하고, 대중교통을 이용함 으로써 휘발유를 절약할 수 있다.

해설 picking과 joining이 동명사이므로 등위접속사 and 다음에도 동명사가 와야 한다. 동명사가 전치사 by의 공통목적어로 쓰였다. 모두 동명사가 동사의 성질을 가지고 있어서 명사 목적어를 취하고 있다.

127 The works of the author Herman Melville are literary creations of a high order, blending fact, fiction, adventure, and subtle [symbolic → symbol].

번역 | Herman Melville의 작품들은 높은 수준의 문학 창작물로, 사실, 허구, 모험, 미묘한 상징을 결합하였다.

해설 | blending은 현재분사로 분사구문이다. fiction과 adventure가 명사이므로 and 다음에도 명사가 와야 한다.

128 The mechanic studied electronics in night school so as to be promoted and [transferring → transferred] to another job.

번역 | 그 기술자는, 승진과 전직을 위해 야간학교에서 전자공학을 공부했다.

해설 | promoted가 과거분사로 수동의 뜻을 나타내는데, 수동의 뜻을 나타내야 하므로 and 다음에도 과거분사가 와야 한다.

129 The photoperiodic response of algae actually depends on the duration of darkness, but [is → ϕ] not on light.

번역 | 녹조의 광주기 반응은 사실 햇빛에 달려 있는 것이 아니라 어둠의 지속 기간에 달려있다.

해설 | but이 등위접속사이므로 동형의 요소가 나타나야 한다. on the duration과 동형을 선택한다.

130 Natural adhesives are primarily of [animals → animal] or vegetable origin.

번역 | 천연접착제는 주로 동식물에서 온 것이다.

해설 | 명사인 origin을 형용사인 vegetable이 수식한다. 명사인 animal이 origin을 수식할 경우 복수를 쓰지 않는다.

131 Why is a man in civil life perpetually slandering and backbiting his fellow men, and [is → ϕ] unable to see good even in his friends?

번역 | 예의바른 삶을 사는 사람이 왜 동료를 비방하고 험담하며, 친구의 장점을 보지 못합니까?

해설 | a man이 주어이고, is slandering and backbiting이 동사이다. and가 등위접속사로 동형의 구조를 연결해야 하므로 is가 불필요하다. 즉 is slandering and backbiting ..., and unable to ...의 구조를 갖는다.

132 Ethics is the branch of philosophy that deals with the values of life in coherent, systematic, and [science → scientific] manner.

번역 | 윤리학은 일관성 있게, 체계적으로, 그리고 과학적으로 삶의 가치를 다루는 철학의 한 분야이다.

해설 | coherent와 systematic이 형용사이므로 and 다음에도 형용사가 와야 한다.

133 Perhaps the most popular film in movie history, *Star Wars* was written and [direction → directed] by George Lucas.

번역 | 아마도 영화 역사상 가장 인기 있었던 Star Wars는 George Lucas가 각본을 쓰고 감독한 것이었다.

written이 과거분사이므로 and 다음에도 과거분사가 와야 한다.

134 "Tom is going fishing tomorrow."
"(A) So am I."

(A) So am I
(B) So Mary is
(C) So I am
(D) So do I

번역 "Tom이 내일 낚시하러 간다." "나도 그래."

해설 앞의 내용을 반복하는 so의 경우 도치가 일어난다. So he is의 경우는 도치가 일어나지 않는다.

135 Unlike hummingbirds, sunbirds tend to perch on the flower they are probing (A) rather than to hover around it.

(A) rather than to hover around it
(B) than rather hover around it
(C) rather than their hovering around it
(D) to hover rather than around it

번역 벌새와 달리 태양새는 꽃의 주위를 맴도는 대신 찾는 꽃 위에 앉는 경향이 있다.

해설 to perch on the flower와 대구를 이루는 표현을 써야 한다. they are probing은 the flower를 수식한다.

136 Congress chartered the first Bank of the United States in 1791 to engage in general commercial banking and (A) to act as a fiscal agent of the federal government.

(A) to act
(B) acting
(C) that has acted
(D) having acted

번역 의회는 일반 상업 은행에 관여하고, 연방정부의 재무 대리 기관의 역할을 할 수 있는 첫번째 미국은행을 1791년에 인가하였다.

해설 to engage ... and to V 구문이다. 이때 to 부정사는 the first Bank of the Untied States를 수식한다.

137 The astronomical unit is the average distance of the Earth from the Sun (A) and is the standard of distances in the Solar System.

(A) and
(B) also
(C) in addition
(D) because

번역 천문학 단위는 지구와 태양의 평균 거리이며, 태양계에서 거리의 기준이다.

The astronomical unit가 주어이며, 두 개의 술부가 and로 연결되어야 한다.

138 The function of Congress is to make laws, but nowhere in the Constitution (D) is a statement about the exact steps that must be taken in the law-making process.

    (A) a statement is there   (B) it is a statement

    (C) there a statement is   (D) is a statement

> 번역 | 의회의 기능은 법을 제정하는 것이지만, 헌법 어디에도 입법과정에서 따라야 할 정확한 단계에 대한 진술이 없다.

> 해설 | 피수식어딘 a statement가 수식어인 about the exact steps 바로 앞에 와야 한다. 부정어구 nowhere in the Constitution이 문두에 있으므로 도치 구문을 써야 한다.

139 (C) Not only does the giraffe's tall neck allow it to reach the highest branches, but also it lets the animal see over long distances.

    (A) Not only the giraffe's tall neck

    (B) The giraffe's tall neck not only

    (C) Not only does the giraffe's tall neck

    (D) Only the giraffe's tall neck does not

> 번역 | 기린의 긴 목은 가장 높은 가지에 도달할 수 있도록 해 줄뿐만 아니라 먼 거리를 볼 수 있도록 해준다.

> 해설 | 뒷 부분의 but also로 보아 앞에 not only가 와야 한다. 부정어인 not only가 문두에 오면 도치가 일어나야 한다.

140 It would be difficult for a man of his political affiliation, (D) however charming and capable, to become a senator from the south.

    (A) though charming and capable is he

    (B) even with charm and so capable

    (C) charming and having capability

    (D) however charming and capable

> 번역 | 아무리 매력적이고 능력이 있다고 하더라도 그의 정치적 동지가 남부에서 상원의원이 되는 것은 어렵다.

> 해설 | 가주어-진주어 구문이며, 의미상의 주어는 a man이다. of his political affiliation은 a man은 수식한다. charming과 capable은 형용사로서 보어 역할을 할 수 있는데 however charming and capable he is에서 he is가 생략된 구문이며, however는 접속사이다.

141 The first tooth usually emerges when an infant [was → is] about six months old.

> 번역 대개 유아가 약 6개월 되었을 때 첫 번째 이가 난다.

> 해설 일반적 사실을 나타내므로 단순현재를 쓴다.

142 During the period of inflation, the value of money drops as prices [rose → rise].

> 번역 인플레이션 기간 동안에는 물가가 오름에 따라 화폐의 가치가 떨어진다.

> 해설 일반적 사실을 나타내므로 단순현재를 쓴다.

143 Kiwi birds mainly eat insects, worms, and snails and [searched → search] for their food by probing the ground with their long bills.

> 번역 키위새는 주로 곤충, 벌레, 달팽이를 먹으며, 긴 부리로 땅을 파서 먹이를 찾는다.

> 해설 일반적 사실을 나타내므로 단순현재를 쓴다.

144 He [commuted → commutes] by subway between Seoul and Incheon every day.

> 번역 그는 서울과 인천을 지하철로 매일 출퇴근한다.

> 해설 습관을 나타내므로 현재시제를 쓴다.

145 Buyers are responsible for supplying the goods and services that an organization [required → requires] for its operations.

> 번역 구매자는 그 조직이 작동하는 데 필요한 상품과 용역을 제공할 책임이 있다.

> 해설 주절이 현재시제로 일반적 사실을 나타내므로 종속절에도 현재시제를 쓴다.

146 Everyone usually leaves the office as soon as the boss (C) goes home.

(A) will go   (B) goes to

(C) goes   (D) went

> 번역 대개 누구나 사장이 퇴근하면 사무실을 나선다.

> 해설 usually는 일반적 사실을 나타내므로 단순현재를 쓴다.

147 One of the essential features of the modern skyscraper [is being → is] the elevator.

> 번역 현대 고층건물의 근본 특징 중의 하나는 엘리베이터이다.

> 해설 be 동사는 상태동사로 진행형을 쓰지 않는다. 다만 You are being silly 와 같이 진행형을 쓰면 일시적인 상태를 나타낸다.

148 Battery-operated reading lamps (B) are selling very well right now.

(A) sale   (B) are selling

(C) were sold   (D) sold

> 번역 | 배터리로 작동되는 독서등이 지금은 잘 팔린다.

> 해설 | sell은 대상이 주어가 되더라도 well/easily와 같은 부사가 있으면 수동태를 쓰지 않는다. right now 때문에 현재진행형을 쓴다.

149 We are (B) expecting David to arrive on the 3:30 flight from Boston.

(A) to expect   (B) expecting

(C) to expecting   (D) expected

> 번역 | 우리는 David가 3시 30분 Boston발 비행기로 도착하기를 기다리고 있다.

> 해설 | be 다음에는 현재분사나 과거분사가 올 수 있는데, 목적어 David가 있으므로 능동형을 써야 한다.

150 During most of this century, A. Philip Randolph struggled for Black rights in the United States and [becomes → became] an important figure in the labor movement.

> 번역 | 지난 세기 내내 A. Philip Randolph는 미국에서 흑인의 권리를 위해 투쟁했으며, 노동운동에서 중요한 인물이 되었다.

> 해설 | struggled가 과거시제이므로 and 다음에 과거시제가 쓰여야 한다.

151 Louis Armstrong quickly won recognition as a trumpeter and vocalist and [has → had] a major influence on the development of jazz in the 1920's.

> 번역 | Louis Armstrong은 트럼펫 연주자와 가수로서 명성을 빨리 얻었으며, 1920년대에 재즈의 발전에 커다란 영향을 미쳤다.

> 해설 | 과거시점을 나타내는 1920's이 있으며, 또한 won이 과거이므로 과거를 쓴다.

152 Once the scientist had figured out the precise path of comet, he [is finding → found] that he was able to predict its next appearance.

> 번역 | 그 과학자는 혜성의 정확한 경로를 파악하고 나면 다음 출현을 예측할 수 있다는 것을 알아 냈다.

> 해설 | 종속절이 과거완료(had figured)로 앞선 사건을 나타내며, 다음에 일어난 일은 단순과거를 쓴다.

153 The French explorers Marquette and Joliet were the first Europeans to explore the region that later [becomes → became] Illinois.

> 번역 | 프랑스의 탐험가 Marquette와 Joliet는 나중에 Illinois가 된 지역을 처음 방문한 유럽인이었다.

> 해설 | were가 과거시제이므로 관계절도 과거시제를 써야 한다.

154 He (C) went out a few minutes ago.

    (A) goes out   (B) has gone out

    (C) went out   (D) will go out

> 번역   그는 몇 분 전에 나갔다.

> 해설   a few minutes ago와 같은 과거 시점을 표시하는 표현이 있으면 단순과거를 쓴다.

155 I (C) made my airline reservation last Monday.

    (A) have made   (B) make

    (C) made   (D) will make

> 번역   나는 지난 월요일에 비행기를 예약했다.

> 해설   last Monday가 과거를 나타내는 표현이므로 단순과거를 쓴다.

156 Do you remember how many years ago (B) we visited the corporation there?

    (A) we visit   (B) we visited

    (C) did you visit   (D) we have visited

> 번역   우리가 거기에 있는 회사를 몇 년 전에 방문했는지 기억하니?

> 해설   과거 시점에 대한 질문이므로 단순과거를 쓴다. When did you meet John?과 같은 과거시점에 대한 질문도 현재완료가 아닌 단순과거를 쓴다.

157 The reception clerk (C) was talking on the telephone when the phone went dead.

    (A) talked   (B) is taking

    (C) was talking   (D) would talk

> 번역   전화기가 고장났을 때 객실 접수원은 통화 중이었다.

> 해설   when절의 단순과거는 짧은 시간 내에 일어난 사건을 나타내며, 주절의 과거진행은 과거에 일정시간 지속된 사건을 나타낸다.

158 Since he went to New York, we have not [hear → heard] of him yet.

> 번역   그가 New York에 간 이후로 아직 그에 관한 소식을 듣지 못했다.

> 해설   현재완료는 have+V-en이다.

159 Baltimore claims to have [being → been] the first city in the U.S. to have streets illuminated by gas light.

번역 Baltimore는 가스등으로 도로를 밝힌 미국의 첫 번째 도시였다고 주장한
다.

해설 현재완료는 have+V-en의 형태이다.

160 The company [doesn't → hasn't] decided yet where to locate the new branch office.

번역 그 회사는 새로운 지점을 어디에 둘 것인지 아직 결정하지 않았다.

해설 과거분사는 완료나 수동에 쓰이는데, 의미상 능동태가 적절하므로 완료형
을 써야 한다. 미래나 과거를 나타내는 시간 표시가 없으므로 현재완료를
쓴다.

161 The job market (C) has been tight recently owing to the depression in business.

(A) is   (B) have been

(C) has been   (D) is become

번역 사업의 불황 때문에 노동시장이 최근에 어려워졌다.

해설 recently는 과거시점을 나타내는 것이 아니라 현재시간이 포함된 기간을
나타내므로 현재완료와 함께 쓰인다.

162 (D) Since the beginning of this century the trumpet has played a leading
role in the development of jazz.

(A) From this century

(B) Since this century has begun

(C) As this century began

(D) Since the beginning of this century

번역 금세기 초에 트럼펫은 재즈의 발전에 주도적 역할을 했다.

해설 현재완료는 since와 함께 쓰이는데, since가 접속사로 쓰였을 때는 과거
시제가 온다.

163 Our company (C) has been using the Metro Messenger Center since 1990.

(A) use   (B) used

(C) has been using   (D) had used

번역 우리 회사는 1990년부터 Metro Messenger Center를 쓰고 있다.

해설 since는 현재완료와 함께 쓰인다. 현재완료진행은 말하는 시점에서 계속
되고 있음을 강조한다.

164 He (B) has attended several sessions of the Board of Directors since he was
promoted to the post of director.

(A) attended   (B) has attended

(C) attends   (D) was attended

> 번역   그는 이사로 승진한 뒤 이사회 회의에 몇 번 참석했다.
> 해설   since는 현재완료와 함께 쓰인다.

165 Ten years (B) has passed since he died of liver cancer.

(A) are   (B) have passed

(C) has passed   (D) passed

> 번역   그가 간암으로 죽은 지 10년이 흘렀다.
> 해설   시간을 나타내는 표현은 형태가 복수라 하더라도 단수 취급한다.

166 It was discovered where he had [was → been] all the while.

> 번역   그가 그동안 내내 있었던 곳에서 그것이 발견되었다.
> 해설   과거완료는 had+V-en의 형태이다. discovered보다 먼저 일어난 일이므로 과거완료를 쓴다.

167 Archaeologists recently unearthed artifacts indicating that the pre-Incan people of South America [developed → had developed] artistic and architectural skills as complex as those of the Incas.

> 번역   고고학자들은 최근에 남미의 잉카 이전의 사람들이 잉카인만큼이나 복잡한 예술적 기교와 건축 기술을 가졌다는 것을 나타내는 인공유물을 발견하였다.
> 해설   developed가 unearthed보다 먼저 일어난 일이므로 과거완료를 쓴다. 과거완료의 소위 대과거 용법이다.

168 By 1988 Gordon Parks had made two documentary films, [wrote → had written] two bestselling books, and had accrued thirty years of experience in still photography.

> 번역   1988년까지 Gordon Parks는 두 개의 기록영화를 제작하였으며, 두 권의 베스트셀러를 썼고, 정물사진에서 30년의 경험을 축적하였다.
> 해설   by+과거표현이 나타나면 주절은 과거완료를 쓴다. had made, had accrued처럼 had+V-en형을 써야 한다.

169 (C) I'd received the message a week before he came.

(A) I'm   (B) I've

(C) I'd   (D) I

> 번역   나는 그가 오기 1주일 전에 메시지를 받았었다.
> 해설   came 보다 먼저 일어난 일이므로 과거완료를 쓴다.

170 Hardly (C) had I arrived at the branch office when I took measures to reform it.

(A) did   (B) have

(C) had   (D) am

| 번역 | 지점에 도착하자마자 나는 지점에 대한 개혁 조치를 취했다. |

| 해설 | hardly *A* when *B*에서 A는 과거완료, B는 단순과거를 쓴다. |

171 Before 1892, the atom (C) had been considered a tiny, unsplittable particle, the smallest portion of matter.

(A) has been considered   (B) were considering

(C) had been considered   (D) had been considering

| 번역 | 1892년 이전에 원자는 조그맣고 더 이상 쪼갤 수 없는 분자, 즉 가장 작은 물질의 부분으로 간주되었다. |

| 해설 | before 1892가 과거 이전을 나타내므로 과거완료를 써야 한다. consider 는 주로 5형식 동사로 쓰이는데 빈칸 뒤에 하나의 명사만 나타났으므로 수동태를 써야 한다. particle과 the smallest portion of matter는 동격 이다. |

172 It is reported that the railroad fare [is → will be] raised by 30% next January.

| 번역 | 철도 요금이 내년 1월에 30% 인상될 것으로 전해졌다. |

| 해설 | next January라는 미래 시간표시어가 있으므로 미래시제를 쓴다. |

173 The girl (D) is going to the movies with her boyfriend this Saturday.

(A) will   (B) she always was

(C) she is   (D) is

| 번역 | 이번 주 토요일에 그 소녀는 남자친구와 영화를 보러 갈 것이다. |

| 해설 | this Saturday는 미래를 나타내며, 예정을 나타내는 be going to를 쓴다. |

174 The spaceship (D) leaves the earth for the moon next Saturday.

(A) leaving   (B) left

(C) leave   (D) leaves

| 번역 | 우주선이 다음주 토요일에 달을 향해 지구를 떠난다. |

| 해설 | next Saturday 때문에 미래시제를 쓴다. start와 leave 등은 현재시제를 써서 미래를 나타낸다. |

175 As soon as the work [will be → is] done, we will have our dinner.

번역	일을 마치자마자 우리는 저녁을 먹을 것이다.
해설	as soon as는 시간부사절을 이끄는 접속사이다.

176 A desert area that has been without water for six years will still bloom when rain [will come → comes].

번역	6개월간 물이 없었던 사막이 비가 오면 여전히 꽃피울 것이다.
해설	when이 이끄는 절은 일반적으로 부사절이다. 따라서 미래를 현재시제로 나타낸다.

177 The paychecks are deposited in the employees' accounts unless the employees [will require → require] otherwise.

번역	급여는 피고용인이 별도로 요구하지 않으면 그의 통장에 입금된다.
해설	unless는 조건을 나타내는 부사절을 이끄는 접속사이다.

178 She is going to buy a hat after she (B) cashes the check.

(A) will cash   (B) cashes

(C) cashed   (D) could cash

번역	그녀는 수표를 현금으로 바꾼 뒤 모자를 사려고 한다.
해설	시간부사절에서는 미래시제는 현재형을 쓴다.

179 By next year, most of our staff will **have been trained** to use the new computer system.

번역	내년까지는 우리 직원 대부분이 새 컴퓨터 시스템을 사용할 수 있도록 훈련되어 있을 것이다.
해설	by next year가 미래를 나타내므로, 미래완료를 쓴다. staff는 단복 동형 명사라는 점에 유의해야 한다.

180 He (D) will have completed one-third of his military service by this time next year.

(A) is completing   (B) completes

(C) will complete   (D) will have completed

번역	그는 내년 이 때쯤이면 군복무의 3분의 1일 마칠 것이다.
해설	'by+미래'가 있는 문장의 주절은 미래완료를 쓴다.

181 This time next month we (A) will have received the result of the market research.

(A) will have received   (B) have received

(C) had received   (D) were receiving

번역	다음 달 이때쯤이면 우리는 시장조사 결과를 받을 것이다.
해설	this time next month는 미래 시점을 나타내는 표현이므로 미래나 미래 완료와 함께 쓰인다.

182 The officials said the leaders [confirm → had confirmed] their commitment to maintain close cooperation.

번역	관료들은 지도자들이 면밀한 협조를 유지하기로 약속하였다고 말했다.
해설	주절이 과거이면 that절은 과거나 과거완료가 온다.

183 Ms. Jenkins knew she [will → would] have to go as soon as possible if she wanted to catch the last flight.

번역	Jenkins 여사는 마지막 비행기를 타고자 한다면 가능한 한 빨리 가야 한다는 것을 알고 있었다.
해설	주절이 과거이므로 종속절에는 과거나 과거완료가 온다. will의 과거를 써야 하는데, 이와 같이 시제의 일치를 위해 들어간 would는 단순과거가 아니라 과거미래(future in the past)를 나타낸다.

184 We expect that he [is → will be] promoted to the manager of the new workshop.

번역	우리는 그가 새로운 직장의 과장으로 승진될 것으로 기대한다.
해설	expect는 미래의 의미를 나타내므로 종속절에 미래시제를 쓴다.

185 After his trips to the west between 1860 and 1872, Ralph Alber Bakelock would often [painted → paint] American Indian encampments on brown-and-yellow-toned canvases.

번역	1890년부터 1872년까지 서부를 여행한 뒤, Ralph Alber Bakelock은 종종 갈색과 노랑색의 캔버스에 미국 인디언 야영지를 그리곤 하였다.
해설	would는 과거의 습관을 나타내며, 서법조동사(modal auxiliary)이므로 다음에 원형부정사가 온다.

186 Over forty years ago, Helen Hall's outstanding contributions as a settlement organizer [catch → caught] the attention of president Franklin Roosevelt, who appointed her to his advisory committee on economic security.

번역	40년전에 Helen Hall의 정착 조직자로서의 놀라운 공헌은 Franklin Roo-sevelt 대통령의 관심을 끌었으며, 그는 그녀를 경제안정 자문위원회에 임명하였다.
해설	ago는 단순과거와 함께 쓰인다.

187 Soil science [begun → began] with the formulation of the theory of humus in 1809.

번역	토양학은 1809년 부식이론의 형성과 함께 시작되었다.

1809가 과거 시점을 나타내므로 단순과거를 쓴다. begun은 과거분사이다.

188 Coal and petroleum resulted when plants [become → became] buried in swamps and decayed.

번역 석탄과 석유는 식물이 습지에 묻혀 썩은 뒤에 생겨난다.

해설 주절의 resulted가 단순과거이므로 종속절도 단순과거를 쓴다.

189 Delaware is known as the "First State" because on December 7, 1787, it [was being → was] the first state to approve the United States Constitution.

번역 Delaware는 1787년 12월 7일에 미국 헌법을 인준한 첫 번째 주였기 때문에 First State로 알려져 있다.

해설 be는 상태동사로 진행형을 쓰지 않는다.

190 In the New England colonies, Chippendale designs [are → were] adapted to local tastes, and beautiful furniture resulted.

번역 New England 정착지에서 Chippendale 디자인이 현지의 취향에 따라 개조되었다.

해설 resulted가 단순과거이므로 단순과거를 쓴다.

191 Some art historians have [say → said] that too many artists have tried only to imitate previous painting styles.

번역 몇몇 미술사가들은 너무 많은 미술가들이 이전의 회화풍을 모방하려고만 했다고 말한다.

해설 현재완료는 have+V-en형이다.

192 (B) About 175 million years ago, Antarctica was part of the giant continent that geologists call Gondwanaland.

(A) In about 175 million years ago

(B) About 175 million years ago

(C) Since about 175 million years ago

(D) For about 175 million years ago

번역 1억 5천만 년 전에 남극은 지질학자들이 Gondwanaland라 부르는 커다란 대륙의 일부였다.

해설 was가 과거이므로 과거를 나타내는 부사구가 적절하다. ago는 부사로 그 앞에 전치사가 쓰이지 않는다.

193 She is one of the few girls who (A) have passed the examination.

(A) have   (B) has

(C) had   (D) was

그녀는 시험을 합격한 몇몇 소녀 가운데 한 명이다.

해설 주절이 현재시제이므로 종속절에는 과거나 현재 모두 올 수 있다. 과거시점을 나타내는 부사가 없으므로 현재완료를 쓰며, 선행사 girls가 복수이므로 복수동사가 쓰여야 한다.

194 Penicillin is perhaps the drug (C) which has saved more lives than any other in the history of medicine.

(A) what has saved   (B) which saved

(C) which has saved   (D) who saves

번역 페니실린은 아마도 의학 역사상 어떤 것보다도 더 많은 생명을 구한 약일 것이다.

해설 in the history of medicine은 과거 시점을 나타내지 않고 기간을 나타내므로 현재완료를 쓴다.

195 The corporation, which underwent a major restructuring seven years ago, has been growing steadily (A) for five years.

(A) for   (B) on

(C) from   (D) since

번역 그 회사가 7년 전에 중요한 구조조정을 하였으며, 5년간 꾸준히 성장하고 있다.

해설 has been이 현재완료이므로 기간을 나타내는 전치사가 필요하다.

196 The board meeting (C) has been going on since nine o'clock in the morning.

(A) is   (B) was

(C) has been   (D) will be

번역 위원회가 오전 9시부터 계속되고 있다.

해설 since는 현재완료와 함께 쓰인다.

197 The people of that country (A) have not been amicable to those of other countries so far.

(A) have not been   (B) are not

(C) has not been   (D) do not

번역 그 나라의 국민은 지금까지 다른 나라의 국민에게 우호적이지 않았다.

해설 so far는 현재의 시간이 포함된 과거이므로 현재완료를 쓴다.

198 Ms. Furtado would help with the program testing if she [is not → were not] supervising the inventory project.

번역	Furtado 여사가 재고 조사를 감독하지 않고 있다면 프로그램 테스트를 도와줄텐데.
해설	would help가 가정법과거 구문을 나타내므로 조건절에는 과거시제가 와야 한다. 직설법에서는 she was이지만 가정법에서는 she were이다.

199
He became, as it [was → were], a hero as he managed to return home from the land where he had lived as a detainee for about forty years.

번역	사실상 그는 40년동안 억류되어 살았던 곳에서 간신히 집에 돌아온 뒤 영웅이 되었다.
해설	as it were는 '사실상'이라는 뜻을 나타내는 숙어이다.

200
If you (A) lived closer to the supermarket, you could walk there.

(A) lived   (B) had lived

(C) live   (D) have lived

번역	만약 네가 수퍼에 더 가까이 산다면 걸어 갈 수 있을 거야.
해설	주절에 과거시제가 왔으므로 가정법과거이며, 따라서 조건절에 과거시제가 온다.

201
If the penalties (D) were tougher, fewer criminals would be on the street and more teenagers would be in school.

(A) are   (B) be

(C) was   (D) were

번역	처벌이 더 심하면, 범죄자들이 길에 덜 있을 것이며, 십대들이 더 많이 학교에 있을 것이다.
해설	would be가 가정법과거이므로 과거형인 were를 쓴다.

202
If he [would have → had] lain quietly as instructed by the doctor, he might not have had a second heart attack.

번역	의사가 지시한대로 조용히 누워 있었더라면 두 번째 심장마미는 일어나지 않았을 것이다.
해설	가정법과거완료는 If S had V-en, S would have V-en의 형태이다.

203
If he had not seen the storekeeper's scissors, he [will → would] have for-gotten to buy a pair.

번역	가게 주인의 가위를 보지 않았더라면 그는 가위를 사야 한다는 것을 잊었을 것이다.
해설	가정법과거완료 구문에서 서법조동사의 과거형이 쓰인다. a pair는 a pair of scissors를 나타낸다.

204 If Watergate [did → had] not occurred, Nixon would not have resigned from the presidency.

> 번역   Watergate 사건이 일어나지 않았더라면 Nixon은 대통령직을 사임하지 않았을 것이다.

> 해설   가정법과거완료의 형태에 관한 문제이다. 조건절은 had V-en의 형태이다.

205 If you [haven't → hadn't] noticed the smoke, the house would have burned down.

> 번역   만약 네가 연기를 보지 못했더라면 그 집은 완전히 타버렸을 것이다.

> 해설   would have burned는 가정법과거완료 구문이므로 조건절에 had+V-en이 온다.

206 He (D) could have doubled his business if he had advertised efficiently.

   (A)   will double   (B)   would double

   (C)   doubled   (D)   could have doubled

> 번역   그가 광고를 더 효과적으로 했더라면 사업이 두 배가 되었을 것이다.

> 해설   had advertised가 과거완료이므로, 조건절에는 would+have+V-en이 온다.

207 The stranger said that if he (A) had been there yesterday, he might have been wounded.

   (A)   had been   (B)   were

   (C)   has been   (D)   was

> 번역   그 낯선 사람은 만약 그가 거기에 어제 왔더라면 상처를 입었을 것이라고 말했다.

> 해설   yesterday로 보아 과거사실의 반대를 나타낸다. 가정법이므로 주절의 said가 과거이지만 시제의 일치는 적용되지 않는다.

208 If he had studied the language before coming here, he (A) wouldn't have so much trouble adjusting to the culture now.

   (A)   wouldn't have   (B)   would have

   (C)   isn't having   (D)   wouldn't be having

> 번역   여기에 오기 전에 그가 언어를 공부했더라면 지금 문화에 적응하는 데 그렇게 어려움은 없을 거야.

> 해설   had studied/before coming here는 가정법과거완료이지만, now로 보아 귀결절은 가정법과거를 써야 한다. 따라서 가정법과거완료＋가정법과거의 혼합가정법을 쓴다.

209 If she (B) were in this town, she would have come to see me by now.

(A) is   (B) were

(C) has been   (D) would be

> **번역**   그녀가 이 마을에 있다면 지금쯤은 나를 만나러 왔을 것이다.
>
> **해설**   조건절은 현재상황에 대한 반대로 가정법과거이며, 귀결절은 by now 로 가정법과거완료를 쓴다. 주의해야 할 점은 by now는 직설법에서 현재완료를 쓰는데, 현재완료도 일종의 과거시제이므로 가정법에서는 가정법과거완료가 된다.

210 The chairman must not have been in his right mind; otherwise he would not [make → have made] such wild statements.

> **번역**   의장이 제정신이 아니었음에 틀림없다. 그렇지 않았다면 그런 거친 말을 하지 않았을 것이다.
>
> **해설**   must have V-en이 과거에 대한 강한 추측을 나타내므로, 가정법과거완료를 써야 한다.

211 The secretary sometimes [wished → wishes] that she were not working in a big corporation.

> **번역**   그 비서는 때로는 대기업에서 일하지 않기를 바란다.
>
> **해설**   sometimes는 단순현재와 함께 쓰인다. were로 보아 가정법과거이다.

212 She has a curious expression on her face as if she [was → were] smiling about something that amused her.

> **번역**   그녀를 즐겁게 하는 뭔가를 본 것처럼 그녀는 묘한 표정을 짓고 있다.
>
> **해설**   as if절에 오는 동사의 시제에 따라 가정법과거, 또는 가정법과거완료가 결정되는데, 주절의 시제가 현재이므로 현재 사실의 반대를 나타내어 가정법과거를 써야 한다.

213 If [they → it] had not been for their wives' understanding, they would not have succeeded in the project.

> **번역**   아내의 이해가 없다면 그들이 그 프로젝트를 성공하지 못했을 것이다.
>
> **해설**   If it had not been for 구문이다.

214 He sometimes wishes he (C) were better qualified for his job.

(A) was   (B) would

(C) were   (D) has been

> **번역**   그는 때로는 자기 일에 더 나은 능력이 있기를 바란다.
>
> **해설**   의미상 가정법 구문이다.

215 I (A) wish sales volume would increase this month.

(A) wish   (B) wish to

(C) know   (D) think

번역 이번 달에는 판매량이 늘어나면 좋을텐데.

해설 this month는 현재나 미래와 함께 쓰여야 하는데, would가 있으므로 가정법과거 구문이다.

216 If it had not (B) been for your help, I should have failed.

(A) have been for   (B) been for

(C) had been for   (D) for

번역 너의 도움이 없었더라면 내가 실패했을 것이다.

해설 If it had not been for는 가정법과거완료에 쓰인다. Without your help, 혹은 But for your help로 바꿔 쓸 수 있다.

217 Mr. Johnson insists that his secretary [is → be] responsible for writing all reports as well as for balancing the books.

번역 Johnson씨는 그의 비서가 결산을 하는 것뿐만 아니라 모든 보고서를 작성할 책임이 있다고 주장한다.

해설 insist는 주장, 요구를 나타내는 동사로 that절에 원형을 쓴다.

218 The prime minister's conviction for improper campaign practices is likely to result in increasing pressure that she [resigns → resign].

번역 수상의 부적절한 선거 운동에 대한 유죄 선고는 사임하라는 압력의 증가를 야기했다.

해설 pressure와 동격절인 that절에 원형을 쓴다.

219 If a severe earthquake [would occur → should occur], survivors would have to be housed in temporary shelters and provided with emergency supplies of food and water.

번역 심한 지진이 일어나면, 생존자들은 임시 거처에 수용되고 비상 식량과 물이 제공된다.

220 If traffic problems are not solved soon, driving in cities [becomes → will become] impossible.

번역 교통문제가 곧 해결되지 않으면 도시에서 운전하는 것은 불가능해질 것이다.

해설 조건절이 현재이므로 단순한 가정이며, 따라서 귀결절에 단순미래를 쓴다.

221 I recommend you hire Andy Roth as your accountant. If Andy (B) should make a mistake, he won't charge you for his time.

(A) making   (B) should make

(C) have made   (D) is making

| 번역 | 나는 Andy Roth를 회계사로 추천합니다. 만약 그가 실수를 저지른다면, 일한 시간에 대한 비용을 청구하지 않을 것입니다. |

| 해설 | won't로 보아 가정법미래이다. |

222 If any signer of the Constitution (B) were to return to life for a day, his opinion of our amendments would be interesting.

(A) was to   (B) were to

(C) should have   (D) had to

| 번역 | 만약 헌법에 서명을 한 사람이 하루 동안 살아난다면, 수정안에 대한 의견이 흥미로울 것이다. |

| 해설 | were to는 미래에 대한 가정으로 가능성이 없을 때 쓴다. would be로 보아 가정법과거이며, 죽은 사람이 살아날 가능성은 없으므로 should 대신 were to를 쓴다. |

223 [The Board of Directors should → Should the Board of Directors] decide to hire him, we should advise the personnel office to prepare all the necessary papers.

| 번역 | 이사회가 그를 고용하기로 결정한다면, 인사과에 필요한 모든 서류를 준비시키도록 해야 한다. |

| 해설 | 두 개의 절이 있으므로 접속사가 필요하다. If the Board of Directors should decide의 도치구문이다. |

224 Had they known the snowstorm would be so treacherous, the hikers [did not venture → would not venture] into it without proper equipment.

| 번역 | 눈보라가 그렇게 위험하다는 것을 알았더라면, 도보여행자들이 적절한 장비도 없이 눈보라 속을 걸을 생각도 안 했을 것이다. |

| 해설 | If they had known에서 Had they known으로 도치된 가정법과거완료이므로 귀결절에 would V가 와야 한다. |

225 (A) Had they not been hunted so ruthlessly for food and ivory for many years, elephants nowadays would have much larger populations.

(A) Had they not been hunted   (B) If they had not hunted

(C) If they didn't hunt   (D) Have they not been hunted

| 번역 | 오랫동안 식량과 상아 때문에 그렇게 무자비하게 사냥을 당하지 않았더라면, 오늘날 코끼리가 훨씬 많을 것이다. |

| 해설 | 조건절은 for many years 때문에 가정법과거완료이고, 귀결절은 nowadays 때문에 가정법과거를 쓰므로, 혼합가정법 구문이다. |

226 Should the quality of your products decline, all our future orders (C) shall be canceled.

    (A) will cancel   (B) cancel

    (C) shall be canceled   (D) will have canceled

> 번역   제품의 질이 떨어진다면 앞으로 주문이 취소될 것이다.

> 해설   If the quality of your products should decline에서 주어와 조동사가 도치된 가정의 구문이다.

227 (C) Were each of the proposals considered separately, there would not be enough time for discussion and voting before the end of the conference.

    (A) Each   (B) If each

    (C) Were each   (D) Since each

> 번역   각 제안을 각각 살핀다면 회의가 끝나기 전에 논의하고 투표할 시간이 없을 것이다.

> 해설   If each of the proposals were에서 If가 생략되고 were가 문두로 이동한 도치구문이다.

228 Mary told me that she would accept the invitation if she [was → were] in my place.

> 번역   Mary는 내 입장이라면 초대에 응할 것이라고 말했다.

> 해설   가정법에서 was 대신 were를 쓴다.

229 Had he told the boss he had a traffic accident the night before, he could [had → have] taken the day off.

> 번역   전날 밤에 교통사고가 있었다는 것을 사장에게 이야기했었다면 휴가를 하루 주었을거야.

> 해설   If he had told는 가정법과거완료이고, 따라서 could have V-en을 쓴다.

230 If you [will → would] have friends, first learn to do without them.

> 번역   만약 친구를 갖고 싶거든 먼저 친구 없이 사는 방법을 배워라.

> 해설   would가 여기서는 '바라다'의 뜻으로 쓰였다.

231 If the organizers of the conference [have → had] spent a little more time preparing, half the problems probably wouldn't have occurred.

> 번역   회의 조직자들이 준비하는 데 좀 더 많은 시간을 할애했더라면 문제의 반은 일어나지 않았을 것이다.

> 해설   wouldn't have occurred가 가정법과거완료이므로 had spent라 해야 한다.

232 [Since → If] you had come on time, we would have been able to see the movie, but we just missed the last showing.

> 번역 만약 네가 제 시간에 왔더라면 우리가 그 영화를 볼 수 있었을 텐데, 금방 마지막 회를 놓쳤어.
>
> 해설 가정법의 부사절은 접속사 if를 쓴다.

233 If they (C) had not overworked in the beginning, the volunteers would have helped finish the project.

(A) were not overworked   (B) was not overworked

(C) had not overworked   (D) have not overworked

> 번역 지원자들이 처음에 과로하지 않았더라면 그 계획을 끝내는 데 도움을 줄 수 있었을 것이다.
>
> 해설 would have helped가 가정법과거완료이다.

234 Some historians say that if the South had not lacked essential industries, it (D) would have won the American Civil War.

(A) won   (B) had won

(C) would win   (D) would have won

> 번역 어떤 역사가들은 남부가 필수 산업이 부족하지 않았더라면 남북전쟁에서 이겼을 것이라고 말한다.
>
> 해설 had not lacked가 가정법과거완료이므로 귀결절은 would have V-en을 쓴다.

235 If the factory had not been damaged by the fire, it (D) would have been completed by the end of the year.

(A) would finish   (B) will be completed

(C) would be completed   (D) would have been completed

> 번역 만약 화재로 공장이 피해를 입지 않았더라면 연말에는 완성되었을 것이다.
>
> 해설 had not been damaged는 가정법과거완료이며, 따라서 they would have completed the factory의 수동형인 it would have been completed가 적절하다.

236 (D) Should she smile at you, I would give you my favorite book.

(A) Not she had smiled   (B) Had she have smiled

(C) That she would smile   (D) Should she smile

> 번역 그녀가 혹시 네게 미소를 짓는다면 네게 내가 좋아하는 책을 줄게.
>
> 해설 If she should smile의 도치구문이다.

237 Had the damage been worse, the insurance company (C) would have paid.

(A) would pay   (B) paid

(C) would have paid   (D) had paid

> 번역   피해가 컸더라면 보험회사가 지불했을 것이다.

> 해설   If the damage had been worse의 도치구문이다.

238 Three months after they have been laid, crocodile eggs are ready [hatched → to be hatched].

> 번역   악어의 알은 낳은 지 3개월 후에 부화될 준비가 된다.

> 해설   be ready to V 구문이다. crocodile eggs가 의미상 목적어이므로 수동태를 쓴다. lay가 '알을 낳다'의 뜻일 때 lay-laid-laid이다.

239 Those who had participated in the negotiation decided not [making → to make] an offer until they looked over the contract.

> 번역   협상에 참여한 사람들이 계약서를 살펴보기 전에는 가격을 제안하지 않기로 결정하였다.

> 해설   decide는 to부정사를 취한다. 부정사의 부정은 to 앞에 not을 쓴다.

240 The mechanics haven't been able (A) to find the problem with the car yet.

(A) to find   (B) find

(C) finding   (D) to found

> 번역   정비공이 아직 차에 어떤 문제가 있는지 알아내지 못했다.

> 해설   be able to V 구문이다.

241 It is difficult (C) to translate a foreign text literally.

(A) for translating   (B) that translating

(C) to translate   (D) to be translated

> 번역   외국어로 된 글을 문자 그대로 번역하는 것은 어렵다.

> 해설   가주어-진주어 구문으로 difficult는 to 부정사를 취한다.

242 In both debate and discussion, opposing ideas are presented (C) in an attempt to persuade people.

(A) an attempt in persuade people

(B) an attempt to persuade people

(C) in an attempt to persuade people

(D) when attempt persuade to people

| 번역 | 논쟁과 토론에서 모두 대립되는 생각은 사람들을 설득하기 위해 제시된다. |
| 해설 | attempt는 동사로 쓰이든 명사로 쓰이든 to 부정사를 취한다. |

243 He advised me [sending → to send] a verbal message to them before making an official complaint against them.

| 번역 | 그는 그들을 공식적으로 고소하기 전에 언어적 메시지를 보내도록 권고하였다. |
| 해설 | advise+목적어+to V 구문이다. |

244 I was [compelled pay → compelled to pay] the bill because my boss did not have enough money to cover it after having dinner at a very fancy restaurant with some clients.

| 번역 | 고객들과 아주 멋진 식당에서 식사를 한 뒤 사장님이 그 비용을 지불할 만한 돈을 가지고 있지 않아서 내가 지불해야 했다. |
| 해설 | be compelled to V 구문으로 수동형을 쓴다. |

245 Acute hearing helps most animals [sensitive → sense] the approach of thunderstorms long before people do.

| 번역 | 민감한 청각은 사람들보다 먼저 대부분의 동물들이 닥쳐오는 뇌우를 느끼도록 도움을 준다. |
| 해설 | help는 목적어 다음에 원형부정사를 취한다. do는 sense the approach of the thunderstorms를 가리킨다. |

246 The purpose of inductive logic is (D) to infer general laws from particular occurrences.

(A) general laws to infer   (B) to inferring general laws

(C) to general laws infer   (D) to infer general laws

| 번역 | 귀납법의 목적은 특정한 발생으로부터 일반적 법칙을 추론해 내는 것이다. |
| 해설 | purpose가 주어로 쓰였을 때 보어 자리에는 to 부정사를 쓴다. |

247 The function of language is to enable (A) people to communicate ideas to one another, primarily through audible speech, and secondarily through written words.

(A) people to communicate ideas

(B) people communicate ideas

(C) ideas to communicate people

(D) people's communication ideas

| 번역 | 언어의 기능은 일차적으로 들을 수 있는 말로, 그리고 이차적으로 쓰여진 언어로 서로 생각을 주고받을 수 있도록 하는 데 있다. |

해설 enable+목적어+to V 구문이다.

248 Although a biography is primarily intended to recount a person's life, many biographers examine the social forces (B) that helped shape it.

(A) that was helped shape it   (B) that helped shape it

(C) that they helped shape it   (D) that helped shaping it

번역 전기가 주로 한 개인의 삶을 자세히 설명하려는 의도이지만 많은 전기작가들은 삶을 이루는 데 도움이 된 사회적 영향을 조사한다.

해설 help 다음에는 목적어가 없더라도 원형부정사를 쓴다.

249 In 1852 Massachusetts passed a law requiring all children from four to eighteen years of age (C) to attend school.

(A) attending   (B) attend

(C) to attend   (D) who attend

번역 1852년에 Massachusetts 주는 4세부터 18세까지의 아이들이 학교에 다니도록 요구하는 법을 통과시켰다.

해설 require+목적어+to V 구문이다.

250 If you use a credit card [paying → to pay] for the meal, you may include the tip on the credit card slip or leave the tip in cash.

번역 식사비를 지불하기 위해 신용카드를 사용한다면 팁을 신용카드전표에 포함시키거나 현금으로 팁을 두고 올 수 있다.

해설 목적을 나타내는 부사적 용법의 to 부정사를 쓴다.

251 The practice of making excellent films based on rather obscure novels has been going on so long in the United States [as for → as to] constitute a tradition.

번역 아주 잘 알려지지 않은 소설에 근거하여 훌륭한 영화를 만드는 관행이 미국에서 전통을 이룰 만큼 아주 오랫동안 이어져 왔다.

해설 so long as to ... ··· 할 만큼 오랫동안

252 A statue, a monument, a building, or a park may be dedicated to [commemoration → commemorate] a distinguished individual.

번역 조각상, 기념비, 건물, 공원 등을 유명한 인물을 기념하기 위해 바칠 수 있다.

해설 dedicated to에서 to가 전치사이지만, 여기서는 to가 목적을 나타내는 부정사의 to이다.

253 (B) To overcome conflict, we must apply the ultimate strength.

(A) If we overcame conflict

(B) To overcome conflict

(C) Though we overcame conflict

(D) Overcoming conflict

번역 ┃ 갈등을 극복하기 위해서는 우리는 최선을 다 해야 한다.

해설 ┃ 목적을 나타내는 부사적 용법의 부정사가 적절하다.

254 When Columbus discovered the New World he was not surprised (B) to find it inhabited; he thought he had landed in India or Japan.

(A) finding it inhabited   (B) to find it inhabited

(C) to find it inhabit   (D) to find inhabited it

번역 ┃ 신세계를 발견했을 때 Columbus는 사람이 거주하고 있다는 것을 발견하고서도 놀라지 않았다. 그는 인도나 일본에 도착했다고 생각했다.

해설 ┃ be surprised to V 구문으로 부사적 용법의 부정사이다. inhabited는 형용사로 목적보어로 쓰였다.

255 Because the arctic regions receive little sunlight, the air there is too cold (C) to hold much moisture.

(A) for hold much moisture

(B) that it cannot hold much moisture

(C) to hold much moisture

(D) of holding much moisture

번역 ┃ 북극 지역이 햇빛을 거의 받지 못하므로 그곳의 공기는 너무 차가워서 많은 수분을 함유하지 못한다.

해설 ┃ too ... to 구문이다. there가 부사이지만 the air를 후치수식하고 있다.

256 Although Canada's Parliament can neither administer or enforce laws nor initiate policy, it does have the power [for making → to make] laws and vote on the allocation of funds.

번역 ┃ 캐나다 의회가 법을 집행하거나 정책을 제안할 수 없지만, 법을 만들거나 자금을 배당하는 데 투표하는 힘을 가지고 있다.

해설 ┃ to make laws가 the power를 수식하는 형용사적 용법의 부정사이다.

257 In 1924 Nellie Taylor Ross of Wyoming became the first woman (D) to be elected governor in the United States.

(A) was   (B) was to

(C) she was   (D) to be

번역	1924년 Wyoming 주의 Nellie Taylor Ross는 미국에서 주지사로 선출된 첫 번째 여성이 되었다.
해설	형용사적 용법의 부정사는 명사가 first나 last의 수식을 받을 때 관계절을 대신하여 쓰인다.

258 It takes several years (C) for bamboo seeds to grow into plants that can be used for commercial purposes.

(A) if bamboo seeds grow into plants

(B) of bamboo seeds to grow into plants

(C) for bamboo seeds to grow into plants

(D) for bamboo seeds while growing into plants

번역	대나무 씨앗이 자라서 상업적 목적으로 쓰일 수 있는 묘목으로 자라려면 수년이 걸린다.
해설	It takes+(사람)+시간+to V 구문으로 의미상의 주어는 for를 써서 나타낸다.

259 (C) It is not unusual for architects to design irregularly shaped buildings when their clients ask for something unique.

(A) Not unusually, architects

(B) It is not unusual that architects

(C) It is not unusual for architects

(D) Architects are not unusually

번역	고객이 뭔가 독창적인 것을 원할 때 건축가가 불규칙적인 모습의 건물을 고안하는 것은 흔한 일이다.
해설	가주어-진주어 구문으로 진주어인 to 부정사의 의미상의 주어를 for로 나타낸다.

260 All airlines have a policy of letting passengers in the lavatory [to move → move] back to their seats when the airplane is about to take off or land.

번역	모든 항공사들은 비행기가 곧 이착륙할 때 화장실의 승객이 좌석으로 돌아가도록 하는 정책을 가지고 있다.
번역	let은 사역동사로 목적어 다음에 원형부정사를 쓴다.

261 The face of the Moon is changed by collisions with meteoroids, causing new craters [appear → to appear].

번역	유성체와 충돌하여 새로운 분화구가 생겨나서 달의 표면이 변화되었다.
해설	cause는 의미상 사역동사와 유사하지만 사역동사가 아니며, 따라서 to 부정사를 취한다. 여기서 causing은 분사로 분사구문을 이루며, and it causes로 바꿔 쓸 수 있다.

262 Daylight saving time came into use in the United States in an effort to conserve electricity by having business hours [to correspond → correspond] to the hours of natural daylight.

> 번역 ┃ 일광 절약 시간은 근무시간을 자연 일광 시간에 일치시킴으로써 전기를 절약하기 위해 미국에서 사용되기 시작하였다.

> 해설 ┃ have가 사역동사이므로 목적어 다음에 원형부정사가 온다.

263 I'll have my secretary (C) make a copy of the fax.

(A) to make   (B) to have made

(C) make   (D) made

> 번역 ┃ 내 비서에게 팩스 복사본을 만들도록 하겠다.

> 해설 ┃ have는 사역동사로 다음의 목적어가 사람이면 원형부정사를 쓰며, 사물이면 과거분사를 쓴다.

264 The company attempts to make all its employees (A) feel like family.

(A) feel   (B) felt

(C) feels   (D) feeling

> 번역 ┃ 그 회사는 모든 직원들이 가족처럼 느끼도록 만들려고 한다.

> 해설 ┃ make도 have와 마찬가지로 사역동사로 사람 목적어 다음에 원형부정사가 온다.

265 Finally, the police (C) let the suspect go.

(A) allowed   (B) permitted

(C) let   (D) wanted

> 번역 ┃ 마침내 경찰은 혐의자가 가도록 허락했다.

> 해설 ┃ go가 원형부정사이므로 앞에는 사역동사나 지각동사가 와야 한다. allow, permit, want는 모두 to 부정사를 취한다.

266 Heating and cooling can cause matter (C) to expand and contract.

(A) expanding and contracting (B) expansion and contract

(C) to expand and contract   (D) expand and contract

> 번역 ┃ 가열과 냉각은 물질이 확장하고 수축하도록 한다.

> 해설 ┃ cause는 to 부정사를 취한다. and 다음에 to를 쓰지 않음으로써 expand와 contract가 밀접한 관계가 있다는 것을 나타낸다.

267 It's no longer important to have the flowers [to bloom → bloom] at the same time I have the baby.

번역	내가 임신함과 동시에 꽃이 피게 하는 것은 이제 더이상 중요하지 않다.
해설	have는 사역동사로 원형부정사나 과거분사가 오는데, the flowers와 bloom은 능동관계이므로 원형부정사를 쓴다. at the same time 다음에는 관계부사 when이 생략되었다.

268 The witness said he saw someone [was placing → placing] the bag on the park bench.

번역	그 증인은 누군가가 공원 벤치에 가방을 놓는 것을 보았다고 말했다.
해설	see는 지각동사로 현재분사나 원형부정사를 취한다.

269 The men in the mines stop work when they hear the whistle (A) blow.

(A) blow   (B) to blow

(C) be blow   (D) to be blowing

번역	탄광 속의 사람들은 휘파람 소리를 들을 때 일을 멈춘다.
해설	hear는 지각동사로 다음에 현재분사나 원형부정사가 온다. stop은 부정사와 동명사를 모두 취할 수 있는데, 여기서 work는 명사이다.

270 [To telling the truth → To tell the truth], so little care have I given to my library's well-being at normal times.

번역	솔직히 말해서 평상시에 도서관의 복지에 대해 관심을 거의 갖지 않았다.
해설	to tell the truth는 숙어로 독립부정사이다.

271 The representative was announced [to be killed → to have been killed] in the car accident.

번역	대표단이 자동차 사고로 죽은 것으로 발표되었다.
해설	They announced someone had killed the representative in the car accident에서 the representative가 두 번의 수동태를 거쳐 만들어진 문장이다. announced보다 had killed가 먼저 일어난 일이므로 완료부정사를 쓴다.

272 We are glad to (C) have helped you when you needed our help.

(A) help you   (B) helping you

(C) have helped you   (D) having helped you

번역	우리의 도움이 필요했을 때 당신을 도울 수 있어서 우리는 즐거웠다.
해설	과거에 도움을 준 것이므로 완료부정사를 쓴다.

273 The hormone insulin, which is produced by specialized cells in the pancreas, enables the body [using → to use] and store glucose quickly.

췌장의 전문화된 세포가 만들어내는 인슐린은 인체가 포도당을 빨리 사용하고 저장할 수 있도록 한다.

enable+목적어+to V 구문이다. store는 use와 마찬가지로 to V의 형태인데 and 다음에 와서 to가 생략되었다.

274 You must warn your soldiers [to not be tempted → not to be tempted] by street girls when your platoon marches through the city.

번역 당신의 부대가 시내를 통과하여 행진할 때 부대원들이 길거리의 여자들에게 유혹되지 말도록 경고해야 한다.

해설 부정사의 부정은 to 앞에 not을 쓴다.

275 Margaret Mead studied many different cultures, and she was one of the first anthropologists (C) to photograph her subjects.

(A) and photograph her subjects

(B) to photograph her subjects

(C) that were photographed her subjects

(D) while photograph her subjects

번역 Margaret Mead가 많은 다른 문화를 연구했으며, 대상을 촬영한 첫 번째 인류학자 중의 한 명이다.

해설 first나 last의 수식을 받는 명사의 경우 관계절 대신 to 부정사를 쓸 수 있다. (A)는 현재시제로 비문법적이며, (C)는 수동태로 목적어가 있으므로 적절하지 못하다. 관계절로 바꾸면 who photographed her subjects가 된다.

276 Henry Ford's introduction of the assembly line vastly reduced the time it took (A) to make a car.

(A) to make a car   (B) for making a car

(C) making a car   (D) a car to make

번역 Henry Ford의 조립 라인 도입으로 차를 만드는 시간이 크게 단축되었다.

해설 it takes 시간+to V 구문인데, the time이 선행사인 관계절로 쓰였다.

277 A footnote is characteristically employed to give information (C) that is too long or too detailed to be included in the body of a text.

(A) and that is too long or too detailed

(B) that is so long or so detailed as

(C) that is too long or too detailed

(D) is too long or too detailed

번역	각주는 특성상 본문에 포함되기에는 너무 길거나 상세한 정보를 제공하기 위해 사용된다.
해설	that절은 information이 선행사인 관계절이며, too+형용사+to V 구문이다.

278 The greater an object's mass, the more difficult it is (A) to speed it up or slow it down.

(A) to speed it up or slow it down

(B) it speeds up or slows down

(C) than speeding it up or slowing it down

(D) than speeding up or slowing down

번역	물체의 질량이 클수록 속도를 증가시키거나 줄이는 것이 그만큼 어렵다.
해설	The+비교급 ..., the+비교급 구문이다. 뒷 부분은 it is difficult to V 구문이다.

279 Identical colors (A) may appear to be quite different when they are viewed against different backgrounds.

(A) may appear to be quite different

(B) may appear being quite different

(C) may appear be quite different

(D) may appear quite different to be

번역	동일한 색상이라 할지라도 다른 배경에서 볼 때 전혀 다르게 보일 수 있다.
해설	It may appear that identical colors are quite different에서 identical colors가 주절의 it 자리로 이동하고 that절이 to 부정사가 된 문장이다.

280 Unless an athlete is physically fit, there is not sense in [him → his] sacrificing himself for victory in any one game and, therefore, facing a lifetime injury.

번역	운동선수가 신체적으로 완전하지 않다면 자신을 희생하여 한 경기에서 이기고 평생 아프다면 무분별한 것이다.
해설	him sacrificing himself는 전치사 in의 목적어로 쓰인 동명사로 그 주어는 소유격을 쓴다.

281 The [land → landing] of a spaceship requires the precise coordination of numerous intricate mechanisms.

번역	우주선의 착륙은 많은 복잡한 장치의 정확한 작동을 필요로 한다.
해설	의미상 spaceship을 land시키는 것으로 동사가 필요하며, 주어자리이므로 동명사를 쓴다. the landing of a spaceship 대신 landing a spaceship 으로 쓸 수 있는데 이때는 the가 쓰이지 않는다는 점에 유의해야 한다.

282 Do you mind (C) my smoking here?

(A) smoking   (B) smoke

(C) my smoking   (D) my smoke

> **번역** 여기서 담배를 피워도 되겠습니까?

> **해설** mind는 동명사를 취하는 동사로 주어는 소유격을 쓴다. Would you mind opening the window? 처럼 소유격 주어를 쓰지 않을 경우 주절의 주어와 동명사의 주어가 동일하며, 주어가 다를 경우 Do you mind my opening the window? 처럼 소유격 주어를 쓴다.

283 My father's hobby is (D) raising roses.

(A) raise   (B) rise

(C) rising   (D) raising

> **번역** 우리 아버지의 취미는 장미를 기르는 것이다.

> **해설** 동명사는 명사의 기능을 가지고 있어서 보어로 쓰일 수 있다. rise는 자동사인 반면, raise는 타동사이다.

284 Scientists think (C) that losing leaves helps some tree to conserve water in the winter.

(A) when losing leaves   (B) leaves are lost

(C) that losing leaves   (D) the leaves losing

> **번역** 과학자들은 낙엽이 지는 것이 나무가 겨울에 물을 보존하는 데 도움이 된다고 생각한다.

> **해설** 시제동사인 helps는 주어가 필요하다. think는 타동사로 명사절을 취하므로 when으로 시작되는 부사절이 올 수 없다. losing leave는 동명사로 helps의 주어로 쓰일 수 있다.

285 Unlike the owl, bats cannot see very well, but they do have (D) very good hearing.

(A) it hears very well   (B) very good to hear

(C) hearing very well   (D) very good hearing

> **번역** 부엉이와 달리 박쥐는 잘 보지 못하지만 청력은 매우 좋다.

> **해설** have는 타동사로 명사 목적어를 취한다. 동명사는 명사적 성격을 가지므로 형용사의 수식을 받을 수 있다.

286 The dictionary functions primarily as a tool for [the definings → defining] the meaning of words.

> **번역** 사전은 주로 단어의 의미를 정의하는 도구 역할을 한다.

전치사 for의 목적어로 쓰이면서 동시에 the meaning of words를 목적어로 취하므로 동명사가 와야 한다. 동명사는 the를 취하지 않으며, 또한 복수형을 취하지 않는다.

287 The primitive men were proud of their masks and laughed at the visitor for [wearing not → not wearing] one.

번역 원시인들은 탈에 자부심을 가졌으며, 방문객들이 탈을 쓰지 않는 것을 우습게 생각했다.

해설 동명사는 명사적 성격과 동사적 성격을 가지고 있는데, 그 부정형은 not+동명사이다. one은 mask를 가리킨다.

288 A complete biography of a person's life is not written by merely (B) listing the pertinent facts in chronological order.

(A) the pertinent facts are to be listed

(B) listing the pertinent facts

(C) list of the pertinent facts

(D) when the pertinent facts are listed

번역 어떤 사람의 삶의 완벽한 전기는 연대순으로 적절한 사실을 나열하기만 함으로써 쓰여지는 것은 아니다.

해설 by는 전치사로 명사나 동명사를 취한다.

289 The participants are committed to dealing (A) fairly with the opponents.

(A) fairly   (B) fair

(C) fairness   (D) fairer

번역 참가자들은 상대에게 정정당당하게 대할 것을 서약한다.

해설 동명사는 동사적 성격과 명사적 성격을 가지고 있으며, 수식어가 뒤에 있는 것으로 보아 동사적으로 쓰인 것이며, 따라서 수식어는 부사라야 한다.

290 We are still in the process [to build → of building] up the data base with a wide range of information.

번역 우리는 다양한 정보를 가지고서 데이터베이스를 구축하는 중이다.

해설 명사의 동격으로 to 부정사, 동명사, that절이 쓰일 수 있는데, 그 선택은 명사의 성격과 관련이 있다. 특별히 지정되지 않은 명사의 경우 of 동격을 쓴다.

291 Translated into terms of psychological theory, association has been thought of as the basis of [to learn → learning], conditioning, and creative thinking.

번역 심리학 이론의 용어로 번역하자면 연상은 학습, 조건화, 창의적 사고의 근거로 생각되어 왔다.

translated 앞에 being이 생략된 분사구문이다. of는 전치사로 명사나 동명사를 취한다.

292 The main purpose of [classified → classifying] animals is to show the most probable evolutionary relationship of the different species to each other.

번역 동물을 분류하는 주요 목적은 서로 다른 종 사이의 가장 가능성이 높은 진화 관계를 보여주는 것이다.

해설 의미상 of 다음에 동격이 와야 한다. 과거분사는 형용사처럼 수식하며 수동의 의미를 갖는다. 동명사는 다음의 명사를 목적어로 취한다.

293 If you are considering [to buy → buying] your house, take advantage of our low rates of interest.

번역 주택을 구입할 생각을 하고 있다면 우리의 낮은 이율을 이용하시기 바랍니다.

해설 consider는 동명사 목적어를 취한다.

294 In England as early as the twelfth century, young boys enjoyed [to play → playing] football.

번역 영국에서는 12세기에 남자 아이들이 축구를 즐겼다.

해설 enjoy는 동명사 목적어를 취하는 동사이다.

295 You have to pay taxes by the end of the month in order to avoid [to pay → paying] an overdue charge.

번역 연체료 지불을 피하려면 월말까지 세금을 내야 한다.

해설 avoid는 동명사 목적어를 취한다.

296 I wish you would mind your own business and stop [interfere → interfering] in the matter.

번역 남의 일에 참견하지 말고 그 문제를 방해하는 것을 그만두길 바란다.

해설 stop 다음에 동명사가 오면 동명사가 목적어 역할을 하며, to 부정사가 오면 부사적 용법의 부정사이다. 의미상 목적어가 필요하므로 동명사를 쓴다.

297 The suspect denied (C) having stolen the money.

(A) stole   (B) steal
(C) having stolen   (D) to steal

번역 용의자는 돈을 훔친 것을 부인하였다.

해설 deny는 동명사 목적어를 취하는 동사이다. steal이 deny보다 먼저 일어난 일이므로 완료동명사를 쓴다.

298 In addition to [spend → spending] time with her family, Pat enjoys knitting, walking, reading and spending time with her group of lady friends.

| 번역 | Pat은 가족과 시간을 보내는 것 뿐만 아니라 뜨개질, 산보, 독서, 여자 친구들과 시간 보내기를 좋아한다. |

| 해설 | in addition to의 to는 전치사로 다음에 (동)명사가 와야 한다. |

299 The woodwind section of an orchestra may enrich the melody by [provide → providing] different tonal qualities.

| 번역 | 오케스트라의 목관 부문은 다른 음색을 제공함으로써 멜로디를 풍요롭게 할 것이다. |

| 해설 | 전치사 다음에는 동명사를 쓴다. |

300 Doing a good deed is like (B) sowing a good seed.

(A) sow   (B) sowing

(C) to sow   (D) to sowing

| 번역 | 선행을 하는 것은 좋은 씨앗을 뿌리는 것과 같다. |

| 해설 | like가 여기서는 전치사로 쓰여 그 다음에 동명사가 온다. |

301 Our landlord insisted (C) on our paying additional cleaning expenses when we moved out of the rented house.

(A) that we paid   (B) us to pay

(C) on our paying   (D) in our paying

| 번역 | 우리 집주인은 셋집을 나올 때 청소 비용을 추가적으로 지불할 것을 강요하였다. |

| 해설 | insist는 자동사로 on과 결합하여 타동사를 이룬다. 동사+전치사 구문의 경우 동명사 목적어를 취한다. |

302 We do not take up a book, either to pass time or for amusement, (C) without getting from it more or less definite instruction.

(A) without get   (B) without to get

(C) without getting   (D) without have got

| 번역 | 시간을 보내기 위해서든, 재미를 위해서든 다소 명확한 지시 없이 책을 집어 들지는 않는다. |

| 해설 | without은 전치사로 다음에 명사나 동명사가 온다. |

303 People may have difficulty [to think → thinking] clearly when overcome by excitement.

번역 흥분을 이기지 못했을 때 사람은 명확히 생각하는 데 어려움이 있을 수 있다.

해설 have difficulty V-ing 구문이다.

304 I had much trouble (B) finding the house.

(A) on finding
(B) finding
(C) find
(D) found

번역 집을 찾는 데 어려움이 많았다.

해설 have trouble V-ing 구문이다.

305 Mariam didn't go to the movies last night because she was so busy (A) preparing for her trip to Guam.

(A) preparing
(B) that prepared
(C) by preparing
(D) to prepare

번역 Mariam은 Guam 여행을 준비하느라고 바빠서 어제 저녁에 극장에 가지 않았다.

해설 be busy V-ing 구문이다.

306 His name sounds familiar, but I don't remember (C) meeting him before.

(A) to meet
(B) of meeting
(C) meeting
(D) that I meet

번역 그의 이름이 낯설지 않지만 전에 그를 만난 기억이 없다.

해설 remember는 to 부정사와 동명사를 모두 취하지만 의미가 다르다. to 부정사는 미래에 해야할 일을 기억하는 것이며, 동명사는 과거에 했던 일을 기억하는 것이다. before로 보아 과거에 대한 기억이다.

307 Her old house needs (C) painting.

(A) to paint
(B) being painted
(C) painting
(D) paint

번역 그녀의 낡은 집은 페인트칠을 해야 한다.

해설 need는 to 부정사와 동명사를 모두 취할 수 있는데, 동명사는 수동의 의미를 갖는다. to 부정사는 수동을 나타내려면 to be painted처럼 수동형을 써야 한다.

308 Engineers and scientists have had no trouble [to find → finding] high-level, high-paying positions.

번역 기술자나 과학자는 높은 지위의 고임금의 직장을 찾는 데 어려움이 없었다.

have trouble V-ing 구문이다. high-paying은 사물 목적어를 수식하는 현재분사이다.

309 Technological innovation has affected our civilization by [change → changing] the nature of technology.

> 번역 | 기술 혁신은 기술의 본질을 바꿈으로써 문명에 영향을 끼쳤다.

> 해설 | 전치사 다음에는 (동)명사를 쓴다.

310 A telescope improves our view of the skies, partly by forming a large image that magnifies the detail in objects, but even more importantly by [gather → gathering] more light than the human eye can.

> 번역 | 망원경은 사물의 사소한 부분을 확대한 커다란 영상을 만들기도 하지만 더 중요한 것은 인간의 눈보다 더 많은 빛을 모음으로써 하늘의 시야를 개선시킨다.

> 해설 | 전치사 다음에는 (동)명사를 쓴다.

311 A commercial embargo may include the official seizure of merchandise or the detention of the persons involved in [transportation → transporting] cargo.

> 번역 | 상업적 교역금지에는 상품의 공식적인 압류나 화물 수송에 연루된 사람의 억류가 포함될 수 있다.

> 해설 | cargo를 목적어로 취하려면 동사가 필요하다. in이 전치사이므로 동명사를 쓰면 전치사의 목적어로 쓰면서 동시에 목적어를 취할 수 있다.

312 Friction can be reduced by [smooth → smoothing] and polishing the surface of contact, by lubricating surfaces with grease or oil, or by rolling instead of sliding.

> 번역 | 접촉 표면을 매끄럽게 하고 닦음으로써, 혹은 그리스나 기름을 표면에 바름으로써, 혹은 미끄는 대신 굴림으로써 마찰이 감소될 수 있다.

> 해설 | by는 전치사로 동사를 쓰려면 동명사로 바꿔 써야 한다.

313 Historians believe that some forms of [an advertising → an advertisement] must be as old as barter and trade.

> 번역 | 역사가들은 어떤 형태의 광고가 물물교환이나 거래만큼이나 오래되었을 것으로 믿는다.

> 해설 | 동명사는 흔히 명사 자리에 동사를 써야 하는 경우에 쓴다. 만약 적절한 명사형이 있으면 동명사를 쓰지 않고 명사를 쓴다.

314 He should stop (B) working and take a rest.

(A) work (B) working

(C) to work (D) to working

> 번역 | 그는 일을 그만하고 쉬어야 한다.

해설 stop 다음에 to부정사가 오면 부사적 용법의 부정사이며, 동명사 목적어를 취한다.

315 A previous engagement prevented him from (C) attending the party.

(A) attend
(B) to attend
(C) attending
(D) the attending

번역 선약 때문에 파티에 참석할 수 없었다.
해설 prevent+목적어+from+V-ing 구문이다.

316 (B) Protecting Florida's coral reefs is difficult because some of the corals are very fragile: even the touch of a diver's hand can kill them.

(A) The protection Florida's coral reefs
(B) Protecting Florida's coral reefs
(C) It is protecting Florida's coral reefs
(D) When protecting Florida's coral reefs

번역 어떤 산호는 매우 부서지기 쉬워서 Florida의 산호초를 보호하는 것이 힘들다. 잠수부의 손이 닿기만 해도 산호가 죽을 수 있다.
해설 is가 시제동사로 그 앞에 주어가 필요하다. (A)는 The protection of Florida's coral reefs처럼 of가 필요하다.

317 Although the many hours of summer sunshine in Canada's Klondike region produce good vegetable crops, the long winters rarely permit (C) the ripening of grain crops.

(A) grain crops ripen
(B) grain crops are ripe
(C) the ripening of grain crops
(D) to ripen grain crops

번역 캐나다의 Klondike의 긴 여름 햇빛이 훌륭한 채소를 생산하지만, 긴 겨울은 곡식이 익는 것을 거의 허락하지 않는다.
해설 permit+목적어+to V 구문으로 쓰이기도 하지만 이때는 목적어가 사람이다. 여기서는 permit가 3형식 동사로 쓰여 (동)명사 목적어를 취한다. 동명사에 the가 붙으면 다음에 of를 쓴다는 점에 유의해야 한다.

318 The president became very [depressing → depressed] because his company couldn't get the bid.

번역 자기 회사가 입찰을 받지 못하였기 때문에 사장은 아주 낙심하였다.
해설 주어(the president)가 사람이므로 과거분사 보어를 쓴다.

319 He thought that it would be [excited → exciting] to see this tree fall with a crash to the ground.

번역	그는 이 나무가 큰 소리를 내며 땅에 쓰러지는 것을 보는 것이 재미있을 것이라고 생각했다.
해설	it은 가주어로 to 부정사가 진주어이다. 주어가 사물일 때 현재분사 보어를 쓴다.

320 As far as I am [concerning → concerned], I have no objection to the bill laid before the House.

번역	나로서는 하원에 제출된 법안에 반대하지 않는다.
해설	concerning은 전치사이다. 주어가 사람이므로 과거분사를 쓴다. the bill which is laid에서 which is가 생략되었다.

321 The executive's [speaking → spoken] messages have always been much more powerful than his published reports.

번역	그 임원의 구두 메시지는 항상 출판된 보고서보다 훨씬 강력하였다.
해설	speak와 messages는 수동관계이므로 과거분사로 수식한다.

322 That was one of the most [interested → interesting] films I have ever seen.

번역	그것은 내가 본 가장 재미있는 영화 가운데 하나였다.
해설	사물인 films를 수식하려면 현재분사가 필요하다.

323 During the Middle Ages, [handwriting → handwritten] notices kept groups of nobles informed of important events.

번역	중세에는 손으로 쓴 쪽지가 귀족들이 중요한 사건을 알 수 있도록 하였다.
해설	notice와 handwrite의 관계는 수동이므로 과거분사를 쓴다.

324 It is believed that people [referring → referred] to as "Vikings" reached North America about the year A.D. 1,000.

번역	바이킹이라 불리는 사람들은 약 서기 1000년경에 북미에 도달한 것으로 믿어진다.
해설	people who were referred to as Vikings에서 who were가 생략된 구문이다. 관계대명사 who는 refer의 목적어로 수동태가 되어 주어자리로 이동하였다.

325 A type of ocean fish (C) living in warm and temperate seas, groupers are born as females and later change into males.

(A) is living   (B) while living

(C) living   (D) that is lived

번역	따뜻하고 온화한 바다에 사는 바닷고기의 일종인 그루퍼는 암컷으로 태어나서 나중에 수컷으로 변한다.
해설	fish which is living in ... 에서 which is가 생략된 구문이다.

326 The United States Constitution provides for a count of the population (C) called a census, every ten years.

    (A) that it is called   (B) when called

    (C) called   (D) as called

> **번역** 미국의 헌법은 매 10년마다 인구조사라 불리는 인구수를 제공한다.

> **해설** which is called a census에서 which is가 생략된 구문이다.

327 The nine-banded armadillo of the southern United States is one of few mammals (D) known to bear identical quadruplets.

    (A) that known   (B) that is known

    (C) which know it   (D) known

> **번역** 아홉 개의 띠를 가진 미국 남부의 아마딜로는 똑같은 네 쌍둥이를 낳는 것으로 알려진 소수의 포유류 가운데 하나이다.

> **해설** 선행사인 mammals가 복수이므로 which are known에서 which are가 생략된 구문이다.

328 [Looking → When I looked] back, the house seemed to have been engulfed by the snow, which fell faster and faster.

> **번역** 뒤돌아 보니 집이 더욱 빨리 내리는 눈에 삼켜져버린 것처럼 보였다.

> **해설** 주절의 주어가 the house이므로 look의 주어가 될 수 없다.

329 (B) He being absent, I took the place of him.

    (A) Being   (B) He being

    (C) Having been   (D) Been

> **번역** 그가 없어서 내가 그를 대신하였다.

> **해설** 의미상 분사구문의 주어는 I가 될 수 없으므로 생략될 수 없다. As he was absent를 분사구문으로 바꾸면 He being absent이며, being을 생략할 수 있다.

330 Although (A) a part of the immune system, skin is often viewed as simply a barrier between the body and the outside world.

    (A) a part of the immune system

    (B) there is a part of the immune system

    (C) it is the part of a immune system

    (D) the immune system is a part of it

> **번역** 피부는 면역체계의 일부이지만 흔히 신체와 외부의 세계 사이의 장벽으로만 바라본다.

해설 Although it is a part of the immune system을 분사구문으로 바꿀 때 접속사, 주어, be를 생략하는데, 의미상 필요할 경우 접속사를 남겨 둘 수 있다.

331 (D) When making ice cream, manufacturers usually use additives to improve keeping qualities and ease of serving.

(A) When make ice cream

(B) When making of ice cream

(C) When they making ice cream

(D) When making ice cream

번역 아이스크림을 만들 때 생산자들은 대개 보존성과 제공의 편의를 위해 첨가제를 사용한다.

해설 When they(=manufacturers) make ice cream을 분사구문으로 전환하면 When making ice cream이다. make는 타동사이므로 목적어를 취할 때 전치사가 필요없다.

332 It has not been determined how many years sea turtles can live in their natural environment, but they will reach a very old age (D) if left undisturbed by humans.

(A) if they left undisturbed by humans

(B) if undisturbed left by humans

(C) if left them undisturbed by humans

(D) if left undisturbed by humans

번역 바다거북이 자연 환경에서 몇 년이나 사는지 알 수 없지만, 인간의 방해를 받지 않는다면 매우 오래 살 것이다.

해설 if humans leave them undisturbed를 수동태로 전환하면 if they are left undisturbed by humans이다. 분사구문에서 if를 생략할 수 없으므로 if being left ...가 되며, being은 생략한다.

333 Throughout her career Georgia O'Keeffe paid meticulous attention to her craft: her brushes were always clean, (A) her colors fresh and bright.

(A) her colors fresh and bright

(B) her colors were fresh and bright

(C) her fresh and bright colors

(D) because her colors fresh and bright

번역 일생동안 Georgia O'Keeffe는 그녀의 공예에 세심한 주의를 기울였다. 그녀의 화풍은 산뜻하였으며, 색상은 신선하고 밝았다.

시제동사를 쓰려면 접속사가 필요하며, 반대로 접속사가 있으면 접속사가 필요하다. her colors were fresh and bright에서 were의 분사형 being 을 생략하였다.

334 When thinking about living abroad, (B) we are concerned about different customs in that country.

(A) it is different customs that we are concerned about

(B) we are concerned about different customs

(C) different customs are being concerned about

(D) different customs concern ourselves

번역 해외에 거주하는 것을 생각할 때 우리는 그 나라의 다른 문화에 대한 걱정을 한다.

해설 주절의 주어가 분사구문의 주어와 동일해야 하므로 주절의 주어가 think 의 주어가 될 수 있는 것을 고른다.

335 [Facing → Faced] with dismissal, he decided to submit his resignation.

번역 면직에 직면하자 그는 사표를 내기로 결심하였다.

해설 As he was faced with dismissal을 분사구문으로 바꾸면 Being faced with dismissal이다.

336 (A) Regarded as the world's foremost linguistic theorist, Noam Chomsky continues to create new theories about language and language learning.

(A) Regarded as   (B) As he regards as

(C) Regarding him as   (D) If regarded as

번역 세계에서 가장 훌륭한 언어학자로 간주되는 Noam Chomsky는 언어와 언어학습에 관한 새로운 이론을 계속하여 만들어 낸다.

해설 주절 주어 Noam Chomsky가 의미상 regard의 목적어로 쓰여야 하므로 과거분사를 쓴다.

337 [Struck → Having struck] an iceberg, the British liner Titanic sank on its first voyage, resulting in the deaths of some 1,500 passengers.

번역 빙산에 부딪힌 후 영국의 여객선 타이타닉호는 첫 번째 항해에서 침몰하여 약 1,500명의 승객을 죽게 만들었다.

해설 배가 가리 앉기 전에 빙산과 부딪혔기 때문에 완료분사를 써야 한다.

338 (A) It having snowed steadily for two weeks, the roads were impassable.

(A) It having snowed   (B) Having snowed

(C) Snowing   (D) Being snowed

| 번역 | 2주동안 계속 눈이 내려서 길이 불통이었다. |

| 해설 | 눈이 이미 내렸으므로 As it had snowed이다. 이를 분사구문으로 바꿀 때 접속사를 생략하고 주절 주어와 다른 it은 생략하지 않는다. |

339 (C) Having received over eighty percent of the vote, Jane M. Byrne became the first woman to be elected mayor of Chicago.

(A) Having been received over eighty percent

(B) After had received over eighty percent

(C) Having received over eighty percent

(D) Have received over eighty percent

| 번역 | 80퍼센트 이상의 득표를 하여 Jane M. Byrne은 여성으로는 처음 시카고의 시장으로 선출되었다. |

| 해설 | 시제동사가 있으면 주어가 필요하므로 (B)와 (D)는 정답에서 제외된다. As she had received over eighty percent를 분사구문으로 바꾸면 Having received …가 된다. |

340 As has been the case with many artistic geniuses, Edgar Allan Poe was not [adequate → adequately] appreciated in his own time: many of his contemporaries criticized him as morbid and excessive.

| 번역 | 많은 천재 예술가의 경우처럼 Edgar Allan Poe는 당시에 제대로 평가받지 못했다. 많은 동시대인들은 그가 병적이며 극단적이라고 비난하였다. |

| 해설 | 분사는 형용사 역할을 하므로 부사로 수식한다. |

341 It is always silly of you to get on the bus with your rain coat (B) on.

(A) in   (B) on

(C) over   (D) off

| 번역 | 네가 비옷을 입고서 버스를 타는 것은 항상 어리석은 것이다. |

| 해설 | with+목적어+현재분사/과거분사/부사 형태의 분사구문이다. |

342 (B) Not knowing what to do, he applied to me for advice.

(A) Knowing not   (B) Not knowing

(C) Not know   (D) Not to know

| 번역 | 어떻게 해야 할지 몰라서 그는 내게 충고를 구했다. |

| 해설 | 분사구문의 부정은 not+분사이다. |

343 Monkeys and apes are extraordinarily communicative, (D) using body language and facial gestures to tell one another how they feel.

(A) they use body language and facial gestures

(B) use body language and facial gestures

(C) used body language and facial gestures

(D) using body language and facial gestures

> 번역 원숭이와 유인원은 매우 대화를 잘하여 몸짓언어와 얼굴 표정으로 감정을 전달할 수 있다.

> 해설 두 문장을 연결하려면 접속사가 필요하다. 분사구문은 접속사와 주어가 생략된 구문이다.

344 Many people living on the North American frontier in the mid-1800's (D) carried a weapon called the bowie knife.

(A) were carried a weapon called

(B) carried a weapon was called

(C) were carried a weapon which called

(D) carried a weapon called

> 번역 1880년대 중반에 북미 국경선에 거주하던 많은 사람들은 보우이 칼이라 불리는 무기를 지니고 다녔다.

> 해설 Many people carried a weapon에서 living … in the mid-1800's가 many people을 수식하며, 또한 (which is) called the bowie knife가 a weapon을 수식한다.

345 One of the great engineering feats of the world, the 44-mile Panama Canal bisects the continents of North and South America, (A) making it possible for ships to sail between the Atlantic and Pacific Oceans.

(A) making it possible for ships

(B) made it possible for ships

(C) it made it possible for ships

(D) making possibility for ships

> 번역 세계에서 가장 훌륭한 토목공사 업적 중의 하나인 44마일의 파나마 운하는 북미와 남미를 양분하며, 선박이 대서양과 태평양 사이를 항해할 수 있도록 하였다.

> 해설 bisects가 주절의 동사이다. 뒷 부분에는 접속사가 없으므로 시제동사가 나타날 수 없으며, make는 5형식동사로 make it possible to V의 형태로 쓰인다.

346 Many writers in the eighteenth century were inspired by the educational and scientific ideas of the Enlightenment, (A) seeing the potential of literature to reach a wide readership.

(A) seeing the potential

(B) saw the potential

(C) which was seen the potential

(D) they saw the potential

번역 18세기의 많은 작가들은 계몽시대의 교육사상과 과학사상의 자극을 받았으며, 광범위한 독자를 가질 문학의 잠재력을 보게 되었다.

해설 시제 동사를 쓰려면 접속사가 필요하다. (C)의 관계대명사가 접속사 역할을 하지만 목적어가 있으므로 과거분사를 쓸 수 없다.

347 Economics as a science is a small subsystem, (A) dealing with the economic behavior of people.

(A) dealing with

(B) in dealt with

(C) which deal with

(D) with which are dealt

번역 학문으로서의 경제학은 조그마한 하위체계로, 사람들의 경제적 행태를 다룬다.

해설 a small subsystem이 단수이므로 which deals with가 되어야 하며, 분사구문으로 바꾸면 dealing with가 된다.

348 While staying in Florence, Italy, in 1894, (A) philanthropist Winifred Holt discovered that she had a talent for sculpture and began taking lessons.

(A) philanthropist Winifred Holt discovered

(B) that the philanthropist Winifred Holt discovered

(C) discovered by philanthropist Winifred Holt

(D) there philanthropist Winifred Holt discovered

번역 박애주의자인 Winifred Holt는 1894년 이탈리아 플로렌스에 머물면서 조각에 대한 재능을 발견하고서 레슨을 받기 시작하였다.

해설 While ... in 1894는 분사구문이므로 뒷 부분에 주어＋시제동사가 와야 한다.

349 (A) Using northern quahog clam shells, Native Americans made beads that they strung together and used as money.

(A) Using northern quahog clam shells

(B) Northern quahog clam shells using

(C) Northern quahog clam shells are used

(D) When using northern quahog clam shells

번역 북부의 대합 껍질을 이용하여 미국 원주민들은 서로 엮어 목걸이로 만들었으며, 화폐로 사용하였다.

해설 시제동사가 있으면 접속사가 필요하다. 분사구문은 접속사와 주어가 생략되고 동사를 분사로 바꾼 구문이다.

350 Chain reactions (C) involving thermal or fast neutrons can be controlled in a reactor.

(A) involve　　　　　　　(B) involved

(C) involving　　　　　　(D) are involved

번역 열중성자나 고속중성자와 관련된 연쇄반응이 원자로에서 통제될 수 있다.

해설 뒤에 목적어가 있으므로 현재분사가 필요하다. involve는 상태동사이므로 which involve로 바꿔 쓸 수 있다.

351 Your great [intelligent → intelligence] and energy will help you solve any problem you encounter if you use these strengths wisely.

번역 당신의 지능과 정력은 현명하게 사용하면 닥치는 어떤 문제도 해결하는 데 도움을 줄 것이다.

해설 주어 자리에는 명사가 와야 한다.

352 The energy needed for animal [grow → growth] is derived primarily from carbohydrates and fats.

번역 동물의 성장에 필요한 에너지는 주로 탄수화물과 지방으로부터 얻는다.

해설 전치사 for 다음에는 명사가 와야 한다. animal은 growth를 수식한다.

353 The [directing → direction] of the wind is indicated by a weather vane.

번역 바람의 방향은 풍향계로 나타내어진다.

해설 the가 있을 때는 동명사를 쓰지 않고 명사를 쓴다. 동사를 명사 자리에 쓰고자 할 때 동명사를 쓴다.

354 Don't forget to note that these pamphlets have minor [revising → revision] from the original pamphlets.

번역 이 팜플렛들은 원본에는 사소한 수정이 있다는 것을 잊지 말고 꼭 유의하세요.

해설 동명사는 근본적으로 동사가 명사적으로 쓰인 것으로 형용사의 수식을 받지 않는다.

355 In the early twentieth century, there was considerable [interesting → interest] among sociologists in the fact that in the United States the family was losing its traditional roles.

번역 20세기에 미국에서 가족이 전통적 역할을 상실하고 있는 사실이 사회학자들 사이에 상당한 흥미를 끌었다.

해설 형용사 다음에는 명사가 와야 한다.

356 In these circumstances, you may only have a partial discount for the (D) remainder of the month or no discount at all.

(A) remain
(B) remaining
(C) remained
(D) remainder

> **번역** 이러한 상황에서 당신은 이달 말까지 할인을 일부만 받거나 전혀 받을 수 없을 겁니다.

> **해설** 전치사 for의 목적어 자리이므로 명사가 와야 한다.

357 He was kind enough to carry the [baggages → baggage] all the way to the train station.

> **번역** 그는 친절하게도 기차역까지 수화물을 운반해 주었다.

> **해설** bag이 가산명사인 반면 baggage는 비가산명사이다.

358 Peas require rich soil, constant [moistures → moisture], and a cool growing season to develop well.

> **번역** 완구콩은 잘 자라기 위해 비옥한 토양, 지속적인 습도, 선선한 성장 계절이 필요하다.

> **해설** moisture는 비가산명사이므로 복수형을 가질 수 없다.

359 Encyclopedias may be used to answer questions, to solve problems, or to obtain [informations → information] on a particular topic.

> **번역** 백과사전은 질문에 답하거나, 문제를 풀거나, 특정한 주제에 대한 정보를 얻는 데 쓰일 수 있다.

> **해설** information은 furniture와 함께 대표적인 비가산명사이다.

360 Langston Hughes always seemed to know exactly who he was, and [those knowledges → that knowledge] helped make him one of the most respected writers in the United States.

> **번역** Langston Hughes는 항상 자신에 대해 알고 있었으며, 그러한 지식은 미국에서 가장 존경 받는 작가가 되는 데 도움이 되었다.

> **해설** knowledge는 비가산명사이다. those는 가산명사와 함께 쓰일 수 있다.

361 Yesterday we saw [the Millet → a Millet] at the exhibition, but it was not a genuine painting.

> **번역** 어제 전시회에서 Millet의 작품을 보았는데, 그것은 원본그림이 아니었다.

> **해설** 고유명사인 Millet를 보통명사화하여 '밀레의 작품 하나'의 뜻을 갖는다.

362 This school has produced many [Einstein → Einsteins] since it was founded.

> **번역** 이 학교는 설립 이래 많은 과학자를 배출했다.

해설 고유명사인 Einstein을 보통 명사화하여 '천재'라는 뜻을 갖는다.

363 Every year Colorado is visited by millions of tourists who come for a variety of [reason → reasons].

번역 매년 다양한 이유로 수백만의 여행객이 Colorado를 방문한다.

해설 reason은 가산명사로 a variety of 때문에 복수형을 쓴다.

364 The importance of mythology within a culture is reflected in the status of [storyteller → storytellers/the storyteller(s)].

번역 어떤 문화에서의 신화의 중요성은 작가의 지위에 반영되어 있다.

해설 storyteller는 가산명사이다.

365 Numerous professional associations have educational [program → programs] for their members.

번역 많은 전문 단체는 회원을 위한 교육 프로그램을 가지고 있다.

해설 program은 가산명사이다.

366 Sprinkler [system → systems] have proven to be the most effective means of fighting hotel fires.

번역 스프링클러는 호텔 화재를 진압하는 데 가장 효과적인 수단으로 증명되었다.

해설 have가 복수동사이므로 주어가 복수형이어야 한다. system은 가산명사이므로 복수형을 쓸 수 있다.

367 Most mammals maintain a relatively constant body [temperatures → temperature], regardless of what the air temperature might be.

번역 대부분의 포유동물은 대기온도와 무관하게 비교적 지속적인 체온을 유지한다.

해설 temperature는 가산명사인데 앞에 부정관사 a가 있으므로 단수형을 써야 한다.

368 Fish are the most ancient form of vertebrate life, and from them evolved all other [vertebrate → vertebrates].

번역 물고기는 가장 오래된 형태의 척추생물이며, 물고기로부터 다른 모든 척추동물이 진화했다.

해설 fish는 단복 동형 명사이다. 단, 종류를 나타낼 때는 복수형이 fishes이다. vertebrate는 가산명사이다. from them evolved all other vertebrates의 원래 어순은 all other vertebrates evolved from them이다.

369 The importance of mythology within a culture is reflected in the status of [storyteller → storytellers/the storyteller(s)].

| 번역 | 어떤 문화에서의 신화의 중요성은 작가의 지위에 반영되어 있다.

| 번역 | 어떤 문화에서의 신화의 중요성은 작가의 지위에 반영되어 있다.
| 해설 | storyteller는 가산명사이다.

370 Numerous professional associations have educational [program → programs] for their members.

| 번역 | 많은 전문 단체는 회원을 위한 교육 프로그램을 가지고 있다.
| 해설 | program은 가산명사이다.

371 Baseball and other popular [sport → sports] have provided a number of new words for the English language.

| 번역 | 야구와 다른 대중 스포츠는 영어에 많은 새로운 단어를 제공하였다.
| 해설 | sport는 주로 복수형을 쓴다.

372 The measures being taken to renovate the company are of great [significant → significance] to the shareholders.

| 번역 | 회사를 개혁하기 위해 취해지고 있는 조치가 주주에게 매우 중요하다.
| 해설 | of great significance는 very significant의 뜻이다.

373 This information is (D) of no use to us.

| (A) much used | (B) able to use |
| (C) of not use | (D) of no use |

| 번역 | 이 정보는 우리에게 별로 소용이 없다.
| 해설 | of no use는 useless의 뜻이다.

374 Capital and labor are of equal (D) importance in the modern corporation.

| (A) import | (B) importantly |
| (C) important | (D) importance |

| 번역 | 자본과 노동은 현대의 기업에서 동일한 중요성을 가진다.
| 해설 | of equal importance는 equally important의 뜻이다.

375 Because the equipment is delicate, it must be handled with (C) care.

| (A) caring | (B) careful |
| (C) care | (D) carefully |

| 번역 | 장비가 정교하기 때문에, 조심히 다루어야 한다.
| 해설 | 전치사+명사는 부사의 역할을 한다.

376 Among Thomas Jefferson's many [accomplishment → accomplishments] was his work to establish the University of Virginia.

> 번역   Thomas Jefferson의 많은 업적 가운데 Virginia 대학교를 설립한 것이 있다.

> 해설   many는 복수 가산명사와 함께 쓰인다. 동사 was 때문에 혼동되는데 주어는 his work이다.

377 [Much → Many] nutritionists argue that people's intake of fat should be reduced.

> 번역   많은 영양학자들은 인간의 지방섭취를 줄여야 한다고 주장한다.

> 해설   nutritionists가 복수 가산명사이므로 much 대신 many를 쓴다. much는 비가산명사와 함께 쓰인다.

378 I got a letter from that company yesterday, but there wasn't [many → much] news in it.

> 번역   나는 어제 그 회사로부터 편지를 받았으나 새로운 소식은 별로 없었다.

> 해설   news는 형용사에 -s가 붙은 형태로 형태는 복수처럼 보이지만 단수이며, 비가산명사이다. 비가산명사는 much와 함께 쓰인다.

379 [Much → Many] unknown plants and animals are disappearing as the tropical forests are destroyed.

> 번역   알려지지 않은 많은 동식물이 열대 숲이 파괴됨에 따라 사라지고 있다.

> 해설   plants와 animals가 가산명사이므로 much 대신 many를 쓴다.

380 It was not so much the [much → many] blows he received as a lack of spirit that led to his losing the fight.

> 번역   그가 싸움에서 진 것은 맞은 주먹 때문이라기보다는 정신력의 부족 때문이다.

> 해설   blows가 복수 가산명사이므로 much 대신 many를 쓴다.

381 Data received from two spacecraft indicate that there is [many evidence → much evidence] that huge thunderstorms are occurring around the equator of the planet Saturn.

> 번역   우주선에서 보낸 정보에 따르면 토성의 적도 부근에 거대한 뇌우가 발생한다는 많은 증거가 있다.

> 해설   data와 spacecraft는 단복 동형이다. evidence는 가산명사로도 비가산명사로도 쓰일 수 있지만 is로 보아 비가산명사로 쓰인 것이다.

382 [Many of → Many] companies have to pay millions of dollars to establish their trademarks as symbols of reliability and value.

> 번역   많은 회사들이 자기 상표를 신뢰와 가치의 상징으로 자리 잡도록 수백만 달러를 지출해야 한다.

해설 many는 수량사로 다음에 of가 오면 한정명사가 와야 한다. 수량사 다음에
명사가 올 수 있다.

383 As a rule, the police don't have (B) much power in a situation like this.

    (A) many   (B) much

    (C) some   (D) big

번역 일반적으로 경찰은 이러한 상황에서 별로 힘이 없다.

해설 power는 비가산명사이다.

384 You should try to have (B) many chances to speak English with native
speakers.

    (A) many times   (B) many chances

    (C) much chances   (D) any chance

번역 원어민과 영어로 말할 수 있는 기회를 많이 가지려고 노력해야 한다.

해설 times는 횟수를 뜻하며, chance는 기회를 뜻한다. 가산명사는 many와
함께 쓰인다.

385 She likes to buy (C) much furniture.

    (A) few   (B) many

    (C) much   (D) several

번역 그녀는 가구를 많이 사기를 좋아한다.

해설 furniture는 비가산명사이다.

386 Flowers make a lot of (A) differences to a room.

    (A) differences   (B) difference

    (C) different   (D) the difference

번역 방에 꽃을 두면 큰 차이가 난다.

해설 difference는 가산명사이다.

387 When a human being walks, he or she exerts a certain [number → amount]
of force on the gland.

번역 사람이 걸을 때 분비기관에서 어느 정도의 힘을 사용한다.

해설 number는 가산명사에 쓰이며, 비가산명사는 amount를 쓴다.

388 (B) A piece of mail travels faster when the zip code is indicated on the
envelope.

(A) A   (B) A piece of

(C) A pack of   (D) A pair of

> 번역   봉투에 우편번호가 적혀 있으면 우편물이 빨리 배달된다.

> 해설   letter는 가산명사이지만, mail은 비가산명사이다. 특정한 표현이 없을 경우에는 a piece of를 쓴다.

389 The writer smokes (D) two packs of cigarettes a day at work.

(A) 20 sticks   (B) 40 pieces

(C) two boxes   (D) two packs

> 번역   그 작가는 매일 작업 중에 두 갑의 담배를 피운다.

> 해설   cigarettes는 세고자 할 때 단위로 pack을 쓴다.

390 I'd like a steak, a salad, and (D) an ear of corn with butter.

(A) a few corns   (B) ears of corns

(C) an ear of corns   (D) an ear of corn

> 번역   스테이크, 샐러드 그리고 버터 바른 옥수수 하나를 먹겠습니다.

> 해설   corn은 단위로 ear를 쓴다.

391 Drying food by means of solar energy is [a → an] ancient process applied wherever food and climatic conditions make it possible.

> 번역   태양에너지에 의한 식량의 건조는 식량과 기후조건이 가능한 곳에서는 어디서나 사용된 오래된 가공법이다.

> 해설   ancient가 모음으로 시작되므로 a 대신 an을 쓴다.

392 Last year [a → an] honor which is rarely conferred was awarded to this scientist, one of the greatest men of our age.

> 번역   작년에는 좀처럼 주어지지 않는 훈장이 우리시대의 가장 위대한 사람 중의 하나인 이 과학자에게 수여되었다.

> 해설   honor의 h가 묵음이므로 부정관사 an을 쓴다.

393 Fiber is [a → an] important element in nutrition, and it aids in protecting the digestive tract as well.

> 번역   섬유소는 영양에서 매우 중요한 요소이며, 소화기를 보호하는 데도 도움을 준다.

> 해설   important가 모음으로 시작되므로 an을 쓴다.

394 Francis Hopkinson, a New Jersey signer of the Declaration of Independence, was an American statesman, artist, writer, lawyer, and [a judge → judge].

| 번역 | New Jersey주를 대표하여 독립선언문에 서명한 Francis Hopkinson은 미국의 정치가, 예술가, 작가, 변호사, 판사였다. |
| 해설 | and로 연결될 때 한 사람인 경우 맨 앞에 관사 하나만 쓴다. |

395 Between the ages of nine and fifteen, almost all young people undergo [rapid → a rapid] series of physiological changes.

| 번역 | 15세부터 19세까지 거의 모든 젊은이들은 빠른 생리적 변화를 겪는다. |
| 해설 | series는 단복 동형 명사이며, 주로 a series of처럼 쓴다. |

396 There is [rumor → a rumor] that the workers are discussing establishing a labor union.

| 번역 | 노동자들이 노동조합을 설립하는 것을 논의하고 있다는 소문이 있다. |
| 해설 | rumor가 비가산명사이지만 여기서는 사건(event)을 나타내므로 가산명사로 쓰였다. |

397 The political party took [the → an] announcement a week ahead of schedule.

| 번역 | 그 정당은 예정보다 일주일 전에 발표하였다. |
| 해설 | anouncement가 여기서 사건을 나타내므로 가산명사로 쓰였으며, 불특정 발표이므로 부정관사를 쓴다. |

398 His decision to retire came as [surprise → a surprise] to everyone in the department.

| 번역 | 퇴임하려는 그의 결정은 학과의 모든 사람을 놀라게 했다. |
| 해설 | 여기서 surprise가 사건을 나타내므로 가산명사로 쓰였다. |

399 The snowy egret is about the size [of large crow → of a large crow].

| 번역 | 새하얀 왜가리는 크기가 커다란 까마귀만 하다. |
| 해설 | crow는 가산명사이다. |

400 [Ruler → A ruler] is mainly used to measure and to draw straight lines on flat surfaces.

| 번역 | 자는 주로 평면에 직선을 긋거나 잴 때 사용된다. |
| 해설 | ruler는 가산명사이므로 단수일 때 부정관사를 쓰거나 the를 쓴다. |

401 [Grass-eating → A grass-eating], river-dwelling mammal, the hippopotamus is related to the pig.

| 번역 | 풀을 먹으며 강에 사는 포유류인 하마는 돼지와 친족이다. |
| 해설 | mammal이 가산명사이므로 부정관사가 필요하다. 총칭표현일 경우 동물은 the+단수명사를 쓸 수 있다. |

402 The victim of the traffic accident sued the bus company for [damage → the damage].

> 번역 교통사고의 희생자가 버스회사에 대해 손해 배상을 요구하는 소송을 하였다.

> 해설 the traffic accident, the bus company로 보아 특정한 사건을 염두에 둔 것이므로 damage도 특정한 것으로 보아야 한다.

403 The sugar the cook left [on shelf → on the shelf] was eaten by a mouse as large as a rat.

> 번역 요리사가 선반위에 둔 설탕은 쥐만큼 큰 생쥐가 먹었다.

> 해설 shelf는 가산명사인데 the sugar, the cook으로 보아 특정 상황을 염두에 둔 것이다.

404 Part of the sunlight that strikes the Earth is reflected into the sky, and [a rest → the rest] is absorbed by the ground.

> 번역 지구에 쏟아지는 햇빛의 일부가 하늘로 반사되고, 나머지는 땅에 흡수된다.

> 해설 rest가 나머지를 가리킬 때는 명확한 것을 나타내므로 the를 쓴다. part는 일반적으로 부정관사를 쓰지 않는다.

405 American manufacturers depend on ocean shipping for most [of trade → of the trade] with other countries.

> 번역 미국의 생산자들은 다른 나라와의 무역에 있어서 대부분 해상 운송에 의존한다.

> 해설 수량사+of+명사의 구조에서 명사는 한정적이므로 the를 쓴다.

406 Lack of animal protein in the human diet is a serious cause of [the malnutrition → malnutrition].

> 번역 식사에서 동물성 단백질의 부족은 영양 결핍의 중요한 원인이다.

> 해설 malnutrition은 비가산명사이며, 여기서는 특정한 것을 가리키지 않으므로 무관사이어야 한다.

407 [The clay → Clay] is a material that has the fundamental characteristic of becoming plastic when moist.

> 번역 점토는 젖었을 때 유연하게 되는 근본적 특성을 가지고 있다.

> 해설 clay는 비가산명사이므로 총칭적 표현으로 쓰더라도 무관사이며 단수이다.

408 When used for studies of learning and memory, the octopus is a more interesting subject than [squid → the squid].

> 번역 학습과 기억에 대한 연구에 사용될 때 문어가 오징어보다 재미있는 대상이다.

> 해설 the octopus에 따라 총칭적 표현으로 the squid를 쓴다.

409 (D) The elephant relies more on its sense of smell than on any other sense.

    (A) The elephants   (B) Elephants

    (C) Elephant   (D) The elephant

> 번역   코끼리는 다른 감각보다는 후각에 의존한다.

> 해설   elephant는 동물이므로 총칭적 표현으로 an elephant, the elephant, elephants를 쓸 수 있다. relies가 단수동사이므로 주어도 단수명사라야 한다.

410 Agriculture is defined as [science → the science] and art of cultivating the soil, growing crops, and raising livestock.

> 번역   농업은 토지를 경작하고, 농작물을 재배하고, 가축을 기르는 과학이자 기술이라고 정의된다.

> 해설   of의 수식을 받으므로 정관사 the가 필요하다.

411 [First → The first] European settlers of Australia left the city of Portsmouth in May 1787.

> 번역   호주의 초기 유럽 정착민은 1787년 5월 Portsmouth시를 떠났다.

> 해설   of Australia의 수식을 받으므로 the를 쓴다.

412 Computers that are not accessed remotely should be turned off [at end of → at the end of] the business day and on weekends.

> 번역   원격으로 접속되지 않는 컴퓨터는 영업시간 후에나 주말에는 꺼야 한다.

> 해설   end가 of 이하의 수식을 받으므로 the를 써야 한다.

413 I want (C) the document that is on the desk.

    (A) document   (B) a document

    (C) the document   (D) a piece of document

> 번역   나는 책상 위에 있는 문서를 원한다.

> 해설   관계절의 수식을 받는 선행사는 the를 쓴다.

414 One of [most → the most] impressive collections of nineteenth-century European paintings in the United States can be found in the Philadelphia Museum of Art.

> 번역   미국에서 가장 인상적인 19세기 유럽 회화 소장품 중의 하나를 Philadel-phia Museum of Art에서 볼 수 있다.

> 해설   최상급에는 the를 쓴다.

415 Of all the Native American in the United States, the Navajos form [largest → the largest] group.

번역	미국 원주민 가운데 나바호족이 가장 큰 집단이다.
해설	최상급 largest 앞에 the가 필요하다.

416 A number of doctors believe that taking an aspirin [the day → a day] can reduce a person's chances of having a heart attack.

번역	많은 의사들은 하루에 한 알의 아스피린을 복용하면 심장마비에 걸릴 가능성이 줄어든다고 믿는다.
해설	a day는 '하루에'의 뜻이다. '일일 단위로'는 by the day라 한다.

417 As a rule, the factory workers get paid (B) by the hour.

(A) by an hour   (B) by the hour

(C) by a hour   (D) by hours

번역	일반적으로 공장 노동자들은 시급을 받는다.
해설	'시간 단위로'는 by the hour라 한다.

418 In an exchange of gunfire, one police officer was wounded in (B) the foot and another was hit in the shoulder.

(A) a foot   (B) the foot

(C) his foot   (D) his feet

번역	교전에서 한 명의 경찰이 발에 부상을 입었고, 다른 한 명은 어깨를 맞았다.
해설	동사+사람+전치사+the+신체부위 구문이다.

419 After [the church → church] the men stood together in the churchyard saying he must be crazy.

번역	예배 후에 사람들은 그가 틀림없이 미쳤다고 말하며 교회 뜰에 서 있었다.
해설	church가 '예배'의 뜻일 때 관사를 쓰지 않는다.

420 [The baseball → Baseball] has been approved as an extracurricular activity.

번역	야구는 과외 활동으로 인정되어 왔다.
해설	악기명에는 the를 쓰며(예, the guitar, the piano), 구기명에서는 the를 쓰지 않는다.

421 The doctor told me that the major's wife had died (C) of pneumonia.

(A) of the pneumonia   (B) of a pneumonia

(C) of pneumonia   (D) with pneumonia

번역	의사는 나에게 소령의 아내가 폐렴으로 죽었다고 말했다.

해설 | 질병명은 보통 관사를 쓰지 않는다. 예외가 많으므로 암기해야 한다(the flu, a cold, measles)

422 Dr. Brown was (B) Minister of Foreign Affairs from 1991 till 1996.

(A) a Minister
(B) Minister
(C) the Minister
(D) Ministerial

번역 | Brown 박사는 1991년부터 1996년까지 외무부 장관이었다.

해설 | 관직을 나타낼 때 보어자리에 오면 무관사이다.

423 Moonquakes originating at [deep → depth] of some 800 kilometers indicate the Moon has considerable rigidity and is not molten at such levels.

번역 | 약 800km의 깊이에서 시작되는 월진은 달이 상당히 단단하며, 그 깊이에서 용해되지 않았음을 보여준다.

해설 | 전치사 at 다음에 명사가 와야 한다.

424 The wide range of elevations in the southern Appalachian Mountains allows for the great [diverse → diversity] of plant life found there.

번역 | 아팔레치아 산맥의 다양한 고도 때문에 거기에서 매우 다양한 식물이 살 수 있다.

해설 | 관사+형용사 다음에는 명사가 와야 한다.

425 The 1897 [discover → discovery] of gold in the Klondike hastened the commercial development of Washington State, as did the increasing trade with Pacific Islands.

번역 | 1897년 Klondike에서의 금의 발견은 태평양 제도와의 무역 증가와 마찬가지로 워싱턴주의 상업적 발달을 촉진하였다.

해설 | 관사와 전치사 사이에는 명사가 와야 한다.

426 Even though they do not have [webbed foot → webbed feet], gallinules are excellent swimmers.

번역 | 쇠물닭은 비록 물갈퀴가 달린 발을 가지고 있지 않지만 수영을 잘한다.

해설 | foot는 가산명사이다. 앞에 부정관사 a가 없으므로 복수를 쓴다.

427 Fossils of [plant → plants] that have been extinct for fifty million years have been found in large deposits of amber near the Baltic Sea.

번역 | 5천만년 전에 사라진 식물의 화석이 발트해 가까이에 있는 호박 매장층에서 발견되었다.

해설 | plant는 가산명사이다. 관계절의 동사 have가 복수동사이므로 선행사인 plant도 복수형을 써야 한다.

428 Approximately one-third of all persons involved in adult education programs in 1970 were enrolled in occupational education [course → courses].

> 번역   1970년대에 성인교육 프로그램에 참여한 사람의 약 3분의 1이 취업 교육 프로그램에 등록하였다.

> 해설   course는 가산명사인데 앞에 부정관사가 없으므로 복수형을 쓴다.

429 You could prove my identity by seeing my [driver → driver's] license or my passport.

> 번역   당신은 운전면허증이나 여권을 봄으로써 내 신분을 증명할 수 있습니다.

> 해설   운전면허증은 driver's license라고 한다. 복합명사는 명사+명사를 쓰지만 복합명사가 아닌 경우에는 명사's 명사를 쓴다.

430 The city of Boston was settled in 1630 on a hilly, wooded peninsula where the Charles River flows into a natural [harbors → harbor].

> 번역   Boston시는 Charles강이 천연 항구로 흐르는, 산이 많고 숲이 우거진 반도에 1630년에 정착되었다.

> 해설   부정관사는 단수명사와 함께 쓰인다.

431 Philosophers are concerned with [the truth → the true], the good, and the beautiful.

> 번역   철학자들은 진·선·미에 관심을 갖는다.

> 해설   'the+형용사'는 추상적 개념을 나타내거나, 사람을 나타낸다.

432 Hickories are medium to large trees common [in eastern → in the eastern] and the central areas of North America.

> 번역   히코리는 북미의 동부와 중부에 흔한 크기가 중간 이상인 나무이다.

> 해설   area를 수식하므로 the central처럼 the가 필요하다.

433 The [cultures early → early cultures] of the genus Homo were generally distinguished by regular use of stone tools and by a hunting and gathering economy.

> 번역   사람속의 초기 문화는 일반적으로 규칙적인 석기의 사용과 사냥 및 수렵 경제로 구별된다.

> 해설   형용사는 일반적으로 수식되는 명사 앞에 온다.

434 Nowadays, [every virtually → virtually every] kind of organization through-out the world conducts business with computers.

> 번역   오늘날 세계적으로 거의 대부분의 조직은 컴퓨터로 사업을 수행한다.

> 해설   한정사는 부사로 수식한다. kind가 명사이므로 부사가 수식할 수 없으며 every kind에서 부사가 한정사 every를 꾸미게 된다.

435 Maryland's economy is based largely on service industries, which account for more than [four-fifth → four-fifths] of Maryland's gross state product.

> 번역 │ Maryland의 경제는 주로 서비스업에 기초하고 있는데, 서비스업은 Maryland주의 총생산량의 5분의 4를 차지한다.

> 해설 │ 분수는 분자가 복수이면 분모도 복수형이 된다.

436 We made a [three weeks → three-week] business trip through America and Europe last fall.

> 번역 │ 우리는 지난 가을에 미국과 유럽을 3주간 사업차 여행하였다.

> 해설 │ 명사가 명사를 수식하는 경우 수식하는 명사는 단수형을 쓴다.

437 There are several [way → ways] to become an office worker without having to take the examination.

> 번역 │ 시험을 보지 않고 사무직원이 되는 몇 가지 방법이 있다.

> 해설 │ several은 복수명사와 함께 쓰인다.

438 After Holmes's departure for the concert, I lay down upon the sofa and endeavored to get (B) a couple of hours' sleep.

(A) a couple of hours   (B) a couple of hours'

(C) a couple of hour   (D) a couple of hour's

> 번역 │ Holmes가 음악회로 떠났을 때, 나는 소파에 누워 두 시간동안 잠을 자려 노력했다.

> 해설 │ a couple of는 two의 뜻으로 다음에 복수가 와야 한다. 복수의 소유격은 hours'처럼 쓴다.

439 (A) The study of mathematics began in ancient Greece thousands of years ago.

(A) The study of mathematics   (B) Study of the mathematics

(C) A study of mathematics   (D) A study of the mathematics

> 번역 │ 수학이라는 학문은 수천년 전에 고대그리스에서 시작되었다.

> 해설 │ the study of mathematics에서 of는 동격이다.

440 (A) Much of our office furniture is uncomfortable.

(A) Much   (B) Many

(C) Several   (D) One

> 번역 │ 우리 사무실의 많은 가구가 불편하다.

수량사가 부정대명사로 쓰일 수 있는데, 비가산명사에는 much를 쓰며, 가산명사에는 many를 쓴다.

441 It is [a such lovely day → such a lovely day] that I'd like to go on a picnic.

번역 날씨가 참 좋아서 소풍을 가고 싶다.

해설 such는 전치한정사로 한정사인 부정관사 앞에 온다.

442 Our manager is a man of character, and yet he is well known as (A) quite a strict manager.

(A) quite a
(B) a quite
(C) the quite
(D) quite the

번역 우리 지배인은 인격자이지만, 잘 알려진 아주 엄격한 지배인이다.

해설 quite는 전치한정사로 부정관사 앞에 온다.

443 An ultrasonic wave has (D) such a high frequency that it is inaudible.

(A) this a
(B) so a
(C) a such
(D) such a

번역 초음파는 아주 높은 주파수를 가지고 있어서 들을 수 없다.

해설 such는 전치한정사로 한정사 앞에 온다.

444 The best known of [the all → all the] Arctic birds, ptarmigans are a favorite of birdwatchers.

번역 북극새들 가운데 가장 잘 알려진 뇌조는 조류 관찰자들이 좋아한다.

해설 all은 전치한정사이므로 한정사 the 앞에 온다.

445 [The all three → All the three] people in the car were seriously injured in the car crash.

번역 차를 탔던 세 명 모두 차량 충돌로 심하게 다쳤다.

해설 all은 전치한정사이며, three는 후치한정사이므로, 전치한정사+한정사+ 후치한정사 어순인 all the three를 쓴다.

446 In 1992, Albert Gore, Jr., the son of a former United States senator, became the [forty-five → forty-fifth] Vice President of the Unites States.

번역 1992년에 미국 전 상원의원의 아들인 Albert Gore, Jr. 는 미국의 45대 부통령이 되었다.

해설 순서를 나타내므로 서수를 쓴다.

447 The bank is the [two → second] largest bank in the country, according to the monthly magazine.

주간 잡지에 따르면 그 은행은 국내에서 두 번째로 큰 은행이다.

해설 largest bank에서 bank가 단수이며, 또한 '두 번째'라는 뜻이 적절하므로 second를 쓴다.

448 (C) Three of every four migrating water birds in North America visit the Gulf of Mexico's winter wetlands.

(A) Four of three every
(B) Three every four
(C) Three of every four
(D) Every four of three

번역 북미의 이주하는 물새의 네 마리 가운데 세 마리가 멕시코만의 겨울 습지대를 방문한다.

해설 every는 전치한정사이고, four는 후치한정사이므로 every four라 해야 한다.

449 Thomas Jefferson's [the → φ] achievements as an architect rival his contributions as a politician.

번역 건축가로서의 Thomas Jefferson의 업적은 정치가로서의 그의 공헌과 맞먹는다.

해설 소유격은 the와 마찬가지로 한정사이다. 하나의 명사는 한정사를 하나만 갖는다.

450 The swamp maple tree grows well in virtually [every → all] kinds of soil.

번역 습지 단풍나무는 거의 모든 종류의 토양에서 잘 자란다.

해설 every는 단수명사와 함께 쓰인다. kinds가 복수이므로 all을 쓴다.

451 The decimal numeral system is one of the (B) world's most useful ways of expressing numbers.

(A) useful most world's
(B) world's most useful
(C) useful world's most
(D) most world's useful

번역 십진법은 숫자를 표현하는 세계에서 가장 유용한 방법 중의 하나이다.

해설 소유격 명사는 한정사이므로 후치한정사인 형용사 앞에 온다. most는 형용사를 수식한다.

452 When you've finished with his proposals, could you write some comments on [it → them]?

번역 그의 제안이 마무리되면, 그에 관한 논평을 써 주실 수 있겠습니까?

해설 his proposals가 복수이므로 it 대신 them을 쓴다.

453 [That dog of Tom → That dog of Tom's] barks more ferociously when it sees a stranger than my neighbor's.

번역	Tom의 저 개는 낯선 사람을 보았을 때 내 이웃집 개보다 사납게 짖는다.
해설	일반적으로 a dog of mine처럼 비한정 명사+of+한정 명사의 형태인데, this와 that은 예외적으로 한정적 표현임에도 불구하고 이 구문에 쓰인다.

454 Mark joined a health club, but (A) he works out irregularly.

(A) he   (B) his

(C) him   (D) himself

번역	Mark는 헬스클럽에 가입했지만, 불규칙적으로 운동을 한다.
해설	Mark는 남성이므로 he를 쓴다.

455 If you need my help, just dial the number written in (B) my phone book.

(A) me   (B) my

(C) mine   (D) myself

번역	내 도움이 필요하면 전화번호부에 적혀 있는 번호로 전화하세요.
해설	명사 앞에는 소유격을 쓴다.

456 As Jack was leaving the house, his wife chased after (D) him with an important document he left behind.

(A) he   (B) his

(C) himself   (D) him

번역	Jack이 집을 떠났을 때, 그의 아내는 그가 잊고 간 중요한 서류를 가지고서 그 뒤를 쫓아갔다.
해설	전치사 다음에는 목적격을 쓴다.

457 If you compare (B) ours with the best of French wines, we are definitely not there. But if you compare it to the worst of French wines, we are definitely better.

(A) us   (B) ours

(C) ourselves   (D) we

번역	우리의 포도주와 가장 훌륭한 프랑스의 포도주를 비교한다면, 우리는 거기에 속하지 않는다. 그러나 최악의 프랑스 포도주와 우리의 포도주를 비교한다면, 우리가 훨씬 낫다.
해설	소유격+명사를 대신해서 소유대명사를 쓴다. ours는 our wines를 대신한다.

458 In spite of his aged appearance, his movements were as spirited as (A) a young man's.

(A)　a young man's　　　　　(B)　young man's

(C)　a young man　　　　　　(D)　young men

번역 나이가 들어 보이기는 하지만 그의 움직임은 젊은이처럼 활기차다.

해설 앞의 내용을 반복할 경우 소유격＋명사의 구조에서 명사를 생략할 수 있다.

459 The greatest natural resource of the state of North Dakota is [their → its] fertile farmland.

번역 North Dakota주의 가장 커다란 천연자원은 비옥한 농지이다.

해설 the state of North Dakota는 3인칭단수이므로 its로 가리킨다.

460 Countries tend to specialize in the production and export of those goods and services that [it → they] can produce relatively cheaply.

번역 어느 국가든 상대적으로 싸게 생산할 수 있는 재화와 서비스를 생산하고 수출하는 것을 특화하는 경향이 있다.

해설 countries가 복수이므로 they로 받는다.

461 A varnish leaves a hard, glossy film when [they → it] dries.

번역 니스는 마를 때 단단하고, 광택이 나는 막을 남긴다.

해설 a varnish는 it으로 받는다.

462 Our urge to classify different life forms and give [it → them] names seems to be as old as the human race.

번역 다른 생명체를 분류하고, 명칭을 부여하려는 우리의 충동은 인류만큼이나 오랜 역사를 가지고 있는 것 같다.

해설 different life forms를 대신하여 them을 쓴다.

463 Robert Frost was not well known as a poet until he reached [the → his] forties.

번역 Robert Frost는 사십대에 이를 때까지 시인으로서 잘 알려지지 않았다.

해설 in the forties는 40년대, in his forties는 40대를 뜻한다.

464 In Africa, the feeding habits of migratory locusts make [it → them] one of the most feared of pests.

번역 아프리카에서 이주하는 메뚜기는 그 섭생 습관 때문에 해충 가운데 가장 두려운 것이다.

해설 make는 5형식동사로 목적어 자리에 migratory locusts를 대신하는 대명사가 의미상 적절하므로 them을 쓴다.

465 [That → It] always seems to be raining harder than it really is when you look through the window.

창문을 통해서 보면 실제보다 항상 비가 더 세차게 오는 것처럼 보인다.

해설 It always seems that it is raining harder를 It always seems to be raining harder로 바꿔 쓸 수 있다.

466 The odd thing about truth is that [one → it] keeps changing its clothes.

번역 진리의 이상한 점은 계속하여 그 옷을 갈아입는다는 것이다.

해설 truth를 가리키므로 it을 쓴다.

467 All cashiers should remember to have (C) their daily transaction sheets approved by the shift supervisor.

(A) they

(B) them

(C) their

(D) theirs

번역 모든 회계원은 일일 거래장을 교대조 감독자로부터 인가를 받는 것을 기억해야 한다.

해설 명사 앞에는 소유격을 쓴다.

468 The American standard of living is still higher than [those → that] of the other countries of the world.

번역 미국의 생활수준은 세계의 다른 국가들보다 훨씬 높다.

해설 standard of living을 대신하므로 단수인 that을 쓴다.

469 Even though San Francisco's harbor is a splendid one, few harbors in the world are as fine and large [as Rio de Janeiro → as that of Rio de Janeiro].

번역 San Francisco의 항구가 훌륭하지만 세계의 어느 항구도 Rio de Janeiro 의 항구만큼 훌륭하고 큰 것은 없다.

해설 샌프란시스코의 항구와 리오데자이네로를 비교하는 것이 아니라, 두 도 시의 항구를 비교하는 것이므로 지시대명사 that을 써야 한다.

470 The dialects of America are not so widely apart as [that → those] of England.

번역 미국의 방언은 영국의 방언과 달리 서로 크게 다르지 않다.

해설 복수인 dialects를 대신하므로 those를 쓴다.

471 As we have finished the first lesson, now we will read the second [ones → one].

번역 첫 번째 과를 마쳤으므로 이제 두 번째 과를 읽을 것이다.

해설 that/those가 앞선 명사의 수에 따라 결정되는 반면, one(s)는 의도된 수에 따른다. 두 번째 과는 하나밖에 없으므로 one을 쓴다. 즉, the second lesson의 뜻이므로 lesson을 대신하여 one을 쓴다.

472 Martha tried to find a good book on astronomy, but the bookstore she went to did not have [none → one].

> 번역 Martha는 천문학에 관한 좋은 책을 찾으려 했으나 그가 간 서점에는 없었다.

> 해설 앞에 not이 있으므로 none은 적절하지 않다. one이 a good book on astronomy를 가리키지만 동일한 것을 가리키지 않으므로 it을 쓰지 않는다.

473 Walt Whitman originated a distinctive form of free verse that sets his work apart from (B) that of all other poets.

(A) what
(B) that
(C) how
(D) it

> 번역 Walt Whitman은 다른 모든 시인들의 작품과 그의 작품을 구별짓는 독특한 형태의 자유시를 고안하였다.

> 해설 work을 대신하므로 단수인 that을 쓴다.

474 To appreciate what the hybrid corn breeder does, it is necessary to understand how corn reproduces [it → itself].

> 번역 옥수수 교배자들이 하는 일을 이해하기 위해서는 옥수수가 어떻게 번식하는지를 이해해야 한다.

> 해설 주어와 목적어가 동일한 것을 가리킬 때 재귀대명사를 쓴다.

475 As the current society is being globalized rapidly, people living today have to adapt [himself → themselves] to such a circumstance.

> 번역 현대사회가 빨리 세계화되고 있으므로 현대인들은 그러한 상황에 적응해야 한다.

> 해설 people을 가리키므로 themselves를 써야 한다.

476 To stay warm in cold weather, cold-blooded animals must expose [itself → themselves] to a source of warmth such as direct sunlight.

> 번역 추운 날씨에 체온을 유지하기 위해 냉혈동물들은 직사광선과 같은 열에 자신을 노출시켜야 한다.

> 해설 cold-blooded animals를 가리키므로 복수형을 써야 한다.

477 The president announced that he himself would act upon the evidence as presented to [himself → him] by the Congressional Committee.

> 번역 대통령은 그 자신이 의회의 위원회가 제시하는 증거에 따라 행동할 것이라고 발표했다.

> 해설 as (it is) presented to의 뜻이므로 주어와 목적어가 서로 다르므로 재귀대명사를 쓸 수 없다.

478 People out of work organized and operated their own group by (D) themselves in oder to overcome unemployment.

  (A) himself   (B) oneself

  (C) theirs   (D) themselves

  번역   실업자들은 실업을 이겨내기 위해 스스로 그룹을 조직하고 운영했다.

  해설   by oneself는 '스스로'를 뜻한다.

479 The senator found the secret, but he has kept it to (C) himself.

  (A) his own   (B) his

  (C) himself   (D) him

  번역   그 상원 의원은 비밀을 알았지만, 비밀을 지켰다.

  번역   to himself는 '독차지하여'의 뜻이다.

480 An oven that cleans (A) itself is very handy.

  (A) itself   (B) it

  (C) in itself   (D) them

  번역   저절로 닦이는 오븐은 매우 편리하다.

  해설   주어와 목적어가 동일하므로 재귀대명사를 쓴다.

481 Plants (B) rid themselves of excess water through transpiration.

  (A) rid them   (B) rid themselves

  (C) rid itself   (D) rid of themselves의

  번역   식물은 필요 이상의 수분을 발산을 통해 제거한다.

  해설   rid oneself of 구문이다.

482 To help policymakers and [another → others], the U.S. government spends as much as 4 billion a year in collecting statistics.

  번역   정책입안자나 다른 사람들을 돕기 위해 미국정부는 통계자료를 모으는 데 연간 40억 달러나 지출한다.

  해설   하나만을 나타내는 것이 아니라 막연한 다른 많은 사람을 나타내므로 others를 쓴다.

483 Lizards lack the built-in body temperature control many [another → other] creatures possess.

  번역   도마뱀은 다른 많은 생명체가 가지고 있는 고유한 체온 조절 장치가 없다.

  해설   복수에는 another가 아니라 other를 쓴다.

484 Though Artist Tatun was totally blind in one eye and had only slight vision in [another → the other], he became an internationally renowned jazz musician.

> 번역 │ 예술가인 Tatun은 한 쪽 눈이 전혀 보이지 않았고, 다른 한 쪽은 약간의 시력만을 가지고 있었지만, 세계적으로 유명한 음악가가 되었다.

> 해설 │ 눈이 두 개이므로 하나는 one, 다른 하나는 the other를 쓴다.

485 Some people argue that atomic bombs should not have been used in the second world war, but [other → others] maintain using them was inevitable so as to put a quick end to the war.

> 번역 │ 어떤 사람들은 2차 세계대전에서 핵폭탄이 사용되지 않았어야 했다고 주장하는 반면, 다른 사람들은 전쟁을 빨리 끝내기 위해 핵폭탄의 사용이 불가피했다고 주장한다.

> 해설 │ some people, other people이므로 other people을 대신하여 others라 쓴다.

486 Lightning is the transfer of electrical current from a cloud to the ground or from one cloud to [the other → another].

> 번역 │ 번개는 구름에서 지면으로 혹은 구름 사이에 전류를 전달하는 것이다.

> 해설 │ 둘 중 하나는 one, 다른 하나는 the other를 쓴다. 여러 개 중의 하나는 one, 다른 하나는 another를 쓴다.

487 Unlike the carnivores of their era, sauropods did not need to take the lives of [another → other] animals to find sustenance.

> 번역 │ 당시의 육식동물과는 달리 초식공룡은 먹이를 위해 다른 동물의 생명을 빼앗을 필요가 없었다.

> 해설 │ 단수명사에는 another를 쓰지만 복수명사에는 other를 쓴다.

488 Copper is a metal which is easily worked and which mixes well with [others → other] metals to form alloys.

> 번역 │ 구리는 쉽게 가공할 수 있으며, 다른 금속과 잘 혼합되어 합금을 만들 수 있는 금속이다.

> 해설 │ others는 대명사인 반면 other는 형용사이다. metals를 수식하므로 other를 쓴다.

489 Was it another [men → man] who had been lost in the middle of the ocean?

> 번역 │ 다른 한 사람이 바다 한 가운데서 실종되었나요?

> 해설 │ another는 단수명사와 함께 쓰인다.

490 Electric lamps came into widespread use during the early 1900's and have replaced other [type → types] of fat, gas, or oil lamps for almost every purpose.

번역 전등이 1900년대 초에 널리 사용되었으며, 거의 모든 목적의 다른 형태의 동물기름등, 가스등, 기름등을 대체하였다.

해설 other는 복수명사와 함께 쓰인다.

491 The ancient Hopewell people of North America probably cultivated corn and (C) other crops, but hunting and gathering were still of critical importance in their economy.

    (A) another   (B) the other's

    (C) other   (D) other than

번역 북미의 고대 Hopewell족은 아마도 옥수수와 다른 농작물을 재배하였으나, 사냥과 채집은 여전히 경제에서 매우 중요하였다.

해설 crops가 복수이므로 other를 쓴다.

492 Everyone in the delegation had (A) his reasons for opposing the measure.

    (A) his   (B) their

    (C) your   (D) its

번역 대표단의 모든 사람은 그 조치를 반대할 만한 이유가 있다.

해설 everyone은 단수이므로 대명사 his를 쓴다.

493 All are thought to have done (D) their best to make the project a success.

    (A) his   (B) her

    (C) our   (D) their

번역 모든 사람이 그 사업을 성공시키기 위해 최선을 다한 것으로 생각된다.

해설 all이 사람을 가리켜 복수를 쓰고 있으므로(are), 대명사 their를 쓴다.

494 (B) Somebody's bag was left here all night. Do you think there is an address written inside?

    (A) Anybody's   (B) Somebody's

    (C) Everybody's   (D) Some people's

번역 누군가의 가방이 밤새 여기에 버려져 있었다. 그 안에 주소가 쓰여 있다고 생각하니?

해설 긍정의 뜻이며, 단수 bag으로 보아 한 명을 가리킨다.

495 There are always (B) some people who will disregard company regulations.

    (A) any   (B) some

    (C) every   (D) few

번역	회사의 법규를 무시하려는 사람이 항상 있다.
해설	긍정문이므로 some을 쓴다. every는 단수명사와 함께 쓰인다.

496 Even though a lot of people offered to help, he decided to do it by [itself → himself].

번역	비록 많은 사람들이 도와 주겠다고 했으나, 그는 혼자 하기로 결정하였다.
해설	he를 가리키므로 himself라 해야 한다.

497 He was stopped [each → every] dozen yards by friends who wanted to congratulate him.

번역	그는 축하하고자 하는 친구들 때문에 12야드마다 멈추어야 했다.
해설	반복의 의미를 나타낼 때는 every를 쓴다.

498 On the one hand, he always does his work on time; on the [second → other] hand, he is very untidy and dirty in his appearance.

번역	그는 한편으로는 항상 제시간에 일을 하지만, 다른 한편으로는 그는 외모가 아주 단정치 못하고, 지저분하다.
해설	on the one hand, on the other hand라 한다.

499 Some scientists predict that, despite greater material output, the people in the year 2,000 will be poorer in many ways than [it is → they are] today.

번역	어떤 과학자들은 커다란 물질적 생산에도 불구하고 2000년에 사람들이 지금보다 여러가지로 더 가난할 것으로 예측한다.
해설	the people are poor today를 대신하므로 they are라고 해야 한다.

500 Yesterday I met an old friend of (C) mine.

   (A) me   (B) my

   (C) mine   (D) them

번역	어제 나는 오랜 친구를 만났다.
해설	비한정 명사+of+한정 명사의 경우 이중소유격 구문을 쓴다.

501 This computer isn't good for my job. I need (B) another one.

   (A) some   (B) another

   (C) other's   (D) any other

번역	이 컴퓨터가 내 일에 적합하지 않으므로, 다른 것이 필요하다.
해설	막연한 다른 하나를 가리키므로 another를 쓴다.

502 To take pride in what deserves boasting is one thing, and to take good care of it is quite (C) another.

(A) others   (B) thing

(C) another   (D) the other

> 번역   자랑할 만한 것에 자부심을 느끼는 것과, 그것을 잘 보살피는 것은 별개다.

> 해설   막연한 다른 하나는 another를 쓴다.

503 Most household appliances emit electromagnetic fields that are basically equivalent to (A) those emitted by high-voltage lines.

(A) those emitted by   (B) what emitted by

(C) they are emitted by   (D) which are emitted by

> 번역   대부분의 가전제품은 근본적으로 고압선이 내뿜는 것과 같은 전자장을 발산한다.

> 해설   electromagnetic fields에 대해 대명사 those를 쓴다. that과 those는 수식을 받을 수 있다.

504 The advisory board had implemented all of his ideas except (D) those that would cause painful cutbacks.

(A) these which   (B) those what

(C) these that   (D) those that

> 번역   자문위원단은 고통스러운 삭감을 야기할 것만을 제외한 그의 방안을 시행하였다.

> 해설   his ideas는 those로 받는다. those를 선행사로 할 경우 what을 쓸 수 없다.

505 Health is more valuable than wealth; (A) this cannot give such true happiness as that.

(A) this   (B) that

(C) it   (D) one

> 번역   건강이 부보다 중요하다. 후자가 전자만큼이나 진정한 행복을 가져다 주지는 못한다.

> 해설   전자는 that, 후자는 this라 한다.

506 His salary as a bus driver is much higher (C) than that of a teacher.

(A) in comparison with the salary of a teacher

(B) than a teacher

(C) than that of a teacher

(D) to compare as a teacher

| 번역 | 버스 기사로서 받는 그의 급여는 교사의 급여보다 훨씬 많다. |
| 해설 | salary가 단수이므로 that으로 받는다. |

507 The growth of such international organization as the United Nations [have → has] changed the meaning of political neutrality.

| 번역 | UN과 같은 국제기구의 성장은 정치적 중립의 의미를 바꾸어 놓았다. |
| 해설 | growth가 주어의 중심 어휘이므로 단수동사를 써야 한다. |

508 In the past, the rulers of the country [has → have] been selfish, but the present king has great respect and concern for his people.

| 번역 | 과거에는 그 나라의 왕이 이기적이었지만, 현재의 왕은 국민에 대한 존경심과 관심이 많다. |
| 해설 | 주어 the rulers of the country에서 중심어는 rulers이므로 복수동사를 쓴다. |

509 It is red blood cells in the bone that [produces → produce] hemoglobin.

| 번역 | 헤모글로빈을 생산하는 것은 뼈 속의 적혈구이다. |
| 해설 | it … that 강조구문으로 red blood cells in the bone이 강조되었다. cells가 중심어이므로 that절에는 복수동사를 쓴다. |

510 Hurricanes are severe cyclones with winds over seventy-five miles an hour which [originates → originate] over tropical ocean waters.

| 번역 | 허리케인은 열대 바다에서 시작되는 시속 75마일 이상의 바람을 가진 회오리바람이다. |
| 해설 | which에 이끌리는 관계절의 선행사는 winds이므로 동사도 복수동사를 써야 한다. |

511 One of the first results of the police investigation [were → was] a redesigning of the whole security system.

| 번역 | 경찰 조사의 첫 번째 결과는 총체적인 안전 체계의 재설계였다. |
| 해설 | 주어인 one of the first results의 중심어는 one이므로 단수동사를 써야 한다. |

512 The applications of mathematics [has → have] undergone a tremendous growth over the past decade.

| 번역 | 지난 10년간 수학의 응용이 상당한 성장을 이루었다. |
| 해설 | the applications of mathematics에서 중심어는 applications이다. |

513 Cars, like any machine, [requires → require] regular maintenance and care in order to run well.

번역	다른 기계와 마찬가지로 자동차도 잘 달리기 위해서는 정기적인 유지와 관리가 필요하다.
해설	cars가 주어이므로 복수동사를 쓴다.

514 The number of people who own a computer **(C) has been** increasing with rapidity.

(A) are (B) have been

(C) has been (D) has

번역	컴퓨터를 소유한 사람의 숫자가 빠른 속도로 증가했다.
해설	the number of + 복수명사는 단수동사를 쓴다.

515 Ensuring an adequate water supply [**have → has**] been a concern ever since people began to live in towns and cities.

번역	적절한 물의 확보는 인간이 도시에서 살기 시작한 이래 관심사였다.
해설	주어 ensuring an adequate water supply가 동명사이므로 단수동사를 쓴다.

516 Making all the national convention arrangements [**were → was**] Mr. Huge's responsibility.

번역	국가의 모든 협정 준비는 Huge씨의 책임이었다.
해설	동명사가 주어이므로 단수동사를 쓴다.

517 Using many symbols [**make → makes**] it difficult to put a large amount of information on a single map.

번역	많은 기호를 사용함으로써 하나의 지도에 많은 양의 정보를 넣을 수 있다.
해설	Using many symbols는 동명사로 단수 동사를 쓴다.

518 **(B) The uneducated are** more to be pitied than blamed.

(A) Uneducated are (B) The uneducated are

(C) The uneducated is (D) The uneducated people

번역	교육을 받지 못한 사람들을 비난할 것이 아니라 불쌍히 여겨야 한다.
해설	the+형용사가 사람을 나타낼 때는 복수동사를 쓴다.

519 **(D) The accused** has been found guilty.

(A) Accused (B) Accused people

(C) An accused (D) The accused

번역	피고가 유죄로 드러났다.

the+형용사가 사람을 나타낼 때는 복수 취급하지만, the accused, the deceased는 단수 취급한다.

520 The planning committee [have → has] finalized the advertising and marketing strategies for next fiscal year.

번역 기획위원회는 다음 회계연도의 광고 및 마케팅 전략을 최종 승인하였다.

해설 committee는 집합명사인데, 의사결정은 위원회가 집단적으로 하는 것이다.

521 The United States [celebrate → celebrates] the birth of its independence every Forth of July.

번역 미국은 매년 7월 4일 독립의 시작을 기념한다.

해설 the Philippines, the United States와 같은 복수형의 국가명은 the를 쓰며, 단수 취급한다.

522 Measles [spread → spreads] easily among individuals who haven't been vaccinated.

번역 홍역은 백신을 맞지 않은 사람들 사이에 쉽게 퍼진다.

해설 measles는 질병명으로 형태는 복수이지만 단수명사이다.

523 Whether we like it or not, it is true that mathematics [are → is] the language of science and the universe.

번역 좋든 싫든, 수학은 과학과 우주의 언어라는 것은 사실이다.

해설 학문명은 비록 형태가 복수이지만 단수 명사이다.

524 The bad news about the new contract [have → has] finally been confirmed.

번역 새로운 계약에 대한 나쁜 소식이 마침내 확인되었다.

해설 news는 형태가 복수이지만 단수 취급한다.

525 Each student may leave the room whenever [they → he] may desire to do so.

번역 모든 학생은 원할 때 방을 나가도 된다.

해설 each+단수명사이므로 대명사는 he를 쓴다.

526 The electronics company along with ELSS [are → is] having trouble preparing its employees for the new millenium.

번역 ELSS와 함께 그 전자회사는 직원들에게 새천년을 준비시키는 데 어려움이 있다.

해설 *A* along with *B*에서 동사는 A의 수를 따른다.

527 (A) Every great chef prepares his or her food in a different way.

(A) Every   (B) Any

(C) All   (D) Some

> 번역   모든 훌륭한 요리사는 다른 방식으로 자신의 요리를 준비한다.

> 해설   every는 단수명사와 쓰인다.

528 Every boy and girl in our class (B) has a camera.

(A) have   (B) has

(C) is having   (D) have had

> 번역   우리 반의 모든 남학생과 여학생은 카메라를 가지고 있다.

> 해설   every나 each의 경우 and와 결합되더라도 단수취급한다.

529 All the people who [is → are] interested in the problem should be invited to tomorrow's meeting.

> 번역   그 문제에 관심이 있는 모든 사람은 내일 회의에 초대되어야 한다.

> 해설   선행사인 all the people이 복수이므로 복수동사를 쓴다.

530 (C) All ballet dancers learn five basic positions for the arms and feet.

(A) All of   (B) Of every

(C) All   (D) Every

> 번역   모든 발레 선수는 팔과 다리의 5가지 기본 위치를 배운다.

> 해설   ballet dancers가 복수이므로 복수와 함께 쓰이는 all을 선택한다. all of 의 경우 다음에 한정명사가 와야 한다.

531 Neither of them [have → has] turned in the report to the person in charge yet.

> 번역   그들 가운데 아무도 아직 책임자에게 보고서를 제출하지 않았다.

> 해설   neither는 단수 취급한다.

532 Neither of the two candidates having applied for admission to the department [were → was] eligible for it.

> 번역   그 학과에 원서를 제출한 두 후보 중 아무도 적격이 아니었다.

> 해설   주어는 neither of the two candidates이며, having applied for admission to the department는 candidates를 수식한다. neither는 단수 취급한다.

533 Neither of them (D) has done satisfactory work.

(A) done   (B) hasn't done

(C) have done   (D) has done

> 번역 그들 어느 누구도 만족스럽게 일을 하지 않았다.

> 해설 neither of them은 단수 취급한다.

534 One-fourth of a worker's income [are paid → is paid] in taxes to the government.

> 번역 노동자의 임금의 4분의 1은 정부에 세금으로 지불한다.

> 해설 분수의 경우 명사의 수를 따르는데, income이 단수이므로 단수동사를 쓴다.

535 Two thirds of women prisoners [has → have] dependent children under the age of 18.

> 번역 여성 재소자의 3분의 2는 18세 이하의 딸린 자식이 있다.

> 해설 분수의 수는 of 다음의 명사의 수를 따른다. prisoners가 복수이므로 복수동사를 쓴다.

536 It has been estimated that only 21 percent of the world's land surface [are → is] cultivatable and that only 7.6 percent is actually under cultivation.

> 번역 지구 표면의 21 퍼센트만이 경작 가능하고, 7.6 퍼센트만이 실제로 경작되고 있는 것으로 추정된다.

> 해설 the world's land surface가 단수이므로 단수 취급한다.

537 Two-thirds of my project (B) is finished.

(A) are   (B) is

(C) am   (D) be

> 번역 내 프로젝트의 3분의 2가 끝났다.

> 해설 my project가 단수이므로 단수 동사를 쓴다.

538 My nose as well as my ears [were → was] bleeding when the doctor was brought in.

> 번역 의사를 불렀을 때 귀 뿐만 아니라 코도 피가 나고 있었다.

> 해설 A as well as B는 A의 수를 따른다.

539 Not only the plant workers but the manager (B) is on strike.

(A) are   (B) is

(C) being   (D) have been

> 번역 공장 노동자 뿐만 아니라 관리자도 파업 중이다.

해설　not only *A* but also *B*는 B의 수를 따른다.

540 Neither you nor he (B) is likely to be present at the meeting.

    (A) are   (B) is

    (C) were   (D) have

번역　너도 그도 회의에 참석하지 않을 것 같다.

해설　neither *A* nor *B*는 B의 수를 따른다.

541 It is the interaction between people, rather than the events that occur in their lives that [are → is] the main focus of social psychology.

번역　사회심리학의 주요 관심사는 살아 가면서 일어나는 사건보다는 사람 사이의 상호작용에 대한 것이다.

해설　강조용법의 it ... that 구문으로 the interaction이 단수이므로 단수 동사를 쓴다.

542 The group of people [have → has] been waiting some two hours in front of the theater before the movie started.

번역　사람들은 영화가 시작되기 전에 극장 앞에서 약 두 시간 기다리고 있었다.

해설　a group of people은 복수이지만, the group of people은 단수이다.

543 The National Cowboy Hall of Fame in Oklahoma City [pay → pays] tribute to everyone associated with what Americans call the "Old West."

번역　Oklamoma시의 카우보이 명예의 전당은 미국인들이 Old West라 부르는 것과 관련된 모든 사람에게 경의를 표한다.

해설　주어 the National Cowboy Hall of Fame이 단수이다.

544 Many people who live in New York City [thinks → think] that life in a large city offers special advantages.

번역　뉴욕시에 사는 많은 사람들은 대도시의 삶이 특별한 이점이 있다고 생각한다.

해설　people이 주어이므로 복수 동사를 쓴다.

545 Many American novelists, such as Gore Vidal, [resides → reside] in other countries.

번역　Gore Vidal과 같은 많은 미국 소설가들은 다른 나라에 거주한다.

해설　novelists가 주어이므로 복수 동사를 쓴다.

546 The information presented [were → was] too technical for any beginning analyst.

번역　제시된 정보는 초보 분석가에게는 너무 전문적이었다.

해설 주어 information이 단수이므로 단수 동사를 쓴다.

547 The first [libraries → library] in the North American colonies was established in Massachusetts in the year 1638.

번역 북미 식민지의 첫 번째 도서관은 1638년에 Massachusetts 주에 설치되었다.

해설 was가 단수 동사이므로 주어도 단수 명사를 쓴다.

548 Paulina Wright Davis was an American social reformer [which → who] worked for the right of women to own property and to vote.

번역 Paulina Wright Davis는 여성이 재산을 소유하고 투표할 권리를 갖도록 힘쓴 미국의 사회개혁가였다.

해설 선행사 reformer가 사람을 나타내므로 who를 쓴다.

549 Anne Elizabeth McDowell is best remembered for a weekly journal, *the Woman's Advocate*, [who → which] she launched in January 1855.

번역 Anne Elizabeth McDowell은 1855년 1월에 출판한 주간잡지 Woman's Advocate로 잘 기억되고 있다.

해설 선행사가 사물인 a weekly journal이므로 which를 쓴다.

550 Plant cuttings [who → which] are placed in water will develop roots and can then be planted in soil.

번역 물 속에 넣어둔 자른 나무 가지는 뿌리가 자랄 것이며, 흙에 심을 수 있다.

해설 선행사 plant cuttings가 사물이므로 which를 쓴다.

551 The job requires an expert (D) who is capable of making the complex program needed for the software.

(A) whom   (B) whose

(C) which   (D) who

번역 그 일은 소프트웨어에 필요한 복잡한 프로그램을 만들 줄 아는 전문가를 필요로 한다.

해설 선행사 expert가 사람이므로 who를 쓴다.

552 Anthony Burgess, (B) who has achieved fame as a novelist, was originally a student of music.

(A) because of being famous

(B) who has achieved fame

(C) who because he was famous

(D) achieved fame

번역 소설가로 명성을 얻은 Anthony Burgess는 원래 음대 학생이었다.

해설 삽입구 이외의 부분이 완전한 문장을 이루므로, 삽입구도 완전한 절을 이루어야 한다. 계속적 용법의 관계절로, 주술 구조를 갖춘 것을 선택한다.

553 Jane Addams, an American social reformer in Chicago, (D) who established a community center for poor people, won the Nobel Peace Prize in 1931.

(A) she established a community center

(B) established a community center

(C) who was established a community center

(D) who established a community center

번역 가난한 사람을 위한 시민 문화 회관을 설립한 시카고의 미국 사회개혁가 Jane Addams는 1931년에 노벨평화상을 받았다.

해설 Jane Addams와 an American social reformer in Chicago는 동격이다. Jane Addams가 주어이며, won이 동사이므로, 삽입구가 주술구조를 갖추어야 한다. 콤마가 있으므로 계속적 용법의 관계절이 오면 된다.

554 Malvin Gray Johnson is noted especially for the pictures (D) which he painted in Brightwood, Virginia, in the late summer of 1934.

(A) which he was painted   (B) in which painted

(C) in which he painted   (D) which he painted

번역 Malvin Gray Johnson은 특히 1934년 늦여름 Virginia주 Brightwood 에서 그가 그린 그림으로 유명하다.

해설 선행사인 the pictures가 관계절의 painted의 목적어 역할을 하므로 목적격 관계대명사를 써야 한다.

555 Rice, (C) which still forms the staple diet of much of the world's population, grows best in hot, wet lands.

(A) still forms the staple diet

(B) which it still forms the staple diet

(C) which still forms the staple diet

(D) which is still formed the staple diet

번역 아직도 많은 세계인의 주식을 이루고 있는 쌀은 고온 다습한 땅에서 잘 자란다.

해설 forms가 타동사로 다음에 the staple diet를 취하고 있으므로 능동태를 써야 하며, 또한 주격 관계대명사를 써야 한다. Rice grows best ...가 완전한 문장을 이루므로 계속적 용법의 관계절이 와야 한다.

556 The director announced the names of those [whom → who] were to be named to the key posts.

번역	감독은 중요 부서에 임명될 사람들의 이름을 발표하였다.
해설	주어 자리이므로 주격관계대명사를 써야 한다.

557 Ripe fruit is often stored in a place [at which → which] contains much carbon dioxide so that the fruit will not decay too rapidly.

번역	익은 과일은 흔히 이산화탄소가 많아서 과일이 너무 빨리 부패하지 않는 곳에 보관된다.
해설	동사 contains의 주어 자리이므로 주격관계대명사가 와야 한다. 전치사＋명사는 주어가 될 수 없다.

558 Mahalia Jackson, [who → whose] singing combined powerful vitality with great dignity, was one of the best-known gospel singers in the United States.

번역	활력과 품위를 가진 노래를 부르는 Mahalia Jackson은 미국에서 가장 잘 알려진 복음 가수이다. 독
해설	명사 앞에는 소유격 관계대명사를 쓴다.

559 A web admin is a system administrator (B) whose job focus is primarily on web technologies such as web hosting on any given platform.

(A) what   (B) whose

(C) whom   (D) when

번역	web admin은 시스템 관리자로 주된 임무는 주어진 플랫폼에 대한 웹호스팅과 같은 웹기술에 관한 것이다.
해설	관계절에 빈 자리가 없으며, his job focus의 his를 대신하는 관계대명사가 필요하다.

560 The earth is the sole planet in the solar system that [it → φ] has appreciable amounts of oxygen gas in its atmosphere.

번역	지구는 대기 중에 상당한 양의 산소를 가진 태양계의 유일한 행성이다.
해설	타동사 has의 목적어가 있으며, 관계대명사 that이 있으므로 주어는 필요 없다.

561 The counselor Ms. Mary talked to [her → φ] was very helpful in her new project because he had been in the business before.

번역	Mary가 대화했던 상담사가 전에 사업을 한 적이 있어서 그녀의 새로운 계획에 매우 도움이 되었다.
해설	the counselor와 Ms. Mary 사이에 있는 관계대명사가 생략되었으며, 이 관계대명사는 her를 대신하는 것이므로 her는 불필요하다.

562 Only the female and the worker wasps are equipped with a sting, which they use [it → φ] to attack their prey or to protect themselves against enemies.

<table>
<tr><td>번역</td><td>암컷 말벌과 일벌만이 침을 가지고 있는데, 먹이를 공격할 때 침을 사용하거나 적으로부터 자신을 보호하기 위해 침을 사용한다.</td></tr>
<tr><td>해설</td><td>타동사인 use가 주어를 가지고 있으며, 따라서 which가 use의 목적어 역할을 하므로 it은 불필요하다.</td></tr>
</table>

563 Our understanding of the past is based on written records, oral traditions, and physical evidence, [all of them → all of which] must be interpreted.

<table>
<tr><td>번역</td><td>과거에 대한 우리의 이해는 쓰여진 기록, 구전, 물리적 증거인데, 이들 모두 해석되어야 한다.</td></tr>
<tr><td>해설</td><td>두 문장을 연결하기 위해서는 접속사가 필요하다. 관계대명사가 접속사의 역할을 할 수 있으므로 them 대신 which를 써야 한다.</td></tr>
</table>

564 The city of Kalamazoo, Michigan, derives its name from a Native American word [means → which means] "bubbling springs."

<table>
<tr><td>번역</td><td>Michigan 주의 Kalamazoo 시는 미원주민어로 '용솟음치는 샘'이란 단어로부터 생겨난 이름이다.</td></tr>
<tr><td>해설</td><td>시제동사인 derives가 주어와 목적어를 가지고 있는데, means는 목적어를 갖는 반면 주어를 가지고 있지 않다. 따라서 means 이하가 수식어 역할을 할 수 있도록 해야 한다.</td></tr>
</table>

565 [That → What] people consider a luxury at one time frequently becomes a necessity; many families find that ownership of two cars is indispensable.

<table>
<tr><td>번역</td><td>사람들이 한 때 사치품으로 여기는 것이 필수품이 된다. 많은 가족들은 두 대의 자동차가 필수적이라는 것은 안다.</td></tr>
<tr><td>해설</td><td>consider의 목적어이면서, becomes의 주어 역할을 하는 요소가 필요하다. what은 선행사를 포함하므로 두 개의 명사 역할을 한다.</td></tr>
</table>

566 Most of the food [what → that/which/ɸ] elephants eat is brought to their mouths by their trunks.

<table>
<tr><td>번역</td><td>코끼리는 대부분의 음식물을 코로 입에 넣는다.</td></tr>
<tr><td>해설</td><td>선행사가 있으므로 what을 쓸 수 없다. eat의 목적어가 없으므로 목적격 관계대명사가 필요하다.</td></tr>
</table>

567 [That → What] is most touching in P. Henry's stories is the gallantry with which ordinary people struggle to maintain their dignity.

<table>
<tr><td>번역</td><td>P. Henry의 소설에서 가장 감동적인 것은 보통 사람들이 자신의 품위를 유지하려고 노력하는 용기이다.</td></tr>
<tr><td>해설</td><td>앞 is의 주어이면서 뒤 is의 주어 역할을 하므로 what을 쓴다.</td></tr>
</table>

568 (D) What would be a fairly long speech in a play is often presented as a reductive in opera.

(A) That   (B) There

(C) It   (D) What

번역	연극에서 매우 긴 연설이 오페라에서는 가끔 간략한 것으로 표현된다.
해설	would be의 주어이면서, is의 주어이므로 what을 써야 한다.

569 As (A) a result of what is now known in physics and chemistry, scientists have been able to make important discoveries in biology and medicine.

(A) a result of what
(B) what a result of
(C) a result what of
(D) a what result of

번역	지금은 물리나 화학에서 알려진 것의 결과로 과학자들은 생물학이나 의학에서 중요한 발견을 할 수 있었다.
해설	of의 목적어이자, is의 주어가 필요하다.

570 The earthworm is a worm [that found → found] in moist, warm soil in many geographical areas.

번역	지렁이는 많은 곳에서 습하고 따뜻한 흙에서 발견되는 벌레이다.
해설	a worm that is found에서 주격관계대명사와 be가 생략될 수 있다.

571 As many as 50 percent of the income from motion pictures (A) produced in the United States comes from marketing the films abroad.

(A) produced in the United States
(B) are produced in the United States
(C) that produced in the United States
(D) and produced in the United States

번역	미국에서 제작되는 영화의 수입 가운데 50%가 해외 영화 마케팅에 의한 것이다.
해설	나머지 부분이 완전한 절을 이루므로 빈칸 부분이 수식어 역할을 해야 한다. motion pictures which are produced in the United States에서 which are가 생략될 수 있다.

572 Before starting on a sea voyage, prudent navigators learn the sea charts, study the sailing directions, and memorize lighthouse locations to prepare themselves for any conditions (A) they might encounter.

(A) they might encounter
(B) or they might encounter
(C) when they might encounter
(D) and they might encounter

번역	신중한 항해사는 항해를 시작하기 전에, 닥치게 될 어떤 상황에 대해서도 대비하기 위해 지도를 익히고, 항해 방향을 연구하고, 등대의 위치를 암기한다.

encounter가 타동사이므로 주어와 목적어가 필요하다. 주어 they가 있으며, 생략된 관계대명사가 목적어 역할을 한다. or나 and는 등위접속사이므로 목적어가 나타나야 한다.

573 John F. Kennedy was only forty-two when he was inaugurated as president of the United States—the youngest person (D) ever elected to the presidency.

(A) ever electing to   (B) ever been elected to

(C) who ever elected to   (D) ever elected to

번역   John F. Kennedy가 미국 대통령 선서를 할 때 겨우 42세였는데, 가장 젊은 나이에 대통령으로 당선된 사람이다.

해설   the youngest person who was ever elected to the presidency에서 who was가 생략되었다.

574 On the 1st floor there is the main hall [which → where/in which] most entrance ceremonies, graduations, official events, parties take place.

번역   대강당이 1층에 있는데, 거기서 입학식, 졸업식, 공식 행사, 파티가 열린다.

해설   관계절에 부사 자리가 비어 있으므로 관계부사를 써야 한다.

575 Last spring, we visited Florida [where → , which] is noted for its beautiful beach.

번역   지난 봄에 우리는 아름다운 해변으로 유명한 플로리다를 방문하였다.

해설   is의 주어가 필요하므로 주격관계대명사가 필요하다.

576 The day will come (B) when my words will come true.

(A) where   (B) when

(C) why   (D) how

번역   내 말이 실현될 날이 올 것이다.

해설   선행사가 the day이므로 when을 쓴다.

577 Dams can be very beneficial to the areas (A) in which they are built.

(A) in which they are built   (B) building them where

(C) which they are built   (D) where are they built

번역   댐은 건설되는 지역에 매우 유익하다.

해설   선행사인 the areas가 built에 대해 목적어 역할을 할 수 없으며, 장소의 의미를 가져야 하므로 in which를 써야 한다. they는 dams를 가리키며, built의 목적어인데 수동태가 되어 주어가 되었다. in which they are built를 where they are built로 바꿀 수 있다.

578 There are very few areas in the world (A) where apricots can be grown successfully.

    (A) where apricots can   (B) which apricots can

    (C) apricots that can   (D) where can apricots

> 번역   세계적으로 살구가 성공적으로 자랄 수 있는 곳이 얼마 되지 않는다.
>
> 해설   apricot이 grow의 목적어인데 수동태가 되어 주어 자리에 있다. 따라서 명사는 필요하지 않으며 부사가 나타나야 한다.

579 Chemistry is concerned with (B) the way substances interact with one another.

    (A) the way of substances   (B) the way substances

    (C) the substances way   (D) way substances

> 번역   화학은 물질이 서로 어떻게 상호 작용을 하는지에 대해 관심을 갖는다.
>
> 해설   the way how substances interact에서 how가 생략된 구문이다.

580 Eastern meadowlarks abound in places (C) where land is cultivated, but eat harmful insects rather than grain.

    (A) land is cultivated there   (B) there is land cultivated

    (C) where land is cultivated   (D) where is cultivated land

> 번역   동부 들종다리는 경작지에 많이 살지만, 곡식을 먹지 않고 해충을 먹는다.
>
> 해설   places가 선행사이므로 where를 쓴다. 관계절에서는 도치가 일어나지 않는다.

581 The columnist feels sure that [who → whoever] wins the election will have the support of both parties.

> 번역   그 컬럼니스트는 선거에서 이기는 사람은 누구든 양당의 지지를 받을 것이라고 확신한다.
>
> 해설   wins의 주어이면서, will의 주어 역할을 할 수 있는 것이 필요하다. 의미상 사람이 필요하므로 whoever를 쓴다. 복합관계대명사는 선행사+ 관계대명사 역할을 한다.

582 A wise administrator will assign a job to [whomever → whoever] is best qualified.

> 번역   현명한 행정가는 누구든지 가장 유능한 사람에게 일을 맡긴다.
>
> 해설   to의 목적어이면서 is의 주어 역할을 하는 관계사가 필요하다. 복합관계사의 격은 관계절에서의 역할을 따른다.

583 The teacher tells the same story to [whomever → whoever] participates in the class.

> 번역 | 선생님은 수업에 참여하는 사람이면 누구든 같은 이야기를 해준다.

> 해설 | to의 목적어 역할과 participates의 주어 역할을 해야 하므로 복합관계대명사를 쓴다. 관계절에서 주어 역할을 하므로 주격을 쓴다.

584 (B) Whoever gets home first starts cooking.

(A) Anyone   (B) Whoever

(C) Who   (D) Those

> 번역 | 집에 먼저 도착하는 사람이 요리를 시작한다.

> 해설 | gets의 주어의 역할을 하면서 starts의 주어 역할을 하는 요소가 필요하다.

585 Send the invitation card (B) to whoever you think is likely to come to the party.

(A) whoever   (B) to whoever

(C) whomever   (D) to whomever

> 번역 | 파티에 올 것 같다고 생각하는 사람에게 초대장을 보내라.

> 해설 | send+직접목적어+to+간접목적어 구문이므로 to가 필요하며, is의 주어가 필요하다. 격은 관계절의 주어에 해당하므로 주격을 쓴다.

586 Please feel free to distribute this program to (C) whomever you like.

(A) whom   (B) whoever

(C) whomever   (D) people

> 번역 | 이 프로그램을 네가 좋아하는 사람이면 누구에게든 마음대로 나누어 주어도 좋다.

> 해설 | to의 목적어 역할과, like의 목적어 역할을 해야 하므로 복합관계대명사가 필요하다. like의 목적어이므로 목적격을 쓴다.

587 The organization asked for more donation [which → than] was necessary.

> 번역 | 그 조직은 필요 이상의 기부를 요구하였다.

> 해설 | 선행사에 more가 포함되어 있으므로 유사관계대명사 than을 쓴다.

588 We are given just as much food (A) as will keep the breath in our bodies.

(A) as   (B) that

(C) what   (D) but

> 번역 | 우리는 신체에서 숨을 쉴만큼의 음식을 제공받는다.

해설　선행사에 as가 포함되어 있으므로 유사관계대명사 as를 쓴다.

589 There is no one (D) but loves his mother.

  (A)　who　　　　　　　　　(B)　as

  (C)　whom　　　　　　　　(D)　but

번역　자기 어머니를 사랑하지 않는 자는 없다.

해설　선행사에 no가 있으므로 유사관계대명사 but을 쓴다.

590 The decade of the 1920's was significant in Georgia's history because of the rapidity with [what → which] agriculture declined in the state.

번역　1920년대는 Georgia주의 역사에서 매우 중요한데, 거기서 농업이 아주 빨리 쇠퇴하였기 때문이다.

해설　선행사가 the rapidity이므로 what 대신 which를 쓴다.

591 Tenant farmers are those [they → who] either rent a farm and work it for themselves or work the farm for the owner and receive payment.

번역　소작농들은 농장을 빌려서 일을 하거나, 소유자를 위해 농장을 돌보고 돈을 받는 사람들이다.

해설　rent의 주어 역할을 하면서 동시에 those와 연결시킬 수 있는 접속사가 필요하므로 관계사를 쓴다.

592 Butterflies and moths undergo complete metamorphosis, [then changing → which change] from caterpillar to adult via one intermediate stage, the pupa.

번역　나비와 나방은 완전변태를 하며, 번데기라는 중간 과정 하나를 거쳐서 애벌레로부터 성충으로 변한다.

해설　선행사가 metamorphosis이므로 분사구문을 쓸 수 없다.

593 A symbol of freedom, the Statue of Liberty represents a woman [has → who has] just escaped from the chains of slavery, which lie at her feet.

번역　자유의 상징인 자유의 여신상은 발에 묶인 노예의 사슬로부터 방금 탈출한 여성을 나타낸다.

해설　a woman이 represents의 목적어로 쓰였으므로 has 이하는 a woman을 수식해야 한다.

594 Mathematics is an indispensable tool for anyone [which → who] desires to do graduate work in the sciences.

번역　수학은 대학원 과정에서 과학을 하고자 하는 사람에게 필수적인 도구이다.

해설　선행사가 사람이므로 who를 쓴다.

595 These guns shoot large shells, any one of [whom → which] would blow up a house or sink a ship.

> 번역 이 총들은 커다란 포탄을 발사하며, 그 가운데 하나가 집을 날려버리고, 배를 가라 앉힐 수 있다.

> 해설 선행사 shells가 사물이므로 which를 쓴다.

596 Antonio Stradivari, [whose generally acknowledged → who is generally acknowledged] to be the greatest violin maker of all time, worked in the Italian town of Cremona and made over 1,000 instruments during the course of his career.

> 번역 역사상 가장 위대한 바이올린 제작자로 인정되고 있는 Antonio Stradivari 는 이태리의 도시 Cremona에서 작업을 하였으며, 일생동안 1,000개 이상의 악기를 제작하였다.

> 해설 주어＋동사＋부사의 어순에 관한 문제이다.

597 Before every presidential election in the United States, the statisticians try to guess the proportion of the population that (D) will vote for each candidate.

(A) are voted   (B) voting

(C) to be voted   (D) will vote

> 번역 미국에서 모든 대통령 선거 전에 통계전문가들이 각 후보자에게 투표할 인구의 비율을 추정하려고 노력한다.

> 해설 관계대명사 that이 주격관계대명사이며, 목적어가 있다는 점을 고려해야 한다.

598 By 1872 the United States had 70 engineering colleges, (B) an astonishing expansion credited largely to the Morrill Act of 1862.

(A) because   (B) an

(C) to which   (D) was

> 번역 1872년까지 미국은 70개의 공과대학이 있었으며, 이는 주로 1862년의 Morill Act에 기인한 놀라운 확장이다.

> 해설 which is an astonishing expansion에서 which is가 생략되었다. which 의 선행사는 앞 문장 전체이다.

599 Since New York City is one of the world's most important centers of business, culture, and trade, (B) much of what happens in the city affects what happens throughout the United States and around the world.

(A) much of happens   (B) much of what happens

(C) much of that happens   (D) much happenings

번역 뉴욕시가 세계에서 가장 중요한 사업, 문화, 무역의 중심지이기 때문에 거기서 일어나는 많은 것이 미국과 세계 전역에 영향을 미친다.
해설 of의 목적어이면서 happens의 주어가 필요하다.

600 New Jersey and Delaware are separated by Delaware Bay, **(D) whose deep channel** connects with the Delaware River and thus enables oceangoing vessels to reach the ports of Wilmington, Del., and Philadelphia.

(A) which deep channel   (B) deep channel of it

(C) that is a deep channel   (D) whose deep channel

번역 New Jersey와 Delaware는 Delaware 만으로 분리되어 있는데, 깊은 해협이 Delaware 강과 연결되어 있으며, 따라서 대양항로선이 Delaware의 Wilmington항과 Philadelphia항에 이를 수 있도록 한다.

해설 동사 connects의 앞에 오므로 명사 역할을 할 수 있는 것이 하나 와야 한다.

Assignment 1

Department _____

Student ID _____

Name _____

Date _____ / _____ / _____

A 문법적으로 틀린 부분을 찾아 고치고, 그 이유를 쓰시오.

> 예 : Baffin Bay played an important role in the exploration of North
> America by Europeans <u>and</u> seeking a trade route to India.
> 삭제
> seeking a trade route to India가 Europeans를 수식하므로 and가
> 불필요하다.

1 That was Shirley S. Chisholm who was the first Black woman to run
for the office of President of the United States in 1972.

2 Unlike carbon monoxide, which it has no odor, hydrogen sulfide
emits a powerful stretch.

3 The term laser stands for light amplification by stimulated emis-
sion of radiation: atoms emit photons of light when some electrons
jumping down to lower energy levels.

4 Charles used to work for a big company in Chicago before his ac-
ceptance a job with Microsoft in Seattle.

5 Bankruptcy legislation is designed to provide an orderly and equi-
tably liquidation of the estate of an insolvent debtor.

6 Nowhere in the world travelers can buy so much beauty for so little
money as in Hawaii.

7 Personnel administration it is the management of the people in or-

ganizations such as corporations.

8 The development of a calendar what is vital for the study of chronol-
   ogy.

9 All things consist of atoms or molecules, which be constantly moving.

10 The adult Pygmy measuring only three and one-half inches in length
    and weighs one-eighth of an ounce.

B 다음 문장에서 주어를 찾아 밑줄을 그으시오.

1 Bevis Hall was closed for repairs during most of October.

2 The headlights of an oncoming car blinded me.

3 Reference materials may not be taken out of the library.

4 Identifying subjects and predicates is the focus of this exercise.

5 Martha's roommate has decided to leave school.

6 Restrictions on automobile imports go into effect next month.

7 The population of the inner city has been decreasing for the past
   fifteen years.

8 Summers in southern Texas are usually hot and dry.

C 주어(S), 동사(V), 목적어(O), 보어(C)를 찾으시오.

1 My favorite musical instruments are the radio, television, and
   stereo.

2   Two popular trees are the linden and the honey locust.

3   The winner will be either Jeff or Will.

4   Are those people our neighbors and friends?

5   Baseball and golf are outdoor sports.

6   Your doctor should be a well-trained individual.

7   Jenny and Emily are close friends.

8   The grand prize was a trip to Hawaii and a cruise to Alaska.

9   Mr. Hatch is a member of congress and a song writer.

10   My wife dusted the furniture and cleaned the floors.

11   Where is the white tablecloth for the table?

12   Well, there are no more candles for sale.

13   The actress was still a very beautiful and lovely person.

14   My mother wanted both flour and sugar from the neighbor.

15   The student knew the answer and was sure of it.

16   The snow storm raged during the night and all day.

17   Jim caught and cleaned both fish quickly.

D   다음 문장은 모두 비문법적이다. 문법적인 문장으로 고치시오.

1   Summers in Arizona very hot.

2   Speaks well but slow.

3   The teacher grew very angrily.

4   Her is getting better.

5   Sitting at home alone not much fun.

E 다음 문장을 괄호 안의 지시대로 고쳐 쓰시오.

1   It appears that he has been ill.(He를 주절의 주어로)

2   It seems that he is rich.(He를 주절의 주어로)

3   A map is on page 33.(There로 시작하여)

4   He showed everyone the letter.(3형식으로)

5   He still owes me a lot of money.(3형식으로)

6   I've bought you some chocolate.(3형식으로)

7   Save me some of them.(3형식으로)

8   I scarcely thought that we would undermine ourselves.(scarcely로 시작하여)

9   He didn't only give me another main meal, but he also passed me the entire tray!(Not only로 시작하여)

Assignment 2

Department _____

Student ID _____

Name _____

Date ____ / ____ / ____

A 문법적으로 틀린 부분을 찾아 고치고, 그 이유를 쓰시오.

1 There is no reliable evidence that aggressive behavior becomes progressively more likely to occur over long periods in which is not provoked.

2 We had plenty of bread, so I need not had bought bread.

3 Coffee is my favorite hot drink, even though it kept me awake at night.

4 He could not but to give his consent to the proposal.

5 I was afraid lest he would come to the conference too late.

6 I had hoped to have learned French before I was sent out to the branch office in Paris.

7 Flotsam includes both goods casted from a vessel in distress and goods that float after a ship sinks.

8 This item is unavailable to you at this price for some coming years, should you miss this golden opportunity.

9 The dam were built in time to protect the inhabitants from the flood: the damage would have been very serious otherwise.

10 He looked as he had been in some strange land where age advanced at a double pace.

11 Our advertising campaign may have been killed if the boss had supported Bernie's idea of TV spots.

12 If he should fail to pass the exam, he were to try again.

13 We suggested that she is the best person for that position.

14 The director insisted that the proceeds of the sale must be devoted to charity.

15 To become a member of the civic association, one need only attend three meetings and to pay his fees regularly.

16 I loved the morning and should go down the dirt road with my tin pain toward the stream where there were gooseberries.

17 Before the invention of the clock, people must depend on the celestial bodies to tell time.

18 I wish I wasn't there the day before yesterday; I could've helped you with the problem.

19 Have we heard about the tragedy, we would never have come without first calling.

20 We have not yet informed them of our decision pulling out of the agreement.

21 Remember mailing the letter on your way home.

22 I was supposed to leaving an hour ago, but I'm still here.

23 All the members except one were in favor of the proposal increasing the dues.

24 The opinion holding by most investors is to buy stocks now.

25 It was considerable of you not to disturb while a guest of honor was at our office.

26 My supervisor had me spent the day taking inventory.

27 The person to answer the phone should always be polite to the caller.

28 The doctor told me checking regularly my pulse and blood pressure when exercising.

29 Explorers were astonished finding that the island was inhabited.

30 In batik, a method of applying colored designs to fabric, design is made on the fabric, and those sections which are to not be dyed are covered with a substance that will not absorb the dye.

31 When overall exports exceed imports, a country said to have a trade surplus.

32 After a lengthy interrogation, the suspect admitted being on the scene of the crime.

33 He spends a solitary time to work by himself as a forest ranger.

34 He regret being idle when he was young.

35 Eliminated problems by transferring the blame to others is often called scapegoating.

36 Why do you object to follow the direction?

37 I am writing with a view to find out whether you have anything wrong with you.

38 Reaching the age of four, Mozart's father gave him harpsichord lessons, and at the age of five he composed two minuets for the instrument.

B 다음 괄호 안의 동사를 적절한 형태로 고치시오.

1 Copernicus maintained that the earth (move) _____ round the sun.

2 It (rain) _____ every day so far this month.

3 "Is there anything wrong?"
"No, so far I (have) _____ no trouble."

4 Although I (live) _____ in this country since last September, I still have trouble getting used to American food.

5 The bus (arrive) _____ at the terminal two hours ago.

6 An Englishman traveling in Africa once (offer) _____ iron to a native tribe in exchange for a canoe.

7 "I don't like to travel."

   "Have you ever (fly) _____ in an airplane?

8 The woman admitted to the doctor that her little boy (sit)
   _____ in the back room and (eat) _____ everything he
   could find.

9 I shall go to Las Vegas before you (come) _____ back next
   week.

10 When he (retire) _____ , Professor Jones will have taught here
   for over thirty years, but his classes are never dull.

11 I think she (study) _____ right now.

12 I recognized Mr. Smith at once, for I (see) _____ him at the
   party.

13 They (take) _____ bath when we went to see them that afternoon.

14 She (live) _____ here for ten years by next March.

15 It is an accepted custom for one to say "Excuse me" when he
   (sneeze) _____ .

16 His father has a flourishing retail business and he (work)
   _____ in the shop for the last 18 months.

17 She could not forgive him for the sacrifice he (make) _____ for
   her sake.

18 Let's start as soon as he (come) _____ .

C 주어진 문장을 if를 사용하여 다시 쓰시오.

e.g. I didn't see the traffic light, so I didn't stop.

→ If I had seen the traffic light, I would have stopped.

1 He eats too much meat; that's why he is so unhealthy.

→ _____

2 I don't have a car so I have to go to work by bus.

→ _____

3 You can speak English perfectly by practicing it everyday.

→ _____

4 It took a long time to find his apartment because I didn't know his address exactly.

→ _____

5 I didn't know your address so I didn't write to you.

→ _____

D 다음 빈칸에 들어갈 적당한 표현을 고르시오.

1 It was an (exciting, excited, to excite) game, and the spectators grew excited.

2 (Writing, Written, To write) in French, the letter is very hard to read.

3 Things (done, doing, to do) by halves are never done right.

4 I'm sorry to have kept you (waiting, waited, to wait) so long.

5 Two men (worked, working, to work) at the factory were seriously injured yesterday afternoon.

6 He appeared (satisfied, satisfying, to satisfy) with my explanation.

7 (Compared, Comparing) (to, with) last year, the prices have risen by ten percent.

8 Everyone (interested, interesting) in music is expected to attend the concert.

9   His success made him (honor, honored, honoring, to honor) by the people around him.

10 The boss is in the habit of standing by the window with his arms (folded, folding, to fold) and watching outside.

11 (Being not, No being, Having not, Not having) found the key, I was a bit confused.

12 It is no good (to tell, telling, having told) me about your having lost your car.

13 I am sure all will go well as (to plan, planning, planned).

14 People are secretly (to arrest, being arrested, having been arrested) throughout the nation for owing minor credit card debts.

15 Our job is (to do, being done, having done) right things and not worry about the results because the results are not in our hands anyway.

E   괄호 안의 동사를 동명사, 부정사, 분사로 고치시오.

1   (Do) it together, for it is not good for man or woman (be) alone.

2   (Look) at the weather forecast, I decided (come) back to the hotel.

3   Human nature is such that most people generally prefer (spend) money to (save) it.

4   Do you feel like (go) out or just (hang) out?

5   After some weeks went by, though, we got tired of (wait) for the record (come) out.

6   I suggested (leave) the car behind and (continue) on foot, before (realize) this meant (walk) for several hours under the (scorch) sun with bags and shoes not (design) for hiking.

7   The IMF offered (lend) instruments (cope) with sunexpected revenue shortfalls beginning in 1963, as did the EU for selected countries.

8 There was now way of (get) out the hotel except by (climb) down a rope and Sue was too scared (do) this.

9 (Be) honest, I didn't know how (do) that and I didn't want (mess) it more. I personally didn't have a problem (delete) it all.

10 Kunal Kapoor was caught (climb) into someone's house (use) a pipleline and was ordered (come) down immediately.

F 다음 문장을 분사구문을 사용하여 다시 쓰시오.

1 Though I live next to his house, I don't know him.

2 After he stole the silver spoon, he looked for a place to hide it.

3 As I didn't receive an answer, I wrote to him again.

4 When our talk was over, we went back to the house.

5 As it was windy, we had to stay we had to stay inside hotel rooms all the time.

G 다음 비문법적인 분사구문을 문법적인 문장으로 바꾸시오.

1 While walking along the street, a car nearly struck me.

2 Comparing with her sister, she looks too plain.

3 When leaving a car in this car park, the brakes must be left off.

4 Tied to a post, the sea was tossing the boat up and down.

5 While cleaning his gun it went off unexpectedly.

Assignment 3

Department _____

Student ID _____

Name _____

Date ____ / ____ / ____

A 문법적으로 틀린 부분을 찾아 고치고, 그 이유를 쓰시오.

1 Helen Traubel, a people of diverse talents, both sang in operas and wrote mystery novels.

2 A deficient of folic acid is rarely found in humans because the vitamin is contained in a wide variety of foods.

3 At birth, an infant exhibits a remarkable number of motor response.

4 First incorporated in 1871, Dallas, Texas, had become the seventh largest cities in the United States by 1976.

5 Scientists have identified several hundred subatomical particle held together by a nuclear force.

6 Today's warplanes carry a wide various of armaments, including fast-firing cannons and sophisticated guided missiles and bombs.

7 It is fortunate that the number of automobile accident in the metropolitan city has decreased recently.

8 In the Middle Ages taxes were paid with good rather than money.

9 After day's pleasure one has a feeling of utter exhaustion.

10 After the church the men stood together in the churchyard saying he must be crazy.

11 There is five sheep on the farm, but there are only three goats.

12 The editors of the weekly *Finance*, which contains financial news, has agreed to accept advertisements.

13 The plane reservations were not so difficult to make as I thought it would be.

14 An enormous variety of informations may be obtained from a large daily newspaper.

15 That clear, perpetual outline of face and limb is but an image of our.

B 다음 빈 칸을 few, a few, little, a little 가운데 적절한 것으로 채우시오.

1 Here are _____ basic rules to make the experience pleasurable and profitable.

2 Many cities have flooding maps, but _____ people know about them.

3 There's always risk involved in investments, but _____ cities and towns would knowingly would invest in something that could eat up 93% of the principal.

4 We didn't think to bring our camera, but I saw _____ people taking MANY snaps.

5 I wasn't hungry but I ate _____ rice.

6 These young people always eat fast food like hamburgers and chips and eat _____ rice, and yet they don't seem to be hungry.

7 This photo was taken shortly after lunch when she drank _____ milk.

C
괄호 안의 표현 가운데 적당한 것을 고르시오.

1 God wanted us to do that by going to (church, the church) to worship him.

2 The plan is for the members of (church, the church) to deliver the food to the community where they live.

3 They are employed and paid by (hour, an hour, the hour), usually on nine-month contracts.

4 I've never played (soccer, a soccer, the soccer) in my life, and I want to know how.

5 When he played (piano, a piano, the piano) in the hospital he didn't play it that well.

6 (Milk, The milk) is very important to growing children.

7 Never force your baby finish all (milk, milks, the milk) in a bottle.

8 She was (beauty, a beauty, the beauty) when she was young.

9 Everyone in the western world knows what it means to be called (an Einstein, the Einstein).

10 I believe that (man, a man, the man) is mortal and has no continuance of life after death.

D 괄호 안의 적당한 동사형을 고르시오.

1 Good communication between layers and clients (is, are) extremely important for the proper treatment of a case.

2 The number of accountants hired by Tax Pros. on a yearly basis (is, are) continuously increasing.

3 This is one of the most sophisticated buildings that (has, have) been put up during the last few years.

4 Mathematics (is, are) considered one of the most important courses that science majors take in college.

5 Two-thirds of my home project (is, are) finished.

6 Not only the plant workers but the manager (is, are) on strike.

E 다음 주어진 두 문장을 관계대명사를 사용하여 한 문장으로 만드시오.

1 He was dancing with a girl. She was at least twice as heavy as the other female dancers.

→ _____

2 He fixed the table. Its leg was broken.

→ _____

3 The bed was thirteen feet long. He slept on it.

→ _____

4 Sally has two close friends. Both of them are interested in fine arts.

→ _____

5 The woman sang and cried aloud all night. This kept us awake.

→ _____